UNIVERSITY OF CALIFORNIA PUBLICATIONS IN ENGLISH

VOLUME XVIII
1947

EDITORS
A. G. BRODEUR, J. R. CALDWELL, W. H. DURHAM

GOTHIC DRAMA FROM WALPOLE TO SHELLEY

BY
BERTRAND EVANS

UNIVERSITY OF CALIFORNIA PRESS
BERKELEY AND LOS ANGELES
1947

UNIVERSITY OF CALIFORNIA PUBLICATIONS IN ENGLISH
EDITORS (BERKELEY): A. G. BRODEUR, J. R. CALDWELL, W. H. DURHAM
Volume 18
Submitted by editors March 1, 1946
Issued October 24, 1947
Price: cloth, $3.50; paper, $2.50

UNIVERSITY OF CALIFORNIA PRESS
BERKELEY AND LOS ANGELES
CALIFORNIA

◆

CAMBRIDGE UNIVERSITY PRESS
LONDON, ENGLAND

ACKNOWLEDGMENTS

I WISH TO express grateful acknowledgment to the librarians of the Henry E. Huntington Library, San Marino, California, for the privilege of examining the Larpent Collection of manuscripts and for their many kindnesses extended me. To my colleagues at the University of California who read my book in its various stages and made invaluable suggestions I am particularly grateful: to Professors Arthur G. Brodeur, James R. Caldwell, and Willard H. Durham, who, as editors of this series, designed many improvements which I have tried to execute; to Professor Bertrand H. Bronson, who has read the book in so many stages as almost to have memorized it; and to Professor Benjamin H. Lehman, without whose encouragement and help from the very inception of the idea there would have been no book.

B. E.

. . . that the eye may look hollow and dark under the shade of its brow; that the shadow of the nose may shorten the upper lip, and give a greater character of sense to the mouth.—JOANNA BAILLIE.

CONTENTS

CHAPTER	PAGE

I. Introduction 1
   The Meaning of Gothic—The Gothic Revival—Eighteenth- and Nineteenth-Century Drama

II. Antecedents and Beginnings 16
   Precursors of the Gothic School—*Douglas*—*The Countess of Salisbury*

III. The First Gothic Plays 31
   The Mysterious Mother—Other Plays of the Decade—*Percy*

IV. Adaptation and Burlesque 49
   The First Adaptation of *Otranto*—*The Count of Narbonne*—Contemporary Original Gothic Plays—*Albina*—Gothic Elements in Comedy—*The Banditti*—Other Comic Plays

V. Full Development of Gothic Drama before 1792 . . 72
   Gothic Plays, 1784-1792—*The Carmelite*—*Vimonda*—*The Regent*—*Kentish Barons*—The Gothic Villain

VI. Ann Radcliffe and Gothic Drama 90
   Boaden and Ann Radcliffe—*Fontainville Forest*—Siddons and Ann Radcliffe—Andrews and Ann Radcliffe

VII. Gothic and German Drama 116
   Types of German Subliterary Fiction—Boaden and a German Motif—The Real German Drama in England

VIII. Lewis and Gothic Drama 132
   The Castle Spectre—Other plays by Lewis—*Adelmorn, the Outlaw*—*The Wood Daemon; or, One O'Clock*—Lesser Plays—The Place of Lewis

IX. Gothic Drama and Melodrama 162
   Gothic Melodramas—*The Foundling of the Forest*—*The Woodman's Hut*—Burlesque Gothic Melodrama

X. Gothic Acting Drama, 1801-1816 177
   Analysis of Four Gothic Acting Plays—*Julian and Agnes*—*The Towers of Urbandine*—*The Curfew*—*Bertram; or The Castle of St. Aldobrand*

CHAPTER	PAGE
XI. Joanna Baillie and Gothic Drama 200
General Characteristics of Joanna Baillie's Plays—*Orra*
XII. Gothic Survival in Literary Drama 216
Literary Plays by Wordsworth and Coleridge—*The Borderers*—*Remorse*—Scott and Gothic Drama—Shelley's *Cenci*—Byron's *Manfred*
Appendix: A List of Gothic Plays 239
Notes 247

CHAPTER I

INTRODUCTION

More than a dozen scholarly volumes and various monographs have been written exclusively on the Gothic novel.[1] Its history, materials, and ramifications have been explored repeatedly. Details of its origins and evolution have been combed and recombed, and the contribution of the genre to early nineteenth-century romanticism has been evaluated and emphatically asserted, not once, but often. Histories of English literature, however brief, find space for a paragraph, a page, or a chapter on the species. Histories of the English novel regularly include several pages on the prose fiction of Horace Walpole, Ann Radcliffe, Clara Reeve, Matthew Gregory Lewis, and Charles Robert Maturin. And, finally, casual students of literature have read *The Castle of Otranto* and know something of *The Mysteries of Udolpho, The Old English Baron, The Monk,* and *Melmoth.*

Through a repetition of study the characteristic elements of the Gothic novel have been made widely familiar. After Walpole the machinery and motifs of the Gothic school swiftly accumulated, swiftly became convention. A standard list of elements serves the historian: the atmosphere of mystery, the spiral staircase, the grated windows, the secret panel, the trapdoor, the antique tapestries, the haunted chamber, the subterranean passage, the gallery, the vault, the turret, the castle itself, the convent, the cavern, the midnight bell, the ancient scroll, the fluttering candle flame, the clank of chains, the gloomy tyrant, the persecuted maiden, the insipid hero, the emaciated "unknown" locked in the dank dungeon. All these we have learned to know well.

It is not a purpose of this study to question the significance of Gothic fiction in the history of English literature or to disparage

---

[1] For notes to chap. i, see pages 247–248.

the value of scholarship in it. The Gothic novel was an expression of the late eighteenth-century *Zeitgeist,* and examination of it illuminates important aspects of an important period. It was instrumental in transforming the Age of Johnson into the Age of Byron, and its history interprets that vital transition.

The part of the Gothic novel in the romantic movement is significant. That the Byronic hero was foreshadowed in Walpole's Manfred and Mrs. Radcliffe's Montoni, and that Mrs. Radcliffe's feeling for nature, her predilection for wild, romantic scenes, and her description of landscapes vitally influenced great poets of the early nineteenth century are facts well known to students of romanticism. Indeed, as one Gothic student writes, we see increasingly in Mrs. Radcliffe "the focus of all the romantic tendencies of her time."[2] The Gothic novel left emphatic marks upon the works of Wordsworth, Coleridge, Scott, Byron, Shelley, and Keats, and any study which throws light upon these is not without excuse for being. In short, the history of the Gothic novel, in its matrix, and in its ramifications, deserves even fuller attention than it has received.

At the same time, however, there is need to explore a new area in order to correct a distorted impression. The emphasis of scholarship upon the Gothic novel has made it appear that the Gothic Revival of the late eighteenth century found literary expression in the novel alone. When we speak of Gothic literature, it is assumed that we mean the Gothic novels; similarly when we speak of Gothic influence upon Byron and Shelley, we mean the influence of the Gothic novels. Scholarship has led everyone to suppose that the Gothic school was composed of novelists only.

Dramatists, however, participated as actively as novelists in the Gothic Revival. Gothic fiction has received elaborate attention; Gothic drama, virtually none.[3]

The plays, as much as the novels, deserve study. There seems little excuse for their not being well known, for they are available in large numbers. Among them are several specimens of the Gothic mode as remarkable as *The Castle of Otranto, The Mysteries of Udolpho,* and *Melmoth.* Though almost without exception poor, the plays are no worse than the novels which have been found significant. The Gothic drama expresses the *Zeitgeist* as revealingly as the Gothic novel and also reflects equally well the transition from the Age of Johnson to the Age of Byron.

Perhaps the primary purpose in examining Gothic literature is to throw light on the greater works it influenced. Gothicists contributed some vital components of romanticism, and studies in fiction have exposed many of these. It is admittedly profitable to examine the crude materials in the novels, and then to detect them again, transformed, among the finer qualities of romantic poetry. Yet the results of scholarship in the novels have not been wholly satisfactory, for little has been revealed of the actual process of transformation. In the novels we see the creaking elements of Gothic machinery; then, in the poetry of the next generation, we confront them again—apparently sea-changed.' The stages of evolution have escaped observation. And, again, scholarship shows us the villains, Manfred, Montoni, and Schedoni, in the novels of Walpole and Mrs. Radcliffe; then, after leaping the gap between the ages—and that greater one between prose and poetry—it shows us the Byronic hero. Resemblances are obvious: yet the one is a villain and the other a hero. When, how, and why did this rather considerable change occur? Gothic fiction has not yielded the answers.

Study of Gothic drama may prove more fruitful than study of Gothic novels in tracing the stages of evolution which hitherto have not been revealed. The medium of dramatic verse remains constant; hence plays afford a bridge between the centuries; they form an unbroken succession from Walpole to Shelley.

Since Gothic literature is chiefly important for the marks it left on the great poets, the plays are especially significant. Except the juvenile Shelley, none of the major romantic poets wrote Gothic prose.[5] But Wordsworth, Coleridge, Scott, Byron, and Shelley wrote plays markedly in the Gothic line of descent. *The Borderers, Remorse, The House of Aspen, Manfred,* and *The Cenci* surely cannot be fully interpreted until they are viewed in relation to the tradition of which they are part. Prose fiction affords an imperfect background, for these are plays and theirs was a dramatic heritage. Yet students of the Gothic have related them to a prose ancestry, ignoring the plays to which, in both form and content, they bear closer affinity.

Another, and related, fact claims special consideration for Gothic drama. A focal center in studies of the Gothic has been the villain who became the Byronic hero. I have stated that the drama reveals the change and that fiction does not. But the fact is even greater than that, for it was the drama, not the novel, which effected the change. It was upon drama that forces operated which inevitably moved the protagonist through stages of villain-hero and hero-villain to the special kind of hero to whom Byron's name has been given. In drama this hero had emerged, with all his characteristic marks upon him, before Byron had published a line of verse. The novel, long before, had created him as an agent of terror; but drama gradually made him a hero and passed him on, laden with agony, to the nineteenth century.

The past neglect of Gothic drama is understandable. Perhaps the most obvious reason is that Horace Walpole attached the epithet "Gothic" to his novel, and the word stuck there, limiting research to the one form. There are other reasons. The inferiority of late eighteenth-century plays, except for those of Goldsmith and Sheridan, has invited general neglect, and it was natural that the Gothic species should have its share of the oblivion. Until Professor Nicoll's volumes[6] appeared, no one since Genest[7] had undertaken more than cursory examination of the field. Students of the late eighteenth century have been mainly interested in prose. Students of drama have been concerned with periods which left better plays, or at least plays less conspicuously bad. Certain conventional terms, too, have hidden the identity of Gothic drama. Many plays of the end of the eighteenth century have been dismissed simply as "German," as "melodrama," or as "romantic."[8] The scarcity of available texts has been another factor. The present account could not have been written without the use of manuscripts preserved in the Larpent Collection of the Henry E. Huntington Library.[9]

The primary task in the following chapters will be to indicate the quantity and describe the nature of Gothic drama over a period of about half a century. It has been necessary to select representative works carefully for description and analysis, and to cite passages liberally, especially from plays not readily available. In the concluding chapter I shall place certain dramatic works of major nineteenth-century poets against the Gothic background for brief reëxamination; I shall not attempt complete studies of these, but may perhaps succeed in laying a foundation on which such studies might be based.

The Meaning of Gothic

Because earlier studies have made the Gothic novel familiar, it seems logical to introduce Gothic drama by relating it to its well-known contemporary. A Gothic play, then, is one marked by features which have long served to identify a Gothic novel. These features include specialized settings, machinery, character types, themes, plots, and techniques selected and combined to serve a primary purpose of exploiting mystery, gloom, and terror. If M. G. Lewis' *Castle Spectre* had been composed as a novel (as indeed the author first intended), we would classify it with *The Monk* as a Gothic novel. If Maturin's *Bertram* were a novel, it would be classified with *Melmoth*. If we accept what have long been accepted as the distinguishing characteristics of Gothic fiction, it is possible to determine what is and what is not a Gothic play. Studies in the one form thus give authority and direction for studies in the other.

Nevertheless, because certain problems about the origins and meaning of Gothic remain vexing after much scholarship in fiction, it seems necessary here to offer some basic explanations. Whatever Walpole intended when he subtitled *Otranto* a "Gothic Story," to his followers, as to students since, the epithet described the most striking features—the secret panels, subterranean passages, midnight bells, and all the rest of the horrific machinery. A novel is Gothic if elements of this kind are assembled in quantity and used to excite feelings of mystery, gloom, and terror. But just why are these elements themselves Gothic? The question "Are the Gothic novels Gothic?"[10] can be answered only by answering that.

If the machinery of Gothic literature consisted merely of castles, convents, subterranean vaults, grated dungeons, and "ruined piles," the answer would be simple: Gothic would be an appropriate name for machinery which consisted exclusively of elements directly associated with medieval architecture. Anyone who scans the "standard" list of elements or reads a Gothic novel is soon aware that much is included which betrays no specific relationship to Gothic architecture or to the age which created it. The full paraphernalia which identifies Gothic literature includes also, to name only a few materials, banditti, caverns, dark forests, midnight bells, wild natural scenes, violent storms, and "ghosts." Obviously, none of these was peculiar to the Gothic age. All existed before and after the medieval period. All have appeared in literature not usually associated with the Gothic school. On what grounds, then, are these to be included among the elements which identify the Gothic species? To find the answer we must look deeper into the Gothic Revival and the origins of its literature.

THE GOTHIC REVIVAL

The Gothic Revival was inspired not by the literature of the medieval romance but by the more conspicuous relic—the architectural ruin.[11] This tangible survival of a past time had been popularized by the "graveyard" poets, whose tradition of "mold'ring walls" and "moss-grown Abbeys" extended from the early decades of the eighteenth century. Through Gray, Blair, Mallet, and others a somber gloom became fashionably associated with ruins. Only after these poets had popularized the musty symbols of the past did architects begin to design new Gothic and "bastard Gothic" edifices;[12] and only after that did attention turn to the old romances—works which ranged from the earliest Middle Ages through the seventeenth century.

As the ruin inspired the Revival, so it became and remained the nucleus around which Gothic writers assembled objects and agents of mystery, gloom, and terror. In 1764 there were three distinct ways of regarding the age which the ruin symbolized. Hurd saw it revealed in the pages of Spenser as a golden age of chivalry, of splendor, and noble manners.[13] The antiquaries saw it as a historical epoch providing wide scope for research. And, finally, a wide circle—the potential public of Walpole—saw it as a dark, barbarous, superstitious time; such was the conventional view from the time of Dryden to the end of the eighteenth century.[14] The ruin itself was identified specifically with this last view.

Horace Walpole has customarily been described as leader of a revolt from the conventional attitude toward medievalism.[15] *The Castle of Otranto* is said to have sprung from a new feeling that the Gothic was not barbarous, and it is this interpretation, I believe, which has been a major source of our confusion about what is and what is not "Gothic" in the novels that followed *Otranto*. An interpretation more in keeping with the facts is that the Gothicists did not rebel against the conventional attitude, but deliberately exploited it. Accepting the Gothicists' intention as one of exploitation of a popular attitude, we can better understand the principle which directed the accumulation of a machinery of mystery, gloom, and terror. And the answer to the question, "Are the Gothic novels Gothic?" waits on a plausible explanation of that unifying principle.

The best evidence—found in the novels themselves—is that *Otranto* and the genre it initiated erupted from two related ideas: first, medieval life was dark, gloomy, and barbarous; second, it would be terrifying if enlightened gentlemen and "sensible" ladies were transported from contemporary society and suddenly thrust into that earlier time.

The ruinous castle, with its turrets, winding staircases, vaults, and secret panels, was the primary object of terror with which to confront these visitors. It is conspicuously anachronistic that, since the scenes are usually set in, or shortly after, the medieval period, the edifices of Gothic literature are almost invariably in an advanced state of decay. We would have expected to find them comparatively new, and certainly not in a condition of crumbled magnificence. But because the architectural relic which survived was the prime mover of the Gothicists' invention, it was shown in ruins even in the period in which it should have been intact.

With one major exception, the figures whom the Gothic writers placed in the medieval setting were their contemporaries. This exception was the villain—a barbarous tyrant whose single function was to strike terror into the hearts of young women suddenly transported to his time and lair. As the heroines—and the heroes—of Gothic literature move about the medieval scene, it is plain that the castles and moats, vaults, turrets, and galleries are strange and awful to them.[16] Why should they not be strange? Walpole's Isabel and Mrs. Radcliffe's Adeline, Emily, and Ellena were no more born to the medieval scene than were Pamela and

Evelina. Enlightened, virtuous, and "sensible," they had been uprooted from their proper society and, with contemporary emotional and intellectual patterns intact, thrust into that era which was "barbarous." Subjected to the various menaces of the Dark Ages, they served as projections of the nervous system of their own time, as sensitive registers of emotional reaction to horrors, and, clearly, as transmitters of the thrills of their exposure. When they shuddered, their home-bound contemporaries shuddered.

The intention of the Gothicists was to select those aspects of medievalism which would prove most terrifying. The primary source, or object of terror, as we have seen, was the ruin itself. The second, naturally, was the tyrant who inhabited it. Of the Gothic villain it has been said that he descended from the machinating villains of Elizabethan drama; that he was derived from the wicked uncle of the folk tale; that he was a reincarnation of Milton's Satan." Such statements suggest ancient and glorious ancestors for the figure who was ultimately to become the Byronic hero and to serve Scott and the Brontes, among others, and that there may be truth in them it is unnecessary to deny. Iago, the wicked uncle, and Satan doubtless lent qualities when it served the Gothicists' interests to borrow; but none of them were vital in the genesis of this special kind of villain.

The Gothic villain was born as adjunct to the ruinous castle. His nature and his function were strictly dictated by his origin. His gloom, which was later to be magnified to an agony that would invite sympathy and make him a hero, was that of the castle he inhabited. His function was to frighten heroines, to pursue them through the vaults and labyrinths of the castle, to harass them at every turn. Whatever the Gothic writers drew from earlier villains was incidental and superficial; it had no effect upon the essential characteristics of the new villain and no force in his evolution. This villain was a new answer to a new need: the need for an active agent of terror to supplement the primary object of terror. Created in the novel, he developed more swiftly in the drama, and there first became a hero. With his evolution and his eventual transformation we shall hereafter be much concerned.

Beginning with a ruin, then, the Gothicists built up an elaborate machinery of mystery, gloom, and terror. The machinery employed by Walpole consisted chiefly of elements closely associated with medievalism—castles, giants, armor, the supernatural (which might be considered legitimately Gothic because superstition was regarded as a medieval characteristic). There can, then, be little doubt that Walpole's novel was Gothic. But after Walpole had established the direction, there began in both novel and drama an accumulation of materials by no means all of which were peculiar to medievalism. To the legitimate materials, centering in the ruin, was added whatever accorded with the mood and furthered the purposes of mystery, gloom, and terror. Soon the castle and the convent were joined by the cavern; the Gothic tyrant by banditti; the vaults and galleries by dark forests at midnight. Caverns, banditti, and forests are not in themselves Gothic. But novels and plays did not cease to be Gothic when, adding these, they retained the nucleus of the accumulation—the architectural ruin—together with other properties immediately associated with medievalism. For decades the driving impulse remained the fact that the Gothic age was considered barbarous. The non-Gothic elements that became attached to the accumulation by the force of this impulse merely built it up on the outside; they did not alter its center. So long as the impulse and the nucleus remained Gothic and directed the accretion of new properties, the entire machinery remained Gothic.

The acquisition of new elements was a natural process. Tyrants pursued heroines outside the walls of the castle into a surrounding forest. Darkness increased the terror of that forest. Banditti increased it still more. Thunder and lightning came to join the tyrant, the darkness, the forest, and the banditti in affrighting the heroine's soul. The banditti naturally required some sort of meeting-place—and thus the cavern, with its gloomy recesses, dank walls, and secret exits and entrances joined castle and convent as an associate fixture of horror. The principle was simple enough: that was added which accorded with the mood and furthered the Gothic purpose.

A knowledge of the process by which these new horrific elements were assembled around an original core makes it possible to acknowledge "Gothic" as an appropriate name for the works which continued the Walpolian tradition. It also throws light on the confused relation of Gothic literature to certain earlier works which have sometimes been considered their sources. Some students of the Gothic, noting that various elements included in the novels of Mrs. Radcliffe and others are not exclusively medieval, have sought the origins of these works elsewhere than in the Gothic Revival. Clara F. McIntyre, for instance, finding that many Gothic trappings appear in Elizabethan drama, has concluded that the Gothic novel was rooted in that drama.[12] Similarly, it has been usual to treat Richardsonian sensibility as a source of the Gothic school. But these are not sources at all. That there are common elements in Gothic literature and Elizabethan plays is indeed evident enough: we need merely remember *Macbeth*. That excessive sensibility is a trait of the Gothic heroine is conspicuously true also. But these facts have nothing to do with sources. Even though some properties were indeed taken by Gothicists directly from Elizabethan dramatists and Richardson, they constituted mere external additions to the growing paraphernalia. Seeking all that would accord with castle ruins and serve the ends of mystery, gloom, and terror, Gothicists seized materials wherever they found them. They took not merely objects of terror, but themes, styles, motifs, even plots, and bent them to the Gothic purpose. In the swift and clutching acquisition it was inevitable that much which had been used in other times by other writers should be gathered into the grab bag. But all these elements were distinct from the source of Gothic literature, which was the attitude of the enlightened eighteenth century toward the Gothic age; thence came the impulse—the urge to Gothicize—which motivated writers to feed a taste for terror and directed the accumulation of appropriate materials.

In the chapters which follow, the process of accretion here outlined is elaborated, and its operation is demonstrated through analysis of representative dramatic works. As successive plays are discussed and the involvement of more and more elements is described, a sharper clarification of the cumulative process may help to illuminate some problems in the history of Gothic literature.

EIGHTEENTH- AND NINETEENTH-CENTURY DRAMA

Before surveying the evolution of the single species which is our subject, we may well review briefly the total dramatic scene in the period in which this species flourished. I wish to avoid distorting the total picture by seeming to suggest that Gothic plays constituted the entire dramatic output of the late eighteenth and early nineteenth centuries, or that they represented the main trend in that time.

In drama the period is one of confusion. Plays are themselves confused, and such study as has been given them is often so. Generalizations have been made and lines of "major trend" drawn on the basis of firsthand examination of too few plays. Much study of the dramatic activity has been directed, not to the plays themselves, but elsewhere. Histories of drama, liberal in their analysis of individual works of other periods, have regularly treated about half a dozen of this period, then have turned to discuss actors, playhouses, and riots.[19] We read repeatedly that theaters were enlarged; that certain actors and actresses rose to surpassing fame; that managers and actors were harassed by a public which was quick to take offense; that the beau monde frequented the theater and the less sophisticated stayed home; that drama strove to compete with fireworks; that the rise of the novel caused the decline of the drama; that theater boxes were used as offices by prostitutes; that "building" on the stage distressed players; and that benefit nights gave rise to intolerable evils. This information, rich with anecdotes drawn from memoirs, autobiographies, theater annals, and letters, holds a fascination unique even for theatrical gossip, but it is scarcely a full substitute for study of the plays.

Three important features are brought out by a preliminary survey of the dramatic literature of the period: first, the prodigiousness of the total output; second, the endless variety of types, themes, materials, and techniques; and, third, the poor quality of all but a few plays.

To be aware of the quantity, the reader needs only note that Professor Nicoll required 416 pages merely to list authors, titles, dates, and places of first performance of theatrical pieces between 1750 and 1850.[20] In relation to the total number of plays of all kinds, the number of Gothic plays between 1768 and 1823 is fractional. Yet it is certain that the period saw as many Gothic plays as any other single kind.

An idea of the infinite variety of types can be gained from the fact that Professor Nicoll listed sixty-six kinds of theatrical entertainments. The exaggeration of Polonius would in this age be gross understatement. And the variety of types is matched by that of subjects, themes, and treatments. I have chosen to trace a specific kind of manifestation; other studies of considerable extent might be given to plays which treat Ossianic materials, Eastern materials, heroic materials, classical materials, and ballad materials. Playwrights dramatized almost anything, in almost any style. Wherever novelists and poets, indeed wherever essayists went, the dramatists kept pace. They turned the philosophy of Rousseau into theatrical spectacle and followed the unities in doing so. They told an antique Greek story so that the effect resembled that of a dramatized Gothic novel. Striving to find something, anything, to catch the public fancy, they rehashed the themes and attempted the dramatic fashions of every age. Shakespearean revivals and publication of Elizabethan dramatists encouraged frequent starts in the Elizabethan manner, many imitations of Shakespeare, and wholesale theft of the master's phrases, lines, and scenes.[21] The result of hurling together clashing materials, motifs, styles, and themes in complete disregard of history or geography was often an incredible mélange: a play set in Anglo-Saxon times, for example, with its scene laid in the great gabled hall, but with warriors who should have been gulping mead and gnawing beef declaiming instead, in late eighteenth-century diction, of patriotism and liberty; with ladies of sensibility asserting their virtue by citing familiar precepts; and, finally, with the whole business tied together by comments on the action from an Aeschylean chorus. Sometimes the stage was peopled by Oscars and Malvinas, talking in the style of "A tale of the times of old! The deeds of days of other years! The murmur of thy streams, O Lora! The sound of thy woods, Germallar!" The ballad materials of Percy, the enchanted woods of Tasso, the adventures of Tom Jones, the opinions of Tristram Shandy—all these were staged in one or the other of Professor Nicoll's sixty-six varieties.

Such heterogeneity makes it apparent that the Gothic was not the sole preoccupation of playwrights or public. But it is true that the Gothic was as prevalent as any interest. The mushrooming of types and the exploitation of varied materials in fact precludes the hasty summarizing and the delineation of main channels that have characterized accounts of the period.[22] Such main channels as sentimental comedy, drama of sensibility, comedy of manners, and romantic drama—convenient when dealing with only a few examples of each—become less certain with each document we find in the Larpent Collection. "Major trends" invented after consideration of Cumberland, Goldsmith, Sheridan, Byron, and Shelley represent the best plays that were written in half a century, but that is all. Discovery of the real major trends—if, indeed, there were any in this period of confusion of minds and spirits when the Age of Johnson yielded to that of Wordsworth and Byron—must await study of many dramatic texts, including some that may not have been read since the Lord Chamberlain's office examined the manuscripts submitted for licensing.

CHAPTER II
ANTECEDENTS AND BEGINNINGS

Though Walpole asserted that he had merely combined two earlier species,[1] and though some of the distinguishing marks of the Gothic novel are apparent in earlier works, *The Castle of Otranto* initiated a new kind of prose fiction. Its newness derived not from the use of new elements, but from new associations of old ones for a new purpose. The new species assembled and exploited those elements, old and new, which would conveniently fit together and serve the ends of mystery, gloom, and terror. Walpole achieved newness by superimposing the attitudes of his own time upon selected aspects of a past age. Neither a sentimental, zealously virtuous heroine nor a medieval castle was new to literature in 1764. But a unique species resulted when the one, furnished with contemporary intellectual and emotional reactions, was thrust into the other in order to capitalize on the conventional attitude toward medievalism. Though Smollett in *Ferdinand, Count Fathom* and Leland in *Longsword, Earl of Salisbury* had anticipated him in the use of some special devices and moods, it has long been accepted that Walpole fathered the Gothic novel with *Otranto*.[2]

The beginning of Gothic drama can be fixed with equal exactness. In 1768 Walpole's *Mysterious Mother* was privately printed and distributed quietly among the author's friends.[3] It was the first work in a genre as distinct as that of the Gothic novel.

But because *The Mysterious Mother* is a play, greater attention must be given to possible antecedents than has been accorded *Ferdinand* and *Longsword* as antecedents of *Otranto*. The novel was a relatively new form when Walpole wrote, but the drama was ancient. The possibility of composing a play not in important respects linked to earlier ones was small. Furthermore, there is

---
[1] For notes to chap. ii, see pages 248–249.

a complication in the relation of Gothic drama to Elizabethan and Jacobean drama that does not exist in the relation of the Gothic novel to that drama. It has been noted that numerous elements used in *Otranto* had appeared in some early tragedies.⁴ These early *plays* obviously cannot be offered as contenders for *Otranto's* title of first Gothic *novel*. But they cannot be thus summarily dismissed as possible antecedents of Gothic plays, and therefore as rivals of *The Mysterious Mother*. It is necessary to pay at least passing attention to them.

We need not bring forward obscure Elizabethan and Jacobean tragedies and tragi-comedies to show that early dramatists employed elements similar to those in the Gothic collection. It is unnecessary even to single out the tragedies of Webster and Tourneur. Shakespeare's plays give evidence enough: *Hamlet, Macbeth, Julius Caesar,* and *Richard III* have ghosts; *Macbeth* and *Julius Caesar* use prophecies and supernatural portents; *King Lear* has a desolate heath and nature at her wildest in thunder, lightning, and rain; *Romeo and Juliet* includes a speech which conjures up images of horror: tombs, vaults, sepulchers, bones, and fumes; *Hamlet* has stark battlements in the dead of night; and various other plays include scenes in and about old castles.

The list might readily be extended, but we need observe only *Macbeth* to see an assortment of elements that have long helped to identify the Gothic novel and are, in the present study, found serviceable in identifying Gothic drama. Besides ghosts and prophecies, *Macbeth* has a variety of apparitions, a signal bell, a forest, thunder and lightning, a cavern, a castle, a murder done in the night to the accompaniment of supernatural sounds, and other striking elements of the same sort.

Though it includes more antecedent elements than perhaps any other Elizabethan or Jacobean tragedy, however, *Macbeth* is not a Gothic play and cannot be claimed as an antecedent of the species. It is not elements alone, but the attitude toward them and the uses made of them that distinguish the Gothic kind. In *Macbeth,* interests and purposes peculiar to the age so engulf even the most horrific features that they do not dominate the total impression; however conspicuous they are, they remain incidentals, not ends. The Elizabethans furnished many elements, seized by Gothicists where they would serve, but wrote no play comparable to the species that arose with *The Mysterious Mother.* This fact will become increasingly evident as Gothic pieces are examined.[5]

No better fortune rewards search for an antecedent in the period of the Restoration. The heroic tragedies, products chiefly of the decade 1664–1674, were frequently imitated in the period covered in succeeding chapters, and the imitations are readily distinguished from Gothic plays. The heroic dramas, marked by preoccupations and uses peculiar to them—by plots contrived and conducted with extreme complication; by ranting speech in rimed couplets; by elaborate scenery and extravagant stage action; by a "tissue of conflicting loves" between the eternal Almanzors and Almahides; and by an avowed aim "to rise as far above the ordinary proportion of the stage as the usual heroic poem soars beyond the common words and actions of human life"—constitute a species distinct from any other. Though a few elements are common to both kinds, the conclusion is inescapable: heroic and Gothic plays bear only such resemblances to each other as either kind bears, for example, to Elizabethan plays.

The nonheroic tragedies of the Restoration and early eighteenth century include nothing that can be remotely considered an antecedent. *Venice Preserved* and *The Orphan,* a historical and a domestic tragedy respectively, are jaded Elizabethan. If mere horror, whatever its source, so long as it existed in quantity, were the distinguishing quality of the Gothic play, Lee's *Caesar Borgia,* bombastic, bloody accumulation of horrors on horror's head, would out-Gothicize anything by Walpole or Lewis. But this tragedy clearly represents a revival of the more grisly features of Elizabethan drama and is no more related to the Gothic school than, say, *Titus Andronicus*. Congreve's *Mourning Bride* is a similar revival.[6]

PRECURSORS OF THE GOTHIC SCHOOL
DOUGLAS

Only in the famous *Douglas* of John Home, the "Scotch Shakespeare," do we find a play which, though it did not fully anticipate the school initiated eight years later, reveals in its spirit, its total effect, and some of its specific properties signs not to be ignored. First acted in Edinburgh in 1756, an enormous success, *Douglas* was brought to the Covent Garden stage the following year. Between 1757 and 1817 it was revived seventeen times at the principal theaters for runs of considerable length.[7] Attracting every famous actress of the period to the role of Lady Randolph—which was ranked without a blush with the great Shakespearean roles—it vied with *Hamlet* as a perennial favorite. *Douglas* created the greatest dramatic stir of the age, not all of which was occasioned by Scotch pamphleteers who cried "shame" on the immorality of the stage in general and on this "masterpiece" by a minister in particular. Certainly some of the explosive reaction resulted from the presence of "new things" which paralleled those in poetry, for the outline of the plot was drawn from an old ballad, *Gil Morrice*. (Percy's *Reliques* was to appear soon.)

The ballad origin relates *Douglas* only loosely to the characteristic dramatic manifestations of the Gothic Revival. Most of the features that came to identify the Gothic school are lacking or dimly foreshadowed. Some of them are included, however, and an atmosphere envelops them which occasionally resembles the pall that hangs over a Gothic scene. It was this atmosphere which led Professor Nicoll to name the play at the head of "Pseudo-Romantic" tragedy.

This false type of romance is exemplified during the period in two distinct ways. On the one hand, there are tragedies which ... show an appreciation of that vague something which we call romantic. On the other hand there are the numerous melodramas, both with and without music, which display the cruder and wilder elements of the same spirit. Unquestionably the latter were more popular; the former seemed constantly between two schools, satisfying neither classicist nor romanticist ... The earliest on the field with this new form was John Home, famous for his Scots tragedy of Douglas. ... There is a genuine passion in many lines, and a distinct love of nature, which show that Home passed beyond the chiller forms of pseudo-classic tragedy. This obscure Scots writer had struck a new note, which but expressed certain latent tendencies in the spirit of his time.[8]

"That vague something which we call romantic" appears conspicuously in the opening soliloquy. Lady Randolph has carried her melancholy into woods that reflect and intensify her mood:

> Ye woods and wilds, whose melancholy gloom
> Accords with my soul's sadness, and draws forth
> The voice of sorrow from my bursting heart,
> Farewell awhile; I will not leave you long;
> For in your shades I deem some spirit dwells,
> Who, from the chiding stream, or groaning oak,
> Still hears and answers to Matilda's moan.
> Oh Douglas! Douglas! if departed ghosts
> Are e'er permitted to review this world,
> Within the circle of that wood thou art,
> And, with the passion of immortals, hear'st
> My lamentation: hear'st thy wretched wife
> Weep for her husband slain, her infant lost.[9]

This passage, for present purposes the most significant in the play, anticipates three characteristic features of Gothic drama. First, it anticipates the *attitude* of the playwrights toward their materials. Several lines suggest, if vaguely, the mood of a Gothic heroine set among medieval wilds. Next, it anticipates a favorite *technique* which, with few modifications, is observable in Gothic plays from Walpole to Byron. This consists in using the opening lines to disclose that a mysterious "past event" has occurred, usually fifteen or twenty years before the opening of the play; thus, often, just enough time has elapsed for an "infant lost" to have grown into a hero or heroine. The perpetrators of the past event—which is nearly always a criminal deed—are unknown. The exact nature of the event is enveloped in mystery at the beginning of the play and is revealed piecemeal through narration spaced at intervals. Dark suggestions intensify the mystery as the action progresses, and often the full truth is disclosed only in the final scene. Finally, the soliloquy introduces a *theme* which came to be used in almost every play. This, the theme of long-lost relatives—or rather, "long-believed-lost" relatives—finds its spring, of course, in the past event. It was employed almost universally in the Gothic school, for it was peculiarly appropriate to plots that involved gloomy castles, tyrant-usurpers, and persecuted ladies.[10]

Besides attitude, technique, and theme, *Douglas* anticipated Gothic settings and character types. It is the settings of Gothic works which establish the most legitimate connection with the Gothic Revival, and, by means of their sets plays could surpass novels in achieving the Gothic purpose. The stage revealed to the outer eye the castles, convents, and caverns that the novel described to the inner eye, and in the play these physical reminders constantly confronted the spectator. The background of ruined buildings was a constant reminder to the audience of the gloom and terror which surrounded the characters. Gothic settings are invariably more than mere fixtures. Not only are they always present, but they are always exploited through dialogue. Often they provide the motivating force in a scene. For the characters, they are the subjects of gnawing preoccupation. Not long after *Douglas* appeared, settings grew increasingly elaborate, covering the stage with the visible survivals of medievalism. The instructions for stage managers, carpenters, and painters became ever more specific. The playwright sometimes specified that the castle, the windows, and even the chairs should be Gothic, that the moon must shine through the branches of trees, that the ruined wall of an old abbey must show between the trunks, and perhaps that a jagged cliff must loom over all. The architectural relics of medievalism, physically represented, came to be as vital in the action as the human figures who moved furtively or menacingly among them.

Toward maximum utilization of specialized settings, *Douglas* moved haltingly. The play opens with "The Court of a Castle, surrounded with Woods." On the surface, this was not new. Earlier plays had employed castles surrounded by woods. But in *Douglas* the setting becomes a motivating force; it determines the mood and expression of Lady Randolph. The fifth act presents "A Grove. Dark. Enter Douglas." Groves, too, had appeared in earlier plays. But here the setting markedly affects the character placed in it; the hero's soliloquy echoes Lady Randolph's and, like hers, is inspired by the place and the time:

> This is the place, the centre of the grove;
> Here stand the oak, the monarch of the wood.
> How sweet and solemn is this midnight scene!
> The silver moon, unclouded, holds her way
> Through skies where I could count each little star.
> The fanning west wind scarcely stirs the leaves;
> The river rushing o'er its pebbled bed,
> Imposes silence with a stilly sound.
> If ancestry can be in aught believed,
> Descending spirits have conversed with man,
> And told the secrets of the world unknown.[11]

Perhaps the most conspicuous fact about both soliloquies is that there is no dramatic reason for their being out of doors. Perhaps deliberately, the author sacrificed probability in order to have his characters react to the solemnity of woods at midnight. The fact suggests the nature of the preoccupations that were to guide the assembling of a complex machinery of gloom and terror. In both speakers the surroundings provoke thoughts of the supernatural, and though the hint of an actual visitation is hesitant and timid (we do not expect a ghost really to show itself either to Lady Randolph or to Douglas) the soliloquies do begin to create an atmosphere into which, in a later decade, genuine phantoms could stalk without appearing incongruous.

Besides the stage sets, the dialogue in *Douglas* emphasizes elements which later playwrights were to exploit. Old Norval, brought prisoner to Lady Randolph, thus describes finding an unknown infant eighteen years before:

> ... Whilst thus we poorly liv'd,
> One stormy night, as I remember well,
> The wind and rain beat hard upon our roof:
> Red came the river down, and loud and oft
> The angry spirit of the water shriek'd.
> At the dead hour of the night was heard the cry
> Of one in jeopardy. I rose, and ran
> To where the circling eddy of a pool
> Beneath the ford, us'd oft to bring within
> My reach whatever floating thing the stream·
> Had caught. The voice was ceas'd; the person lost:
> But looking sad and earnest on the waters,
> By the moon's light I saw, whirl'd round and round,
> A basket; soon I drew it to the bank,
> And nestled curious there an infant lay.[12]

In fifteen lines, Home included a storm, the shrieking of the water spirit, the dead hour of night, a cry of fear, and the moon. All the elements were to become familiarly associated with castles, convents, and caverns. In *Douglas*, conspicuous but not obtrusive in the passage, they are potentially Gothic; they betray a dormant urge to "Gothicize," but little more.

Douglas also sketches the typical Gothic hero and the heroine. Let us look first at the hero.

Douglas is introduced in an aura of mystery. Lord Randolph and a "Young Man" enter, their swords drawn and bloody. "How fares my lord?" asks Lady Randolph.

Lord R.   That it fares well, thanks to this gallant youth,
          Whose valor saved me from a wretched death!
          As down the winding dale I walk'd alone,
          At the cross way four armed men attack'd me:
          Rovers, I judge, from the licentious camp;
          Who would have quickly laid Lord Randolph low,
          Had not this brave and generous stranger come,
          Like my good angel, in the hour of fate,
          And, mocking danger, made my foes his own
          They turn'd upon him; but his active arm
          Struck to the ground, from whence they rose no more,
          The fiercest two; the others fled amain;
          And left him master of the bloody field ...
Lady R.   Have you yet learn'd of him whom we should thank?
          Whom call the saviour of Lord Randolph's life?
Lord R.   I ask'd that question, and he answer'd not;
          But I must know who my deliverer is.
Stranger. A low-born man, of parentage obscure,
          Who nought can boast but his desire to be
          A soldier, and to gain a name in arms.[13]

The "Stranger," who identifies himself as young "Norval," tells of his life on the Grampian Hills, his departure from home, his encounters with rovers, and his meeting with Lord Randolph. Then,

Norval.   I know not how to thank you. Rude I am
          In speech and manners; never till this hour
          Stood I in such a presence; yet, my lord,
          There's something in my breast, which makes me bold
          To say, that Noval ne'er will shame thy favour.[14]

Perhaps the Covent Garden audience which saw *Douglas* in 1757, having learned in the first soliloquy that an infant had disappeared years before, failed to guess that the "Stranger" was that infant grown to manhood. But two decades later the relation between a past event and a "Stranger" was fixed. Early mention that a child had vanished served notice that soon a man would appear whom patches of narration would prove to be that child, appropriately aged.

Home's Douglas resembles the heroes of all Gothic novels and plays until about 1800. Like Walpole's Theodore he enters mysteriously at a critical moment. Like Theodore he is slow to expose his identity—his true origin, indeed, being unknown to himself. Like Theodore he is in the garb of a peasant, but has "something in my breast" which hints that he is no common man. Like Theodore he is reported to have done brave deeds offstage, but he is never actually shown acting heroically. Off the stage, he is related to the Almanzors of the Restoration; on it, he is perpetually *hors de combat*. With the characteristics of this important type I shall be especially concerned.

The Gothic heroine is similarly sketched in Lady Randolph. Obviously a contemporary of Home's, she views her medieval surroundings as though not well acquainted with them. Her emotional, intellectual, and moral complexes are strictly those of a lady of sensibility. Melancholy and harassed, she foreshadows a type persecuted on the stage for decades. For eighteen years she has kept the cause of her grief even from Anna, her constant attendant. Why does she choose the precise moments described in the opening scene to disclose her secret? This question was asked by David Hume,[15] and the play contains no answer. Has her agony been so intense that she has fled to the woods each evening for eighteen years to cry out "Oh Douglas! Douglas!" Or, after those years, does she now first rush to the woods? The questions are directed at the opening motivation, and though unconvincingness is not in itself Gothic, this particular weakness invariably afflicts the typical Gothic plot and action.

Whether or not her motives are peculiarly Gothic, the lady corresponds to the typical heroine in other respects. It is she who has the hidden past, the "sad, sequester'd virtue," she who is the victim of endless machinations, and, finally, she who ends the play with a spectacular dash to the brink of a precipice, where she poses for a moment before plunging to destruction. A distressed Radcliffean maiden, though the Gothic machinery assembled to frighten her is more complex, could be and do no more.

Not present in *Douglas* is a sketch of the typical Gothic protagonist. Home found his villain, Glenalvon, in the Iago tradition. Lacking the tyrant, the Gothic formula was incomplete.

In summary, *Douglas* is an antecedent of Gothic drama in that it contains some qualities of setting, theme, and character which later became associated with specialized machinery in a singular devotion to the ends of mystery, gloom, and terror. The Gothic attitude toward materials is in *Douglas* merely suggested, not exploited. Though Home's "Pseudo-Romantic" tragedy shows an interest in objects and words that impels the spectator to a feeling of mystery and gloom, it reveals no exploitation of the barbarous aspects of medievalism for the specific purpose that distinguishes Gothic plays.

THE COUNTESS OF SALISBURY

Douglas remained isolated in its time as an antecedent of Gothic drama. Neither Home nor any other dramatist wrote another play sufficiently relevant for discussion here. Then, in 1765, Hall Hartson, Irish author of a single play, submitted *The Countess of Salisbury* to the Crow-Street Theatre in Dublin.

Hartson's "tragedy" is nearer than *Douglas* to the Gothic species. Though it does not conform perfectly to the pattern of the typical Gothic play, it must be described as the best representative of one kind of dramatic manifestation of the Gothic Revival. In order to interpret this manifestation, it is necessary to refer once more to the Gothic novel.

It has sometimes been suggested that Dr. Leland's *Longsword, Earl of Salisbury* (1762) should be named with Gothic novels because its scene is medieval and its atmosphere occasionally similar to that of Walpole's "Gothic Story." Both Walpole's and

Leland's novels, it is true, directly represent interest in medievalism, but there is a fundamental difference in the kinds of interest, and, accordingly, in emphases. Attention has already been called to three distinct ways in which medievalism was regarded by 1764. One of these was given expression in Hurd's *Letters on Chivalry and Romance*. Hurd saw in the early romances, and especially in Spenser, a medieval age characterized by nobility of manners, high virtues, and general magnificence. This view gave the primary impetus to Leland's *Longsword*, and it later was reflected, not in the Walpolian Gothic school, but in the romances of Sir Walter Scott and in some nineteenth-century poems of high romance. Quite different was the conventional view which, as I have pointed out, gave rise to *Otranto* and its breed. Walpole's emphasis upon the barbarous aspects of medievalism struck a responsive chord in the late eighteenth century, which continued to prefer this dark view. Therefore most novelists and dramatists followed Walpole's lead, and the characteristic manifestation of the Gothic Revival in literature was of the kind initiated by *The Castle of Otranto. Longsword,* though as truly expressive of the Revival, was neither republished nor imitated in an age which preferred to regard medievalism as barbarous. Leland's (and Hurd's) view had to await a new century.[16]

The Countess of Salisbury, adapted from *Longsword,* bears to the first characteristic Gothic play the same relationship that *Longsword* bears to the first characteristic Gothic novel. Leland's novel and Hartson's play antedated respectively Walpole's novel and play, and both truly represented a view of medievalism. Both, however, fall largely outside the Gothic school as scholarship has defined that school.

Nevertheless, like Scott in the next century, Leland partly reflected the conventional attitude that Walpole's school exploited. Most of *Longsword* concerns the efforts of Salisbury to escape the traps of many enemies on the Continent and to return to his castle in England. In these efforts he is befriended by one Les Roches, who glides in and out of the story, arriving at critical moments to save Salisbury's life. Salisbury, in turn, repeatedly befriends the harassed daughter of Les Roches. In the course of his narrative, the author exposes his characters to various terrors in and around castles, convents, chapels, and dark forests. It is in these episodes—usually limited to passages of paragraph length—that resemblance to the Walpolian school exists.

In dramatizing *Longsword,* Hartson did not overlook those aspects that relate the novel to the horrific school. Indeed, he shifted the emphasis of the novel so that the Gothic elements seem more prominent. The second half of the novel tells of the efforts of Salisbury, who has escaped from the Continent, to recover his castle and his wife from a usurper. On this part the dramatist concentrated. Furthermore, Hartson made another shift of especial importance. In the novel, the central figure is Salisbury; in the play, it is the countess. Hartson emphasized her plight, and thus threw into prominence the persecution theme that was to become so characteristic of Gothic novels and plays.

Nor is this theme the only feature which relates the tragedy to the typical school. By omitting the Continental adventures and centering on the tyrant-heroine situation, the adapter created a need for some special devices of a kind that later playwrights found indispensable. Not many such devices appear, it is true; full accumulation required a generation. Hartson did not attempt to exploit terror by heaping one contrivance on another in order to harass his heroine at every turn. The countess is subjected chiefly to the villain's threats. She is not pursued, like later heroines, through forests where banditti lurk. She is not frozen in terror by supernatural visitors and inexplicable sounds from vacant chambers. She does not flee through subterranean corridors (her lamp extinguished by a sudden gust) to seek refuge in an "antient Abbey"—only to find the prior a menace also.

She is, however, placed in an ancient castle, and Hartson, going beyond Home, specified that it should be in the Gothic style. Act I has "An Avenue leading to a Gothic Castle"; here, and in the dungeons beneath and the forest surrounding, the action takes place. Dark recesses of the castle, though conspicuous in both setting and dialogue, are scarcely exploited as sources of terror, and only one important element of the elaborate machinery that later Gothicists deemed essential is included. Lord Salisbury, in a dungeon, is joined by his wife and Leroches (Leland's Les Roches). Desperate to escape the villain's clutches, he thinks of a means—and thereby opens a way through which a generation of heroines, heroes, and old men similarly incarcerated were to follow him:

> Hear, then. Deep underneath this vaulted ground,
> Curious and close, by our forefathers scooped,
> I do remember me there is a dark
> And secret mine, which leads, by many a maze,
> Without the castle. Not far thence there stands
> An house, for pious uses set apart,
> The hallowed seat of godly brethren: there,
> I fear not, we shall rest secure of ill."

Such a "secret mine" came to appear in almost every Gothic play. Its prevalence was not simply the result of chance or imitation. The device filled a need which was inevitably created by the Gothicists' conception of atmosphere, situation, and action. The problem which Hartson, like a long succession of playwrights after him, posed for his characters was such as could be solved by mechanical expedients. Action in Gothic plays became a matter of tumultuous activity, of assaults and withdrawals, fresh assaults and fresh withdrawals, of flights through horrific machinery, of imprisonment, escape, and pursuit. In conducting these affairs with which he was preoccupied, the Gothicist had urgent need for a battery of physical devices that would aid the flight on the one hand and the pursuit on the other and thus make the spectacle more exciting. Therefore, once the new dramatic species had established the direction it was to take, a machinery of terror accumulated rapidly and grew into a vast paraphernalia.

In addition to introducing an important element of Gothic machinery, Hartson outlined in his Raymond a first dramatic Gothic villain. Though he is to the fully developed villain only as a single subterranean passage is to the fully developed machinery of a Gothic play, Raymond bears certain marks which were to distinguish this special kind of protagonist for at least half a century. His henchman, Grey, who is himself thoroughly in the Iago tradition, comments contemptuously as Raymond enters:

> I hate those motleyed characters;
> Something, I know not what, 'twixt good and ill,
> Yet neither absolute; all good, all ill,
> For me ... This way he moves;
> And, by his gait and gesture, ill at ease.[18]

Here, significantly, the villain of a past age took the measure of the villain of a coming age. Grey describes the central conflict which, from his first appearance on the stage, characterized the Gothic tyrant. This conflict, intensified as decades passed, was ultimately to be resolved in favor of the "good," and thus to transform the villain to hero. There was a long road of torment between Raymond, "ill at ease," and Byron's Manfred, poised to leap from the Jungfrau precipice, but a step on it had been taken.

Brought to the Haymarket stage on August 31, 1767, Hartson's tragedy was well received. Though the novel from which it was taken was never reprinted, the play was revived repeatedly in the next thirty years. It is the nearest antecedent of the Gothic plays which exploited elements it merely suggested. Though analysis shows it to have some qualities that relate it to the Walpolian school, these are employed incidentally. Primarily, *The Countess of Salisbury* represents a rare, not a typical dramatic manifestation of the Gothic Revival.

CHAPTER III

THE FIRST GOTHIC PLAYS

B<small>Y CONSIDERING</small> both the ways in which *Douglas* and *The Countess of Salisbury* foreshadow typical Gothic plays and the ways in which they fail to do so, we have gained a preliminary conception of the species. In this chapter I shall fill in some details of the sketch by describing *The Mysterious Mother* and a few other plays of the decade 1768-1778.

Walpole's tragedy was not quite to Gothic drama as his novel was to Gothic fiction. *The Castle of Otranto* was at once the first Gothic novel and the fount of both Gothic fiction and drama. *The Mysterious Mother* was merely the first Gothic play. Without the novel there might have been no Gothic school. Without the play it is probable that later Gothic plays would have been written essentially as they were and in the number they were.[1]

The dictates of dramatic form which lay heavily upon Walpole, a classicist, tended to curb the excess of horrific elements which characterizes *Otranto*.[2] Though as novelist rules had restrained him not at all, as dramatist he respected and observed the unities, aimed at tragic dignity, and suppressed any lurking impulses to represent such monstrosities as he had assembled in his novel.

> Our Bard, whose head is fill'd with Gothic fancies,
> And teems with ghosts and giants and romances...[3]

exploited, certainly, the attitude of his time toward the barbarous age, played exclusively with mystery, gloom, and terror, and indulged his Gothic propensity from beginning to end, but accomplished all in good "form." *The Mysterious Mother* is sound evidence that Walpole was not a rebel. It is a picture of the barbarous time as seen through the eyes of a classicist and painted in tones of horror for an age which viewed it similarly.

---

[1] For notes to chap. iii, see page 249.

Later playwrights, some of whom knew little and cared less about the "rules," came nearer the excesses of *Otranto* than did its author in his play. Nevertheless, this work represents the true beginning of the Gothic school of drama, and to describe it is, with allowances for later expansion, to describe that school. Its predominant feature is its unrelieved atmosphere of mystery, gloom, and terror. Settings, characters, machinery, theme, and technique are singularly devoted to manufacturing this atmosphere.

THE MYSTERIOUS MOTHER

Of real plot there is little. Sixteen years before the play begins, the husband of the countess was killed while returning home after long absence. The countess learned simultaneously that her husband was dead and that her son Edmund was on that very night to have an assignation with a young woman. She resolved to replace the woman in order to upbraid her son. Overcome by pent-up emotion, however, she failed to identify herself. The fruit of the incestuous union was Adeliza, who at the end of the play is Edmund's sister, daughter, and wife.

To develop and prolong a central mystery, Gothic playwrights characteristically withheld secrets as long as their inventiveness could devise provocative but unrevealing hints. The reader of *The Mysterious Mother* learns nothing of the past event summarized above until the end of the last scene of Walpole's five acts. Scraps of information, scattered throughout, intensify but do not solve the mystery. We learn that for sixteen years, sunk in gloom, the countess has occupied her lonely castle. Inexplicably, she has been generous to the poor and devout in prayer, but has refused the pleas of friars, whose convent adjoins her estate, to receive confession and absolution. She has provided lavishly for Edmund, who lives abroad, but has forbidden him access to the castle. She has reared a "ward," Adeliza.

As the play opens, Florian, Edmund's friend, seeks entrance at the gate and is denied. To his demand for knowledge of the countess, the porter replies enigmatically, himself knowing only that some inscrutable horror hangs over the castle. Florian reports Edmund's death on a battlefield, and a friar conveys the information to the countess, who rejoices. We learn that Edmund has really returned home in secret and has won Adeliza's love. He confronts his mother with protestations of devotion, but is violently repulsed. Friar Benedict, guessing at the cause of the countess' agony and hating her because she has refused confession, vows revenge. He arranges the marriage of Edmund and Adeliza after the mother, thinking Florian was to be the bridegroom, has sanctioned the match. When her son and Adeliza come before her as husband and wife, she falls into successive fits of swooning and madness. Finally, in bursts of coherent utterance, she exposes her secret guilt. Edmund draws his dagger to slay her, but she seizes it and stabs herself. Edmund instructs Adeliza to "take the veil" and announces his intention to seek death in war.

The play was never acted. Though he permitted Mason to make alterations to fit it for the stage, Walpole continued to believe his play too disgusting for representation:

From the time that I first undertook the foregoing scenes, I never flattered myself that they would be proper to appear on the stage. The subject is so horrid, that I thought it would shock, rather than give satisfaction to an audience... The subject is more truly horrid than even that of Oedipus.[4]

Walpole did not invent the "horrid" subject. He had once heard that a despairing woman had confessed the substance of the story to Archbishop Tillotson.[5] But he did choose it for his one serious attempt at drama, and, in view of his stated awareness that it was unfit for the stage, the choice at first seems unexplainable. His remarks on this point, however, are very enlightening.

... I found it so truly tragic in the essential springs of terror and pity, that I could not resist the impulse of adapting it to the scene, though it could never be practicable to produce it there. I saw, too, that it would admit of great situation, of lofty characters, of those unforeseen strokes, which have a singular effect in operating a revolution in the passions, and in interesting the spectator: it was capable of furnishing not only a contrast of characters, but *a contrast of virtue and vice in the same character;* and *by laying the scene in what age and country I pleased pictures of ancient manners might be drawn*, and many allusions to historic events introduced....[6]

Perhaps—in view of the completed work—we may question Walpole's statements as to the opportunity to deal with a great situation, lofty characters, and allusions to historic events. It may be suspected that the choice was made chiefly because the author could lay the scene "in what age and country I pleased." Free choice of time and place was highly attractive to the author of *Otranto*. We can sense the fundamental differences in preoccupation by considering how an Elizabethan dramatist, for example, would have treated the subject. Shakespeare or Webster would have chosen Rennaissance Italy, and would have depicted the people and scenes in which Elizabethan dramatists and their public were interested.[7] But before reading his version, we might know the setting exploited by the inveterate Gothicist.

The theme of incest, which had been treated on the English stage by Beaumont and Fletcher, Ford, and Dryden, among others, and which was to be treated again by Byron and Shelley, is itself little relevant in an analysis of the play. The point of significance is that the reader cannot guess until the last scene that the theme *is* incest. The tragedy is constructed like a sentence in which each word until the last deepens the mystery. Walpole's skill in handling this technique—which obviously was eminently suited to a kind of drama that specialized in mystery, gloom, and terror—was not equaled by any of the later playwrights who gave their best talents to its perfection.

To the end, the play sustains the mood of Florian as he mounts the platform before the castle:

> What awful silence! how these antique towers
> And vacant courts dull the suspended soul,
> Till expectation wears the cast of fear;
> And fear, half-ready to become devotion,
> Mumbles a kind of mental orison,
> It knows not wherefore:—
> What a kind of being is circumstance!
> I am a soldier, and were yonder battlements
> Garnish'd with combatants, and cannon-mouthed,
> My daring breast would bound with exultation,
> And glorious hopes enliven this drear scene.
> Now dare not I scarce tread to my own hearing,
> Lest Echo borrow Superstition's tongue,
> And seem to answer me, like one departed.
> I met a peasant, and inquir'd the way:
> The carle, not rude of speech, but like the tenant
> Of some night-haunted ruin, bore an aspect
> Of horror, worn to habitude. He bade
> God bless me; and pass'd on. I urg'd him farther:
> Good master, cried he, go not to the castle;
> There sorrow ever dwells, and moping misery.
> I press'd him yet—None there, said he, are welcome,
> But now and then a mass-priest, and the poor,
> To whom the pious countess deals her alms,
> On covenant, that each revolving night
> They beg of heaven the health of her son's soul,
> And of her own: But often as returns
> The twentieth of September, they are bound
> Fast from the midnight watch to pray till morn.
> More would he not disclose, or knew not more.[8]

What is the mystery of this place? Until the end nothing is known by the reader or by any character except her who for sixteen years has borne some heavy secret. With each additional scrap of intelligence, the mystery deepens and the air oppresses more. Dark word piled on dark word, as in the passage quoted, contributes to a mounting sense of gloom and terror.

Following Florian's soliloquy, the simple porter intimates that the castle, its mistress, and the behavior within the walls are yet more awful than the visitor has instinctively felt them to be:

> Canst thou in hair-cloths vex those dainty limbs?
> Canst thou on reeking pavements and cold marble,
> In meditation pass the live-long night?
> ...
> These are the deeds, my youngster, must draw down
> My lady's ever heaven-directed eye.'

When Florian replies jauntily, the porter expresses shock and apprehension:

> Angels defend us!
> Yon mould'ring porch, for sixteen years and more,
> Has not been struck with such unhallow'd sounds.

Their conversation is interrupted as, silent, in weeds, crucifix in hand, the countess crosses the stage. The porter then confides his own awe:

> ...But if cold moonshine, deepening every frown
> Of these impending towers, invite her steps,
> She issues forth.—Beshrew me, but I tremble,
> When my own keys discharge the draw-bridge chains,
> And rattle through the castle's farmost vaults.

What ails the countess? Martin, a friar who for sixteen years has vainly sought the cause of her gloom, states the problem of the play:

> What is this secret sin, this untold tale,
> That art cannot extract, nor penance cleanse?[10]

And again he urges:

> Then whither turn
> To worm her secret out?[11]

Half a century later, when Byron's tortured Manfred climbs the Jungfrau and calls up demons, the problem is the same. Between the countess and Manfred fifty years of Gothic protagonists were inwardly consumed for causes which it was the business of the drama ultimately to reveal.

The most casual examination of the vocabulary alone betrays the fact that Walpole's primary interest lay not where that of earlier tragic dramatists lay—in character, delineation of passion, and portrayal of action consequent upon a tragic flaw and leading to catastrophe—but in manufacturing mystery, gloom, and terror. Conspicuous in the passages I have cited are expressions that are loaded with dark suggestion: "antique towers," "vacant courts," "drear scene," "night-haunted ruin," "moping misery," "midnight watch," "cold marble," "mould'ring porch," "unhallow'd sounds," "cold moonshine," "impending towers," "farmost vaults," and "secret sin." Language, characters, setting, and action are combined in a pattern of horror.

Employed with these is a specialized dramatic technique which involves repeated hints and veiled comments which goad the search for the protagonist's secret. Thus the gloom of the castle is intended to suggest the presence of an unknown evil. The porter is made to whisper his secret dread. Supernatural portents spell impending doom. Storms of thunder and lightning and the incoherent ravings of the countess indicate but do not name a mortal sin. The technique of mystification was introduced in *The Mysterious Mother* and practiced by Gothic playwrights for half a century. It is found so universally in the plays to be discussed that it may be well to characterize it further by contrasting it with the technique of another age and another kind of drama. Shakespeare—or indeed any Elizabethan tragic writer—followed a quite different method which required that the audience always know the secret.[12] Even in *Macbeth* it is impossible for a reader or spectator to ask, "What ails Macbeth?" Other characters, to be sure, observing the tyrant during the banquet scene, strive to imagine the cause of his agitation; but the audience, from its vantage point, is preadvised, and its attention is drawn not to a mystery but to the destructive force asserting itself in the protagonist. Similarly, in *Hamlet* we are never tempted and teased into guessing that Claudius bears a black secret; he betrays no marks of villainy until we have been told that he is a villain. On the other hand, the "tragic" writers of Walpole's school invariably brought their criminals to the stage wrapped in mysterious gloom and loudly prompted the audience to find the cause. The original impulse to Gothicize, an impulse arising from the dark ruins of a barbarous time, dictated the nature of the dramatic technique just as it did the accumulation of special machinery. Technique and machinery were devised to accord with the castles and convents which had suggested a species concentrated on exploiting mystery, gloom, and terror.

Some horrific elements were certain to appear in a play by the author of *Otranto*. As we have seen, Walpole was careful to remind his reader through dialogue that the castle is complete with vaults, dark towers, and vacant courts, and of course some of these were physically represented. No sliding panels are in the play, no heroine flees through underground passages, and there is no actual visitation of the supernatural. But the supernatural is nevertheless conspicuous in narrative passages, and must be accounted a major element of the machinery. Martin, having ordered a group of orphans to march ahead to the spot where the count fell, "sixteen years ago this day," hears one of them speak the terror of all:

> Oh, father, but I dare not pass without you
> By the church-porch. They say the Count sits there,
> With clotted locks, and eyes like burning stars.[13]

Urged further, the children go on. In a moment a violent storm strikes, and they rush back, crying that demons rode the air, that lightning struck the ruined monument, that the shield of arms was shivered to splinters, and that the cross itself crashed to earth.

Later dramatists boldly stage such scenes. Walpole's respect for convention relegated the incident to off-stage action.

The movement of *The Mysterious Mother* is not, like that of Elizabethan tragedy, a forward movement. It is a movement backward in time, since the whole problem is to find the truth of a past event. Though later Gothic playwrights conducted forward action, we are repeatedly reminded, even in all the tumult, that the real center of interest lies behind, not ahead.

Elements of setting, character, machinery, and technique, combined for a single purpose, make *The Mysterious Mother* the first play in the Gothic tradition. To be sure, it lacks much of the full paraphernalia assembled as the years passed. Yet it is evident that Walpole found the right working combination for a Gothic drama, just as he had found it four years earlier for a Gothic novel. *Douglas* had anticipated an attitude toward materials, and *The Countess of Salisbury* had struck the theme that was to become most prevalent; *The Mysterious Mother* devised a plan for exploiting selected materials, and established a new species.

OTHER PLAYS OF THE DECADE

After an interval of fourteen years, in which no Gothic novel followed *The Castle of Otranto,* Clara Reeve's *The Old English Baron; A Gothic Story* was published in 1778. Furthermore, no great amount of Gothic prose fiction appeared until Mrs. Radcliffe's *The Castles of Athlin and Dunbayne* (1789); from that time on the flood surged through the final decade of the century. Therefore the fact that the decade after *The Mysterious Mother* showed little activity in Gothic drama does not indicate that dramatists lagged behind novelists in expressing the Gothic Revival. On the contrary, dramatists showed the keener interest up to 1789.

The fact remains, however, that for ten years after *The Mysterious Mother* no play evinces primary concern with Gothic exploitation. Neither do we find that dramatic interest in any other particular materials crystallized during that period. Heterogeneity, chief characteristic of drama in the age as a whole, seems especially conspicuous during these years, which found playwrights experimenting wildly in their haste to discover the subjects which would catch on. Most notable in the time, of course, were the masterpieces of Goldsmith and Sheridan. Besides these, the period saw several sentimental comedies by Cumberland and many farces by Foote. But the great mass of dramatic literature was of such varied sorts as to make impossible any assertion of a dominant trend. The types written included everything from tragedy to extravaganza; the themes indicate frantic groping. Scenes were laid in ancient Syracuse and in contemporary England, in the Far East and in Squire Western's mansion. On every side was evidence that dramatists were struggling to free themselves from pseudoclassic shackles. In all the confusion the Gothic impulse was perhaps no more vital than any other, but there is evidence that it was growing.

Playwrights revealed awareness of a new spirit, and their works suggest that Gothic materials were circulating actively enough to draw attention. *Zenobia* (D. L. Feb. 1768), Murphy's attempt at a Roman subject, includes a note of romance in both theme and setting. Home's *Fatal Discovery* (D. L. Feb. 1769), a treatment of Ossianic material, includes a scene in a "Romantic Cave"—a setting later prevalent in Gothic plays; castle, convent, and cavern, indeed, became inseparable trio. Bickerstaffe's gloomy farce called *'Tis Well 'Tis No Worse* (D. L. 1770), has as a prominent feature a sliding secret panel possibly picked from *Otranto*. *Almida* (D. L. Jan. 1771), by Dorothy Celesia, the daughter of a cult-of-the-ruin poet, David Mallet, has medieval knights for male characters, though the scene is ancient Syracuse; the incongruity epitomizes the general bewilderment of playwrights.[14] The significance of these plays lies in the fact that although they are *not*

Gothic yet Gothic elements from the *Zeitgeist* appeared even in plays where they obviously did not belong.

Perhaps the most remarkable insinuation of Gothic elements into a play in which they were grossly inappropriate to both time and place occurred in Murphy's *Grecian Daughter* (D. L. Feb. 1772), a work which perfectly exemplifies the desperate cross-purposes of the age. In it the clash of ill-assorted elements in theme, form, setting, and characters is astonishing.

The Grecian Daughter is a pseudoclassic tragedy. Its scene is laid in ancient Syracuse, and its plot, the *Biographia Dramatica* advises, was taken from Valerius Maximus' *De Pietate in Parentes*. Nothing Gothic belonged to this combination, certainly; but Gothic properties appear, principally in settings and vocabulary. There is frequent evidence of preoccupation with those objects which, in poetry of the ruin, had heralded the Gothic Revival. Murphy, like Walpole, chose words loaded with suggestion; thus, for example, Philotas explains the fate of Evander:

> At the midnight hour,
> Silent conveyed him up the steep ascent,
> To where the elder Dionysius formed,
> On the sharp summit of the pointed rock,
> Which overhangs the deep, a dungeon drear;
> Cell within cell, a labyrinth of horror,
> Deep caverned in the cliff....[15]

The setting is "A Wild Romantic Scene amidst overhanging Rocks; a Cavern on one side." Almost every descriptive passage is laden with terms like "craggy cliffs," "pointed rocks," "midnight gloom," "dead hour of night," "hallow'd mould," and "dismal sepulchre." The atmosphere becomes so heavy with Gothic associations that the audience would perhaps sense no impropriety if suddenly the turrets of a Gothic castle or convent should protrude above the trees of ancient Syracuse.

The play is not Gothic, but Gothic properties have so far intruded as to give it almost a legitimate claim to inclusion in the

Gothic drama. "A sound comes hollow murmuring through the vaulted aisles," says Euphrasia—and an audience which had read *Otranto* must have forgotten that the time was ancient and the temple Grecian. Euphrasia resembles no antique heroine so much as she resembles the Gothic Isabellas and Emilies in harassed flight through secret door, labyrinth, and forest. Evander, emerging specterlike from his gloomy cavern, must be identified with the countless old men imprisoned in the haunted chambers of the Gothic castles. Dionysius, Greek in name only, is the haughty, erratic, gloomy tyrant who rushes in and out calling threats and ultimatums. Like all the Gothic protagonists, he is disturbed by conscience:

> ... With the scorpion stings
> Of conscience lashed, despair and horror seize him,
> And guilt but serves to goad his tortured mind
> To blacker crimes...[16]

Though an incredible mélange of motifs, *The Grecian Daughter* includes more Gothic elements than any other single kind. That fact may account for its popularity—a popularity which grew while the Gothic craze was rampant. In number of revivals and sustained runs it vied with *Douglas* and even *Hamlet*. Certainly none of its success can be attributed to its merits as tragedy. After a dignified opening, the action degenerates, all sense of inevitability gone, to the scuffling and rushing that characterized "tragic" pieces from *The Countess of Salisbury* to Maturin's *Bertram*. Nor can the many revivals be accounted for by any predilection of star actors for the principal male role. The emaciated, sick, and drooping Evander, half dead at the opening of the play and, after being suckled by his daughter, grotesquely revitalized near the end to a last spasm of agility, was not a part which actors who desired to roar and brandish swords could have relished. Very possibly the success resulted from the fact that Murphy, testing for the winds of fashion, had clutched, among others, the

Gothic elements floating in the air of his time. Thus, perhaps accidentally, he insured the popularity of his play in the next forty years.

Several playwrights between 1768 and 1778 treated English and Scottish history, and the choice of materials suggests possible Gothic interests. In none of these plays is the emphasis on the historical events with which the principal characters are customarily associated. It is on the personal trials of kings and queens, knights and ladies. Dr. Franklin's *Matilda* (D. L. Jan. 1775), set in the time of William the Conqueror, introduces some natural settings and betrays a feeling for romance not apparent in the same author's *Earl of Warwick*, ten years earlier. The fact suggests that *Douglas*, frequently revived, had in the interim spread its "melancholy gloom" over other dramatists. Similar settings and notes of romance are found in Henry Hull's *Henry Second; or, The Fall of Rosamond* (C. G. May 1773), in John Jackson's *Eldred, or The British Father* (Hay. July 1775), and in the same author's *British Heroine* (C. G. May 1778). In none of these is there conspicuous use of Gothic machinery, and rarely is there exploitation of Gothic settings. Occasionally the dramatist has specified Gothic architecture, but there is no appreciable use of it to arouse emotions of characters transported to the medieval scene. Of this group *The British Father*, mildly Gothic in its total effect, is the most relevant here. Its scenes lie in dark groves, among trees and rocks; some use is made of natural settings to evoke expressions of gloom. Edwena, who before the play begins had been saved by Elidure and had married him, opens the dialogue in a grove at dusk; she anticipated by fourteen years the Radcliffean maiden with her lute:

> Peace, cease my song; in vain thy charms attempt
> To chase away this melancholy gloom,
> Whose sable mantle shadowing the soul
> Presents a dreary prospect to the sight
> And spreads o'er nature's works a dusky hue.[17]

Act III presents "A Wood, with a Romantic Rock." It was perhaps the very first dramatic use of this particular setting, introduction of which meant the beginning of a clearing out of Augustan stage sets and the inauguration of a period of new painting and carpentry. This particular "Romantic Rock" was a towering one that cast a "frown" over the landscape; thus Edwena:

> There tow'rs the cliff that frowns upon the vale,
> Striking a sable tinge through twilight gloom;
> All still! all hushed!—no footsteps but my own
> Disturb the silent horrors of the place.[18]

Though talky, actionless, and stilted, the play strives to break its pseudoclassic bonds. Though it betrays no especial interest in Gothic terrors, it does leave the impression that the playwright deliberately laid scenes where cliffs and rocks loom high, where trees cast gloomy shadows, and where footsteps resound in vaulted halls.

PERCY

Another play which depicted an earlier time is *Percy* (C. G. Dec. 1777), Hannah More's discussion, in medieval setting, of a contemporary ethical problem. It may seem surprising to find Mrs. More in an account of Gothic drama; indeed, there is some incongruity in her trafficking with any other than sacred drama, for her remarks on the theater ally her with Gosson, Prynne, and Collier. Anticipating criticism from the publication of her plays in a volume with these comments, she explained her dramatic activity:

I was led to flatter myself it might be rendering that inferior service to society which the fabricator of safe and innocent amusements may be reasonably supposed to confer, to attempt some theatrical compositions, which, whatever other defects might be justly imputable to them, should at least be found to have been written on the side of virtue and modesty; and which should neither hold out any corrupt image to the mind nor any impure description to the fancy.[19]

The plays were products of her idealistic youth; she had believed that her efforts might turn the drama into a more "proper" channel:

> I had been led to entertain that common, but, as I now must think, delusive and groundless hope, that the stage, under certain regulations, might be converted into a school of virtue; and thus, like many others, inferred, by a seemingly reasonable conclusion, that though a bad play would always be a bad thing, yet the representation of a good one might become not only harmless, but useful; and that it required nothing more than a correct judgment and a critical selection, to transform a pernicious pleasure into a profitable entertainment.[20]

The significance of Mrs. More's comments will appear hereafter, when I discuss at length the vital relation between moral solicitude and Gothic drama. For the present, it will suffice to call attention to the fact that this reformer, intent on writing *moral* drama, composed a play which must be included in an account of *Gothic* drama. Almost twenty years later, Joanna Baillie, who positively had no thought that plays should have other than a purely moral purpose, published a collection of her own, no fewer than ten of which are Gothic. As we examine the species, it will become increasingly clear that Gothic drama—even plays like those by Lewis, which contain an elaborate diablerie—is thoroughly moral; indeed, we shall see that the Gothic was virtually "converted into a school of virtue" such as Mrs. More had imagined might be established.

Mrs. More's *Percy*, like Home's *Douglas*, is related primarily to ballad material and secondarily to the Gothic. The past event which underlies the action of most Gothic plays was here a border dispute between Douglas and Percy. In the aftermath which forms the tragedy, the son of Douglas and the son of Percy, together with young Douglas' wife, meet death. Young Percy had been betrothed to Elwina until her father, Lord Raby, enraged at insults received while hunting in the Cheviot Hills, had forbidden them to meet. Percy had gone thereafter to fight the Saracens, and Lord Raby had sought revenge by compelling his daughter to marry Douglas, who was kept ignorant of the true reason for the match. But in the years following the marriage, Elwina had been cold to her husband, and he, grown suspicious, had become a tyrant. The opening scene finds Douglas doubting his wife's virtue. News comes of Percy's death, and Elwina faints in the presence of her husband and her father. As she revives, she calls on Percy, and thus multiplies her husband's suspicions. Percy, escaped from captivity, directly appears, unaware that Elwina has married. They meet, part, and meet again, innocently. At the final meeting, Douglas traps Percy, and they withdraw to fight outdoors. Presently news is brought that Douglas has been killed and that he had ordered poison given his wife in event of his death. Elwina dutifully accepts the command, but Douglas enters, states that in reality Percy had fallen, and accuses his wife of weeping for her lover's death. Elwina retires to her chamber and drinks the poison. Lord Raby then discloses the truth, that Elwina and Percy had been betrothed, that Percy was unaware of her marriage, and that the meetings were innocent. Filled with remorse, Douglas stabs himself.

The author's purpose was to deal, in the light of contemporary social ethics, with the conflict between a woman's passion for her lover and her duty to the husband she had been forced to marry. The subject might have been worked out more convincingly in a modern setting, but Mrs. More, evidently responding to a fashion now widespread, turned to the late medieval period and opened her first scene in "A Gothic Hall." And just as more typical Gothicists carried eighteenth-century ladies of high virtue and sensibility to medieval scenes for the thrilling registration of their reactions, so she thrust Elwina, an intellectual contemporary with a contemporary problem, into a Gothic castle and the affairs of the Douglas and Percy families.

Besides the settings, all of which represent the Gothic castle or the gardens with "the turrets visible through the trees," some characters are Gothic types. Elwina is the persecuted heroine—though indeed the greatest Gothic crisis in her persecution had occurred before the opening of the play; she tells how her father, angered at Percy, had forced her to marry Douglas:

> But who shall tell the agonies I felt?
> My barbarous father forc'd me to dissolve
> The tender vows himself had bid me form—
> He dragg'd me trembling, dying, to the altar,
> I sigh'd, I struggled, fainted, and complied.[21]

Later such scenes were staged, not reported, and an elaborate machinery was devised to introduce and accompany the action. Elwina behaves in her medieval setting not as a medieval bride might be expected to act, but as one born to another manner. Her fear of the surroundings and of her barbarous father reflects the eighteenth-century reaction to the age in which her author has placed her. She solves her medieval problems with full benefit of the later enlightenment. For example, when her lover arrives and asserts his prior claim to her, Elwina answers:

> Percy, hear me.
> When I was robb'd of all my peace of mind,
> My cruel fortune left me still one blessing,
> One solitary blessing, to console me:
> It was my fame.—'Tis a rich jewel, Percy,
> And I must keep it spotless, and unsoil'd;
> But thou wouldst plunder what e'en Douglas spar'd,
> And rob this single gem of all its brightness.[22]

Here Pamela, Clarissa, Evelina, and others form an invisible chorus.

Some of the mystery of the typical tyrant envelops Douglas. Before his first appearance, Edric and Birtha discuss him. Gothic playwrights came infallibly to prepare the entrance of their villains by means of some such dialogue as the following.

Birtha. What may this mean? Earl Douglas has enjoin'd thee
    To meet him here in private?
Edric. Yes, my sister,
    And this injunction I have oft receiv'd:
    But when he comes, big with some painful secret,
    He starts, looks wild, then drops ambiguous hints,
    Frowns, hesitates, turns pale, and says 'twas nothing;
    Then feigns to smile, and by his anxious care
    To prove himself at ease, betrays his pain.
Birtha. Since my short sojourn here, I've mark'd this earl,
    And though the ties of blood unite us closely,
    I shudder at his haughtiness of temper,
    Which not his gentle wife, the bright Elwina,
    Can charm to rest.[28]

Birtha pointedly summarizes the relations of Douglas and Elwina: "Yet some dark mystery involves their fate." As in *The Mysterious Mother,* the problem is posed for the reader or spectator to concentrate on. What ails Douglas? Mrs. More does not withhold the answer for so long as Walpole had, but the essential technique of mystification is the same. Douglas differs from the typical villain in one respect: he bears no knowledge of an evil deed, but is himself the victim of Lord Raby's plan for revenge. If the cause of his gloom differs, however, the effects do not. He shows unstable emotions, makes abrupt decisions, and abuses himself and others by violent changes of mind and mood. At one moment he exits in kindness and humility; at the very next, he reënters "in great agitation," a state which we shall find quite "normal" in later villains. Breaking in, breaking out, breaking in again with mounting desperation, Douglas has scarcely time even to pause in that theatrical "musing posture" which came to be the habitual pose of the Gothic villain—and of the Byronic hero—when not in motion.

CHAPTER IV

ADAPTATION AND BURLESQUE

TWELVE YEARS separated *The Castle of Otranto* from *The Champion of Virtue; A Gothic Story*. Another twelve passed before publication of Mrs. Radcliffe's *Castles of Athlin and Dunbayne*. Not until 1789, nearly a quarter of a century after its first start, did Gothic fiction begin to flourish. Mrs. Radcliffe's four major works and Lewis' *Monk* were all products of the last decade of the century.

Gothic drama had an earlier, somewhat swifter growth. Dramatic exploitation of Gothic elements began in earnest within ten years after *The Mysterious Mother*. By 1792, the date of the first English translation of Schiller's *Die Räuber*—after which the history of Gothic plays becomes somewhat complicated by the intrusion of foreign materials—dramatists had written a number of plays as outstanding in their way as were the novels of Mrs. Radcliffe and Lewis in theirs. In short, Gothic drama flowered a full decade earlier than Gothic fiction. Examination of the more outstanding specimens is postponed to the following chapter to permit immediate discussion of the first adaptation of *Otranto* and the earliest burlesques.

THE FIRST ADAPTATION OF OTRANTO
THE COUNT OF NARBONNE

Although Gothic plays became numerous earlier than Gothic novels, it is not to be forgotten that they owed their original debt to the novel. From *The Castle of Otranto* the dramatic school took its primary impetus, its essential characteristics, and the direction of its development. The extent of influence exerted by the first Gothic novel upon drama is difficult to estimate. Well before 1790 an accumulated stock of Gothic elements had become the common property of the age. To this paraphernalia, which

Walpole had begun, other writers contributed, and from it they borrowed. The identity of individual contribution was lost in the mass, and precise debts of playwrights and novelists to one another are difficult to trace. We can be certain only that all of them were ultimately indebted to Walpole. The fixing of immediate debts becomes even more uncertain as we examine the plays written in the last ten years of the century. By 1795 even so-called adaptations of particular novels included so much of the common pool of materials and motifs that we cannot always guess what has been adapted; sometimes even an explicit acknowledgment of source proves false.

However, the direct impact of *The Castle of Otranto* in the form of dramatic adaptation can be dealt with confidently. The first dramatization of the novel was *The Count of Narbonne* (C. G. Nov. 1781), by Robert Jephson. Examination of this work, involving as it does several comparisons with the important original, must be somewhat detailed.

Jephson undertook to discover how successfully the scenes of *Otranto* could be represented on the stage. He thought of himself as a pioneer Gothic dramatist, and accordingly proceeded with cautious respect for the theater.[1] The gigantic helmet which drops from the ceiling, the portraits which bleed at the nose, sigh, and descend to the floor, the giant arms and legs deposited about the castle, the genuine apparitions, the "clank of more than mortal armor," the final catastrophe which begins with a clap of thunder and ends with the appearance of "the form of Alfonso, dilated to an immense magnitude" in the center of the ruins—these, and other features not so gross, the first adapter of the first Gothic novel discreetly omitted.

Critics and public were pleased, and Walpole, who had been active in advising Jephson, wrote to a correspondent thus:

---

[1] For notes to chap. iv, see pages 249–250.

The Count of Narbonne was played last night with great applause and without a single murmur of disapprobation. Miss Younge charmed me. She played with intelligence that was quite surprising. The applause of one of her speeches lasted a minute, and recommenced twice before the play could go on. I am sure you will be pleased with the conduct, and the easy beautiful language of the play, and struck with her acting.[2]

I shall quote at length from the critical account of the play published in *The London Chronicle,* for it both indicates the general approval of the work and suggests how far critics were willing to go in accepting a theatrical piece made of Gothic materials:

The play is opened by Manfred, now Raymond, Count of Narbonne, in the most interesting period of the story. He has just received the challenge, in which his rights to Narbonne are questioned; and whilst he laments, to his confidant, the prophetic curse that had been denounced against his family, which appeared to be confirmed by a divorce from Hortensia, and a marriage with Isabella, the contracted bride of his deceased son. This is opposed by the good Priest, whose character is given with increased display, and is finely written throughout. Theodore is introduced with more favorable circumstances, and his love for Adelaide originates in an encounter, wherein he saves her from ruffians, who had attempted to carry her off. The successive discoveries of his birth, of his rights to the province, unjustly usurped by the father of Raymond; and of his resemblance to his murdered grandfather, all produced a striking theatrical effect; and the last was greatly heightened, as by an easy and natural event he appears in the real armour of Alphonso. These with the agitations of the Count, whose afflictions deserve consideration, as he suffers for the crime of his father rather than his own—the patient yet dignified fortitude of the injured Hortensia—and the tender attachment of the unfortunate Adelaide form the principal circumstances of the dramatic action. Isabella, though still an object in the drama, does not appear from her messages from the sanctuary delivered by Austin; and her father, with his train of knights, is totally discarded. Amidst so many objects in the original tale, all would not be adopted, as they were much too numerous for a tragedy; but more might have been given in event, the fewer in narrative. The author was probably conscious that his strength lay in narratives, and every figure, every ornamental flower of descriptive poetry is exhausted to advise them. The catastrophe is greatly heightened, and the circumstances managed with better attention to the character of the Count. He thinks he sees the hand of Isabella joined by Austin to Theodore; this fatal sight, which extinguishes at once all hopes of his love and ambition, inflames him to madness, and he draws his sword, though in a place of sanctuary, and rushes on Theodore, who is defended by the armour of Alphonso. Disappointed in his principal object, he darts the vengeful blow, as he thinks, at Isabella, but it penetrates to the bosom of his daughter. At this fatal moment, Hortensia appears, and Raymond, unable to bear her anguish and his own stabs himself and expires, imploring pardon at her feet. Hortensia, overborne by the horrid sight of her murdered daughter and husband at her feet, sinks in the agonies of despair, and a deathlike stupor which precedes dissolution. The race of the usurper being thus extinct puts a period to the portentous calamities with which the state has been inflicted, and Theodore peaceably succeeds to the possession of his ancestors. The dresses and scenery were happily adapted throughout, and the play went off with warm and general applause.[3]

This detailed review indicates the extent of the alterations and additions employed by the adapter. It is perfectly apparent that the reviewer took the work seriously; there is even an indication that he regarded it as a great play. Another note of real approval, written later, comes from Mrs. Inchbald, who was one of those who regarded Jephson as "warm from Shakespeare's school":

The Count of Narbonne proved to be his last, and his best composition.—Terror is here ably excited by descriptions of the preternatural. Horror, by the portraiture of guilt, and passion by the view of suffering innocence. These are three passions which, divided, might each constitute a tragedy; and all these powerful engines of the mind and heart are here most happily combined to produce that end,—and each forms a lesson of morality.[4]

Though mistaken in naming this Jephson's last play,[5] Mrs. Inchbald, writing twenty-two years after the initial performance, at a time when Gothic playwrights had become infinitely bolder and the display of horrific effects accordingly fuller, accurately named the main principles on which Gothic plays were constructed. Terror excited by the preternatural and the supernatural in a setting of medieval barbarous ruins, horror by the depiction of the gloomy tyrant inwardly consumed by secret guilt, and passion aroused by the plight of the persecuted maiden: these were the means and ends of the playwrights of the Gothic school. The implications of Mrs. Inchbald's final sentence—"and each forms a lesson of morality"—must await discussion in a later chapter.[8] The influence of moral purpose on the development of Gothic drama, as I have suggested in connection with *Percy*, was vital.

Though the adapter eliminated its grossest elements, the essential qualities of Walpole's novel were retained. The darkness and gloom of the medieval scene are recreated in the atmosphere of the play. The castle, over which hangs a prophetic curse, remains prominent, as does the convent, with its vaults, aisles, and robed figures. The tormented tyrant-usurper and the persecuted trio of two women and a man are Walpole's. Other features include a subterranean passage (though no scene actually shows it); a vocabulary which denotes preoccupation with medieval objects of terror; and numerous narrative passages in the style of the original. In short, those characteristics of *Otranto* remain that a cautious author and a cautious theater manager of 1781 thought compatible with the conventions of drama and the taste of an audience.

Raymond, Count of Narbonne (the Manfred of Walpole's novel), represents to 1781 an outstanding development of the Gothic stage villain and offers us a first opportunity to expand acquaintance with this, the most significant Gothic type. Rash and often raging, wrapped in mysterious gloom, Raymond is a tyrant of wicked purposes, yet, for all this, a man who in his agony appears more sinned against than sinning. He differs from the typical Gothic villain only in the fact that when the action begins he does not himself know the truth of the evil past event. He suspects that an ancestor had been guilty of crime, for the descendants are afflicted by a curse. Tortured by doubt, he demands that a servant tell him the truth:

> But, prythee, tell,
> (Nor let a fear to wound thy master's pride
> Restrain thy licens'd speech), hast thou e'er heard
> My father Raymond—cast not down thy eye!—
> By any indirect or bloody means,
> Procur'd that instrument, Alphonso's will,
> That made him heir to Narbonne?[7]

At length he learns that his father had gained title to Narbonne by murder; the consequent curse has wiped out Raymond's descendants and left him unable to perpetuate his claim. Thus, laden with grief that two sons have died in infancy and the third at maturity, Raymond is at the outset a guiltless man on whom afflictions for another's crimes have been visited.

In desperation, he sends for Austin, a holy man, and reveals his torment:

> Oh, father, did you know the conflict here,
> How love and conscience are at war within me...[8]

To escape the curse, he resolves to divorce the barren Hortensia and marry Isabel, his son's intended bride. Thereafter the pangs of conscience increase, and his actions grow ever more vicious. In scene after scene he rushes to confront his wife, Austin, or Theodore, issues an ultimatum, and abruptly wheels and departs. He develops the fierce and sudden temper of all the barbarous tyrants created to terrify heroines in the medieval castles of Gothic literature. When Theodore crosses him, he cries instantly, "Away with him!" When he suddenly guesses that Isabel loves Theodore, he exclaims his immediate purpose to kill the hero and carry his heart to Isabel. Finally, when he reaches the convent where Adelaide (Walpole's Matilda) and Theodore are being married, his blind rage mistakes Adelaide for Isabel, and he murders his own daughter. As suddenly, finding his error, he begs Theodore to kill him, and, when the hero declines, instantly dispatches himself.

In depicting the strokes of conscience that torture Raymond, Jephson introduced a dramatic technique that soon became conventional. This consists in confronting a villain with something he cannot bear to see. Theatrically spectacular, the device often gave the audience its very first clue that a certain character was a man of evil. One who suddenly halted, started back, his face ashen and his entire body "in great agitation," thus exposed his wicked past as clearly as though he had stated it. The list of objects a Gothic villain could not abide grew long as decades passed; it came to include a certain spot in the castle, a certain tree in the forest, a certain precipice, a suit of armor, a portrait, a statue, a shield, a sword, a dagger, a birthmark, and many other objects innocuous to the innocent but appalling to the guilty eye.[9] Jephson employed the device first in a narrative passage; Raymond, questioning Hortensia to find whether she knows of his father's guilt, hears this account of an incident that had long disturbed her:

> Your absence on the Italian embassy
> Left him, you know, alone to my fond care.
> Long had some hidden grief, like a slow fire,
> Wasted his vitals; on the bed of death,
> One object seem'd to harrow up his soul,
> The picture of Alphonso in the chamber:
> On that his eye was set. Methinks I see him:
> His ashy hue, his grizzled, bristling hair,
> His palms wide-spread. For ever would he cry,
> "That awful form—how terrible he frowns!
> See how he bares his livid, leprous breast,
> And points the deadly chalice!"[10]

The second use of the technique, which involves Raymond himself, is dramatically represented. Theodore, going to help repel the attack on the castle, had seized the first suit of armor at hand—by chance, that of the assassinated Alphonso. Suddenly confronted by the hero in this armor, Raymond takes him for a specter.

Count. (starting) Ha! angels, shelter me!
Theo. Why starts he thus?
Count. Art miracles renew'd?
Art thou not risen from the mould'ring grave?
And in the awful majesty of death,
'Gainst nature, and the course of mortal thought,
Assum'st the likeness of a living form,
To blast my soul with horror?"[11]

The very obvious echo of *Hamlet* illustrates how playwrights "borrowed" striking utterances in moments of crisis.[12]

Theodore is a first clear sketch of the type that was to remain "hero" until the end of the century. Douglas, in Home's play, gave opportunity for a preliminary description of Gothic heroes; Theodore enables us to expand the previous discussion. Up to 1800, the hero of Gothic plays was the weakest of the characters. Villains became increasingly powerful; heroes, steadily more helpless. Theodore is even less effectual than Douglas. In words, as in action accomplished before the play began and in action off the stage, a Gothic hero is magnificent. But in the fracas on the stage it is invariably he who is first disarmed, seized, and incarcerated. If a secret tunnel (frequently pointed out to him by some older inhabitant of the dungeon) leads him to freedom and permits continuation of his efforts to save the heroine and right all general wrongs, he is yet, by some means, convincing or otherwise, rendered utterly useless, and the ultimate reversal of fortunes is accomplished without his aid. Though Gothic plays almost always end with villainy overthrown and virtue triumphant, it is never the hero who effects the happy outcome. He is perpetually *hors de combat*. In a crisis he finds that his sword is broken or mislaid; or if by chance he has it in good condition in his hand, something prevents his striking a blow with it. What we hear that he has done and what we see him do are irreconcilable.

Theodore appears first as a peasant, led in by guards and accused of aiding Isabel's escape. So Gothic heroes usually are first presented—in a moment of crisis, in humble garb, yet with "something" in their mien and bearing that bespeaks extraordinary qualities. Thus the mystery of the hero's true identity contributes to the total mystery which characterizes the kind of drama. Theodore's true identity is at first a mystery to the audience, to the count, and, as it turns out, to himself, since he discovers only at the end that he is Alphonso's heir. Why had not the guards slain him, a stranger, found wandering where he had no right to be? In Raymond's castle he might have expected to be instantly dispatched; but he was not slain, says a guard, because,

> My arm was rais'd to smite him, but respect
> For something in his aspect check'd the blow.[12]

Thereafter, when the unyielding youth has boldly confessed his aid to Isabel, the count, striking that inevitable "musing posture" in the shadows, observes darkly:

> I must know more of this. His phrase, his look,
> His steady countenance, raise something here,
> Bids me beware of him.

Earlier, Theodore had heroically defended Adelaide from ruffians in the forest; thus, like Douglas, he is reportedly a man of action, superior to a whole band of robbers. Yet the reputation for heroism fails to prove that he—or any representative of the type before 1800—is really a champion. Once the play begins, he is clapped into a dungeon, out of sight and out of the action until the end of the fourth act. He emerges in time to subdue assailants of the castle—in an off-stage combat.

A related characteristic of the hero appears near the end of *The Count of Narbonne,* when Raymond interrupts the marriage ceremony and stabs his daughter. Theodore has opportunity to slay the murderer, but though he brandishes his sword he does not let it fall. The case is typical and highly significant: Gothic heroes never kill villains, no matter what they themselves, their mothers, brides, fathers, or sisters have suffered at the villains' hands. A villain meets his end by any other means, but not by that; he may take his own life, be struck by lightning, buried or burned in the ruins of his castle, drowned in a flood, slain by a henchman, or seized by higher powers and sent to prison. But the hero ends the play with hands unstained even by the blood of villainy."[24] Indeed, the force of good which finally thwarts the force of evil in Gothic drama is never vested in the hero; where an active human agent of good is employed at all, it is usually as a *deus ex machina,* perhaps a good uncle with an army or a beneficent duke with higher authority than that of the villain. We learn early in Gothic literature that no persecuted innocent can rely on the hero for effective aid.

The reason for the hero's unvarying ineffectuality seems to have been chiefly one of dramatic expedience. From the beginning, the nature of Gothic drama committed it to the development of a strong villain. Conversely, the increasing emphasis on the function of the villain and the demands of a theme of persecution committed it to tolerance of a weak hero. The typical Gothic plot involves oppression of a terrified heroine. The primary aim is to excite a maximum of terror. If the hero were permitted to block the villain, the terror of both heroine and spectator would be diminished, and the purpose of the play—the very purpose for which the Gothic species was devised—would fail. Therefore, though the hero must be reputed to have great prowess in order to gain acceptance as a hero, he cannot be allowed to demonstrate it at the right time and place. In moments of peril for the innocent, he must somehow be removed from the scene. Clever playwrights could handle the subterfuge so that an audience would overlook the fact that reports of heroism were not borne out by what the hero did to thwart the villain. Only after we have read many plays does it become obvious that the "Theodores" were consistently sacrificed to dramatic expediency.

The fuller implications of the hero's impotence will be discussed later. For the present, it is enough to suggest that in this inadequacy lay one reason for the gradual transformation of the villain and his assumption of the hero's title. The "Theodores" were at best flat and unpromising; at worst, they appeared utterly stupid. More than traces of their ineffectuality remain in some early nineteenth-century heroes, but in the main the romantic writers found the most striking qualities for their protagonists in the compounded agony, dark mystery, and grandeur that made up the Gothic villain.[15] Perhaps those who have had occasion to deplore the inconsequence of the Gothic hero before 1800 can most appreciate the Master of Ravenswood, Mr. Rochester, and Heathcliff.

Narration occupies some space in dramas of any kind. In Gothic plays, where it serves several purposes, it is especially prominent. *The Count of Narbonne* has many long narrative passages because the dramatist lacked courage to bring "more than mortal" events upon the stage; furthermore, the stage in Jephson's time was not equipped to represent all of the startling scenes described in *Otranto*. Narration continued to solve problems for later dramatists who sought sensational effects without the risk of disbelief and displeasure that actual staging might have invited. As the writers grew bolder and the carpenters more skillful, elaborate and preposterous spectacles were actually shown; but narration always remained as a way to introduce the grossest of gross elements.

Jephson's treatment of his heroine illustrates how effectively narration could be used. It is startling to realize at the end of the play that the much-harassed heroine has not once appeared on the stage. She is a major character by virtue of reports alone. Before the play begins, she has fled the castle, via subterranean channel, to a neighboring convent. By the time the pursuit has reached that refuge, she has moved on. The pursuers—and the scene— never catch her. All that we know of her comes through brief comments and longer narrative passages. "Not to be found!" Raymond rages in the opening line, and at intervals until the end similar remarks tell that the heroine's flight continues. The best picture of her is given by Theodore, who was seized at the trapdoor through which she had escaped. This brief passage describes the plight not only of Isabel, but of most Gothic maidens:

> Theo. In a dim passage of the castle aisles,
> Musing alone, I heard a hasty tread,
> And breath drawn short, like one in fear of peril.
> A lady enter'd; fair she seem'd, and young,
> Guiding her timorous footsteps by a lamp;
> "The lord, the tyrant of this place," she cried,
> "For a detested purpose follows me;
> "Aid me, good youth!" Then, pointing to the ground,
> "That door," she added, "leads to sanctuary."
> I seiz'd an iron hold, and, while I tugg'd
> To heave the unwilling weight, I learn'd her title.
> Count. The lady Isabel?
> Theo. The same. A gleam
> Shot from their torches who pursued her track,
> Prevented more; she hasten'd to the cave,
> And vanish'd from my sight.[16]

It will, perhaps, not be out of place to observe that opening the trapdoor was as much as a hero did for a heroine in a whole generation.

The effective presentation of a principal character through descriptive passages alone suggests the technique by which Gothic playwrights were able to handle other elements which for one reason or another they did not represent physically. Jephson, like Walpole in *The Mysterious Mother,* created Gothic atmosphere through dialogue. Conspicuous in the vocabulary of *The Count of Narbonne* are "gloom," "dismal," "dark," "terrible," and similarly suggestive words. Such barbarous parts of the castle as he did not represent in the settings, the playwright worked into the dialogue:

> Near the cloister,
> From whence, by the flat door's descent, a passage
> Beneath the ground leads onward to the convent,
> We heard the echo of a falling weight.[17]

Theodore's account of his meeting with Isabel in the "dim passage" is almost equivalent to staging the scene. Similarly, Hortensia includes in one short speech numerous reminders that a medieval castle was forbidding:

> ... spectres glide,
> Gibbering and pointing as we pass along,
> While the deep earth's unorganized caves
> Send forth wild sounds, and clamours terrible;
> These towers shake round us, though the untroubled air
> Stagnates to lethargy.[18]

The dialogue includes repeated mention of aisles, trapdoors, corridors, winding staircases, subterranean passages, sliding panels, and galleries. It is laden with the idea of the supernatural. Jephson's main contribution to the Gothic school was his demonstration that the full paraphernalia of the Gothic novel, if it could not quite all be staged, could be represented to the ear and the inner eye.

CONTEMPORARY ORIGINAL GOTHIC PLAYS

Because it was peculiarly helpful in preparing for discussion of typical Gothic plays, *The Count of Narbonne* has been examined before some earlier original plays. It is necessary now to look at some of these, which, if they have little real claim to originality, are nevertheless not mere adaptations.

ALBINA

Albina, Countess of Raimond (Hay. July 1779), a tragedy by Hannah Cowley, displays more Gothic elements than any other play between *The Mysterious Mother* and *The Count of Narbonne*. It opens in "A magnificent Gothic Hall," has one scene in "A Ruined Gothic Colonnade," and another in a garden with "The Towers in the Background." Its dialogue draws repetitiously on these settings and on the "aisles" and "vaulted ceilings" of the castle for atmosphere. Two typical elements of machinery, a grotto and a secret gate, figure prominently in the action.

Of the characters, Gondibert and Albina most resemble perennial Gothic types. It is the former who is the more striking. Though often he suggests the machinating Elizabethan, Gondibert primarily represents the conscience-stricken, gloomy villain. After the second act the play becomes the exploitation of his remorse. In this respect, the play is truly typical, for Gothic plays came to concentrate upon the character of the villain, and more specifically upon his special agony. Successive scenes find Gondibert in a more frightful paroxysm of remorse. Yet he continues, with mounting violence, to assail the heroine and to attempt destruction of her indestructible virtue.

Besides these types, *Albina* includes the first female villain in Gothic drama, unless, of course, we grant that title to Walpole's countess in *The Mysterious Mother*. Editha, who conspires with Gondibert, represents an infrequent type. Ultimately "Monk" Lewis, in novel and drama, and Keats and Coleridge, in poetry, were to make famous the cruel figure which is somewhat clumsily represented by Editha. The female villain in Gothic plays, unlike the male, is an utterly abandoned fiend who knows no remorse. Her commitment to evil is unlimited, and she is unrepentant to the end.

But far the most significant fact is that in *Albina* the wicked Gondibert receives, as he lies dying, complete forgiveness from both the hero and the heroine whom he has strenuously endeavored to injure. It is also noteworthy that the playwright called the work tragedy though only the villain dies. In the agony of the very first Gothic villains—in that central conflict " 'twixt good and ill"—were planted the seeds of sympathy and ultimate hero worship. In later plays, whatever the foul deeds they had perpetrated, villains were to gain not merely wholehearted forgiveness, but affection and tears.

GOTHIC ELEMENTS IN COMEDY

Gothic elements did not respect dramatic forms. Early in the period we find them chiefly where they might be expected—accompanying the somber mood of what the authors called tragedy. Later, just before 1800, they appeared frequently in dramatic romance. After 1802 they were most at home in melodrama. These were their natural lurking places. Sometimes, however, they were exploited in the countless subdivisions of comedy that flourished in the late eighteenth century. In farce, burletta, comic opera, and other bastard varieties of comedy they were introduced occasionally with burlesque intent, occasionally to startle the audience with the sensational thrills of the popular tragedy.

BANDITTI

John O'Keefe, in his comic opera of *Banditti; or, Love in a Labyrinth* (C. G. Nov. 1781), seems to have been the first playwright to mix Gothic materials and comedy. One of the century's most prolific writers of dramatic entertainments, O'Keefe has not a serious play to his name. Nearly all other playwrights attempted tragedy at some time, but O'Keefe's bibliography consists entirely of comic operas, farces, pantomimes, entertainments, burlettas, interludes, operatic farces, and occasional plain comedies. Perhaps in the works of no other playwright would we think it less likely to find Gothic elements, yet *Banditti* not only includes much that had already appeared in serious plays, but anticipated so much more of the full paraphernalia familiar a decade later that O'Keefe requires recognition as a major innovator. His comic opera acted in 1781 reads as though Ann Radcliffe had already published her novels and the era of the so-called German drama had begun. Actually, Mrs. Radcliffe's first novel was eight years in the future, and the era of German drama was not due for more than a dozen years.

These will seem strange comments on a play which resembles both Shakespeare's *Comedy of Errors* and Goldsmith's *She Stoops to Conquer*. A nobleman, with his foolish servant, arrives at the home of his intended bride. A prankster has told the girl's father that the arrivals have exchanged clothing and ranks in order to hoax the family. This, with the resulting confusion, is the main business of the play. The debt to Goldsmith (O'Keefe had earlier written a piece called *Tony Lumpkin's Rambles*) is especially obvious.

The Gothic appears in this comedy of mistaken identity because O'Keefe, a shrewd playwright, was alert to exploit the comic potentialities of effects currently popular. The Gothic elements in *Banditti* are primarily trappings to deck out a trite comic situation and to capitalize on a dramatic fashion. Perhaps it is more indicative of fashion to discover Gothic elements in a play in which they do not belong than to find them in such a play as *Albina*, where they do belong. Their presence in *Banditti* signifies that they were receiving widespread and pressing circulation.

The play was nevertheless damned on its first performance. One year later it was offered again, this time under the title of *The Castle of Andalusia* (C. G. Nov. 1782). Immediately successful, it played thirty-seven nights—almost a record in its time. It was revived often and was acted as late as 1826. A comparison of the printed text of *The Castle of Andalusia* with the Larpent manuscript of *Banditti* shows trifling alterations, and we can only guess why the original production failed and the later succeeded. Perhaps an audience in 1781 was not ready for comic treatment of the Gothic, but was ready in 1782, after *The Count of Narbonne* had made horrific materials and motifs conspicuous. Or, perhaps, the first performance failed simply because of a bad night at the theater. In this period the temporary unpopularity of one member of a cast could provoke such howls, hisses, and more violent responses that even *Hamlet* might be denied a hearing. Any such circumstance, may have caused *Banditti* to fail.[19]

Unlike Goldsmith, who laid his scene in Hardcastle's house and gave the characters thoroughly English names, O'Keefe chose an old castle, a cave, and a dark forest and named his characters Don Alphonso, Don Scipio, Don Fernando, Don Juan, Don Caesar, Donna Isabella, Donna Lorenza, and Sanguino. The principal business—that of confusing master and servant—is conducted partly in the castle, with "an antique Apartment" and a sliding panel, and partly in the countryside with "A view of the outside of the Castle, with Moat and Drawbridge." Certain atmospheric parts of the castle which do not appear in settings are heavily emphasized in dialogue. Says Sanguino, after popping through a secret panel:

I was formerly Master of the Horse to Count D'Olivi, the last resident here, so am well acquainted with the galleries, lobbies, windings, turnings, and every secret lurking-place in the castle.[20]

The exaggerated list of Gothic fixtures, proceeding from the mouth of a comic character with his head protruding from a secret panel, bears the unmistakable appearance of burlesque. Repeatedly, O'Keefe mentions those aspects of medievalism which serious Gothicists exploited. One of his characters refers to "this gloomy mansion"—though there is nothing in the least gloomy in the scene. The atmosphere is that of farce, and references to gloom, galleries, and windings were introduced apparently to make fun of a mounting craze.

But *The Castle of Andalusia* is also significant for a fact other than that it shows that in 1781 the Gothic school had attracted enough attention to provoke comic treatment. It anticipated an important motif usually considered to have been introduced to the English stage more than ten years later. Attached to the main theme of mistaken identities there is, as the original title of *Banditti* indicates, another and quite different one. This, the nobleman-turned-outlaw theme, is usually identified with *Schiller's Die Räuber,* which was published in Germany in 1781 but had no English translation and probably no influence in England until 1792. Thereafter numerous English playwrights used it, and thereby invited attachment of the erroneous label "German" to Gothic plays in general. Certainly *Die Räuber* gave the impetus for exploitation of the motif, but the fact remains that O'Keefe used it eleven years before Schiller's play was translated.

O'Keefe introduced yet other innovations scarcely less important. In developing the robber theme, he had occasion to use two settings that were destined to become almost as closely associated with Gothic plays as were castles and convents. Act I has "A Cavern, with winding stairs, and recesses cut in the rock—a large lamp hanging . . . Don Caesar discovered sitting at the head of the table . . . Spado, Sanguino, Rapino, and others of the Banditti." This setting, like the banditti, was new. Another scene has "A Forest. A stormy night. Thunder." The forest, on the edge of which is the castle of Don Scipio, was an addition also. The time was near when a banditti-infested wood would become a familiar part of the machinery of terror. Don Fernando, on his way to Don Scipio's castle, became the first character in Gothic drama to lose his way, benighted, in a forest overrun by robbers. Here O'Keefe anticipated by eight years a favorite motif of Ann Radcliffe, many of whose "good" characters lose themselves, at one time or another, in a dark wood on a stormy night.

Because it introduced Gothic elements primarily for comic effect, anticipated the Karl Moor motif, and added the cavern-forest-banditti combination, O'Keefe's very slight and very foolish piece is important in the history of Gothic drama. No later playwright, except perhaps "Monk" Lewis, wrote a play that added so much to the Gothicists' paraphernalia.

OTHER COMIC PLAYS

Three plays before 1792 followed O'Keefe's comic treatment of Gothic materials: *The Nunnery* (C. G. April 1785), a silly musical farce by William Pearce; *The Enchanted Castle* (C. G. Dec. 1786), by Miles Peter Andrews; and *The Haunted Tower* (D. L. Nov. 1789), by James Cobb. The latter two are worth brief attention.

Pantomime and horrific trappings on an absurd scale are combined in *The Enchanted Castle,* an unpublished pantomime preserved in the Larpent Collection under the title *The Castle of Wonders*.[21] Andrews—unquestionably one of the worst playwrights of any period—attempted to adapt Walpole's *Otranto;* but even that romance failed to provide absurdities enough for his two-act piece. Perhaps the most efficient way to deal with the concoction is to quote from its preface:

> The novelty attempted to be dramatized tonight takes its rise from the writings of Miss Aikin and the Hon. Horace Walpole. The Castle of Otranto and the fragment of Sir Bertrand form the basis of an endeavor to bring upon the stage somewhat of the effects which may be produced by midnight horror or agency supernatural. What may be the result of this experiment, tonight must determine, for hitherto the experiment has not been made. The ghost of Hamlet and the witches of Macbeth do not militate against this assertion. Their appearance, though out of nature, was simple and not combined. The clank of chains, the whistling of hollow winds, the clapping of door, gigantic forms, and visionary gleams of light attended not their effects upon the stage.[22]

The preface is, of course, incorrect in stating that there had been no previous effort to achieve Gothic effects on the stage; Andrews' awareness of recent dramatic history evidently was no greater than his knowledge of dramatic craftsmanship. The assertion that the supernatural manifestations in *Hamlet* and *Macbeth* differ from the Gothic use is nevertheless well observed. I have earlier shown that the Gothic play was a unique dramatic kind, distinct from even those Elizabethan tragedies in which the supernatural plays a conspicuous role. Andrews' comment that the appearance of Shakespeare's supernatural figures "though out of nature, was simple and not combined" emphasizes the essential point of contrast. It will be necessary to discuss this playwright's Gothic efforts more extensively in a later chapter,[23] since it was he who first adapted Mrs. Radcliffe's *The Mysteries of Udolpho*.

Cobb's three-act opera, *The Haunted Tower*, a compound of nonsense and music, was acted "above eighty times."[24] Perhaps it was the music, supplied by Stephen Storace, which was chiefly responsible for its continued success. Boaden says of the work, "There was a business in this opera just enough to carry the singers into their places on the stage."[25]

Like *Banditti*, this piece looks suspiciously like burlesque. O'Keefe had composed a recipe for comic treatment of Gothic machinery, and Cobb seems to have exaggerated all the ingredients of the formula. Like many a serious play in the Gothic genre, *The Haunted Tower* relates the attempts of a nobleman to recover his usurped title. The old Baron of Oakland, wrongly accused of conspiracy, had been deprived of his estate and banished. This was the past event. Later, when the error had been discovered, he was not to be found, and a foolish peasant, a distant relative, had been created new Baron of Oakland. The problem of the play is to get the usurper out and Lord William, the true heir, in.

Gothic settings predominate. Act I has "The Sea. Dover Cliffs and an Ancient Castle. Thunder and Lightning." Other scenes include "an antique Apartment," "a Chamber in the Tower,"—the haunted chamber—and "the Castle Hall." Of especial interest is the ridicule of the typical tyrant-usurper-villain. The foolish peasant, elevated to high rank, strives to maintain the mystery, gloom, and terror which always envelop the Gothic protagonist. Instructing his son, Edward, also a booby, to cultivate a baronial gloom, he blusters:

> Sirrah, sirrah, don't put me in a passion. You have been civil to those rascals—I know you have; why don't you frown at them as I do? How often have I told you there's nothing supports dignity like ill-humor... I'll defy the best friend I have to say I have given him a civil word since I have been Baron of Oakland: an't I the terror of the neighborhood?[25]

The first of Mrs. Radcliffe's novels had appeared early in 1789, and some of the scenes of *The Haunted Tower* seem to poke fun at one of her favorite motifs—the idea of a haunted wing or chamber. I shall quote from two of these scenes, to show the effects the playwright produced by depicting the reactions, not of a frightened heroine, but of comic figures to Gothic sources of terror.

Hugo. ... I'll go and get on my armour.
Lord W. It is not yet time; the tolling of the curfew will give me notice when all is ready; but tell me, Hugo, was not my father's armour kept in that tower?
Hugo. Yes, my lord, in that very apartment.
Lord W. And has the armour ever been removed from thence?
Hugo. Never, I'll answer for that; the room has been shut up these ten years past to my knowledge. I have still preserved my key to the door which leads to it through the long gallery.
Lord W. Give it me. (Hugo gives key.) Now let us be gone.
Hugo. Excuse me, my lord; I'll follow you to battle, but not to that apartment.
Lord W. Why not?
Hugo. Ah, my lord! I tremble at the thoughts of it; no living soul has entered that room for these ten years; voices have been heard and lights seen—in short, it is haunted. And though I loved your worthy father when he was alive, I-I-I—
Lord W. By Heaven! a light appears through the casement at this moment!
Hugo. And so there does! My dear master, don't be rash.

Lord W. Hark! I hear a noise from the tower; wait for me here (draws), and beware your fears do not betray you. (unlocks door and exit)

Hugo. My lord, my dear lord William, don't leave me alone. He's gone! Oh! that cursed haunted chamber! I can't stay near it; I—I find the only means of preserving my courage is to carry it along with me. (exit)

(Enter Baron of Oakland)

Baron. Why, sure, that was old Hugo; yes, and with his sword drawn. Oh! Oh! lord, oh lord! There's the spirit playing his illumination tricks in the haunted chamber again...."[97]

The next scene is laid in this haunted tower, with its various secret panels and a trapdoor. The audience now learns that the chamber is situated above the wine cellar in which the baron keeps his stock. The effect of burlesque arises with the discovery that the haunted room is a resort for the quite mortal servants of the castle, who spend their nights in hilarious consumption of "the scurvy old knave's" liquor, which they bring up via the trapdoor. Their light has given currency to the superstition that the tower is haunted, and this they have encouraged in order to forestall discovery. In the next scene, however, the baron ventures through the trapdoor and surprises the "ghosts" at his wine. Thereafter the comedy gets a new twist—a favorite of later playwrights, especially Lewis—when the culprits who have perpetrated the "supernatural" hoax are themselves affrighted by what seems a real visitation in the form and habit of the old Baron of Oakland, "dead these ten years."

Robert. Indeed, my lord, we heard an echo.
Baron. Did you? Well, sing again, then, and let me hear it.
Robert. Now mark, my lord, (Sings) "And we'll be wond'rous merry!"
Lord W. (Behind, in Robert's voice) "And we'll be wond'rous merry!"
Baron. (Alarmed) Egad! but it's an odd sort of an echo.
Robert. Suppose your honour was to speak to it, perhaps it would answer you civilly.

Baron.   Oh, I dare say that it will have a proper respect for my dignity. What are you—ghost or spirit?
Lord W. (In the Baron's voice) "Ghost or spirit?"
Baron.   (Very much agitated) Oh, Lord—oh, Lord! Why—why don't some of you speak to me? What—what are you afraid of? Robert, what makes you look so pale? For my part, I-I-I don't believe in apparitions.... Oh, I'm a lost man. But why do you all tremble so? (A bell tolls) Oh, Lord! There's the curfew going at this hour!

(Lord William throws open the doors, and walks with great solemnity in his father's armour, and exit.)

Oh, dear me! It is the old Baron's ghost! I have seen him wear that shield and helmet a thousand times![28]

Viewed as a whole, *The Haunted Tower* is a comic opera-comedy of manners affair furnished with a medieval setting and Gothic machinery. All the characters are contemporary, and the title—which actually names only the two brief scenes from which I have quoted—is misleading, for these scenes are irrelevant to the main plot. It is likely that the title and the scenes were used to catch the public eye. The comic treatment of Gothic elements and motifs, which in 1789 were approaching their period of greatest popularity, may perhaps have accounted, in part at least, for the record number of performances.

CHAPTER V

FULL DEVELOPMENT OF GOTHIC DRAMA BEFORE 1792

IN ORDER to describe early experiments in the comic treatment of Gothic materials, it was necessary in the preceding chapter to depart from a strictly chronological method. I return now to 1784 to discuss some plays which included the fullest accumulation of horrific elements before the first translation of *Die Räuber*. The plays examined in this chapter show conclusively that the English stage, quite without foreign assistance, developed a species to which German writers merely contributed additional elements.

The plays which will best illuminate this period of development are Cumberland's *The Carmelite* (D. L. Dec. 1784), Andrew McDonald's *Vimonda* (Hay. Sept. 1787), Bertie Greatheed's *The Regent* (D. L. March 1778), and Francis North's *Kentish Barons* (Hay. June 1790). Other plays, several of which are excellent specimens of the Gothic species, are necessarily relegated to the appended list of dramatic pieces.[1]

GOTHIC PLAYS, 1784-1792

THE CARMELITE

A prolific playwright, Cumberland wrote three plays besides *The Carmelite* which belong in a Gothic bibliography.[2] But this one best represents his participation in the Gothic Revival and stands as an excellent example of Gothic drama. Though the author asserted that his plot was original, he was clearly indebted to the entire development of Gothic literature which preceded him. There are indications, as we shall see, that he borrowed especially from *Douglas, The Countess of Salisbury,* and *The Mysterious*

---
[1] For notes to chap. v, see pages 250-251.

Mother, but by 1784 the accumulated materials were in such general circulation that it is conceivable Cumberland was indebted to these works without realizing the fact or even being familiar with them.

The Carmelite opens on a scene that became common in later decades. It shows "A Rocky Shore, with a view of the Sea at break of day." Perhaps it was inevitable that the Gothic settings which had begun with castle and convent and extended to cavern and dark forest should have spread to include the cliffs by the sea. A ship has been wrecked, and Montgomeri advises his companions that only two strangers have survived:

> Alas! 'tis now too late:
> I had not left the beach but all was lost;
> The elements had mercy, man had none.
> Two I have sav'd; the one a Carmelite,
> Noble the other in his mien and habit;
> I left them in the outskirts of the grove.

As they leave, the survivors enter. The Carmelite is in good spirits, but the other is wretched. The former notes that they have been cast ashore near a castle:

> Bear up, Lord Hildebrand; there's hope in view.
> See'st thou yon turrets, that o'ertop the wood?
> There we may shelter from the storm.

Few "strangers" after *The Carmelite* were shipwrecked and thrown upon a coast without perceiving the turrets of castle or convent reaching upward through the trees. Moreover, later survivors were to find access to the castle as difficult as do the Carmelite and Lord Hildebrand. Montgomeri, returning, answers their request for shelter:

Carm. Whose is that castle?
Mont. A lady's, whom we serve, of Norman birth.
Carm. Then lead us to her gates, for we are Normans.
      Poor, helpless men, fainting with want of food
      And over-watching: tedious nights and days

>   We struggled with the storm: the greedy deep
>   Has swallow'd up our ship, our friends, our all,
>   And left us to your mercy. Sure, your lady,
>   Who owns so fair a mansion, owns withal
>   A heart to give us welcome. You are silent.
> Mont.   To save you, and supply your pressing wants
>   With food and raiment, and what else you need,
>   We promise, nothing doubting; more than this
>   Stands not within our privilege: No stranger
>   Enters her castle.

The Carmelite's bitter comment that the lady must indeed be merciless provokes a denial and raises the problem of the play:

> Mont.   Your saints in bliss,
>   Your calendar of martyrs does not own
>   A soul more pure, a virtue more sublime;
>   Her very·name will strike defamers dumb.
> Carm.   Speak it.
> Mont.   Saint Valori!
> Carm.   Uphold me, heaven!
>   The ways of Providence are full of wonder,
>   And all its works are mercy. How now, sir! (to Hildebrand)
>   Will you betray yourself? What shakes you thus?
> Hild.   I sicken at the heart: let me go hence,
>   And make myself a grave!
> Carm.   Be patient—stay!
>   And has your lady here consum'd her youth
>   In pensive solitude? Twenty long years,
>   And still a widow?
> Mont.   Still a mournful widow.

We have met earlier the technique which envelopes an opening scene in complex mystery and raises the major questions of the play. What secret reconciles the conflicting conduct and character of the "mournful widow"? What happened twenty years ago that has turned her to "pensive solitude," saintly, yet determined to bar strangers from her castle? Who is the Carmelite from whom the name "St. Valori!" compels an exclamation? Finally, what ails Lord Hildebrand?

As the play continues, we piece together hints that ultimately solve the mysteries. Again a past event is the key. Twenty years before, Lord Hildebrand had—as he believed—slain St. Valori:

> ... from the holy wars returning home,
> Within the rugged Pyrenaean pass.[4]

He had seized his victim's rights and inherited his title; in consequence, for twenty years he has experienced growing remorse, and is now driven to confess his crime. Early stricken by conscience, he says, he had reared "a stately tomb" to St. Valori, endowed an abbey in his name, and even "purchas'd perpetual masses to reclaim his soul" from purgatory. All had been insufficient; even yet, he tells the Carmelite,

> ... I do perceive
> The hand of heav'n hangs o'er me and my house;
> Why am I childless else? seven sons swept off
> To their untimely graves; their wretched mother
> By her own hand in raging frenzy died;
> At last, behold me here, forlorn, abandon'd,
> At life's last hour, before her surly gates,
> Deaf to my hungry cries....

Such is Lord Hildebrand's secret, but what is the Carmelite's? By the end of the first act we have learned that he is in reality the St. Valori supposedly slain by the villain now groveling at the gates of the "widow's" castle. In his disguise as a Carmelite he is an early representative of a frequent type—the holy-man-not-a-holy-man, of which Austin, who at last proved to be Theodore's father and the assassinated Alphonso's son in *The Count of Narbonne*, was the prototype.

The complications which arise after the strangers have gained Lady St. Valori's hospitality are interesting and typical. Lord Hildebrand takes to his bed, dying from remorse, and refuses food from her he had injured. A theme of jealousy motivates much of the action after the second act. The Carmelite believes that Montgomeri is Lady St. Valori's lover, "a minion with whom she wantons." Cumberland devised a highly spectacular scene for the final unveiling of all secrets. It is laid in "A Chapel, with an Altar decorated with funeral Trophies of St. Valori. Matilda discovered kneeling at the Altar." Here, still believing his wife false, the Carmelite melodramatically discloses his true identity. After a long story in which he tells how St. Valori, returning home from war with the Saracens, was waylaid by Hildebrand and left for dead, he adds:

> 'Twas not his lot to find a distant grave.
> Lady. Where? where? Oh! speak! release me from the rack! Where did he fall?
> Val. Nor pagan swords, nor slavery's galling chain,
> Nor murderer's dagger, Afric's burning clime,
> Toils, storms, nor shipwreck, kill'd him—here he fell!
> Grief burst his heart—here in this spot he fell!
> (He falls to the ground.)[5]

It is in this scene, too, reviving and ready to stab Montgomeri, that he discovers the minion to be his son.

The Carmelite, well saturated with Cumberland's usual sentimentalism, is one of the most "moving" Gothic plays. Its initial run of thirteen nights is understandable, especially when we learn that "every feature of the principal character was addressed to Mrs. Siddons,"[6] who evidently carried off such parts with great force. Yet the striking effects for which *The Carmelite* is remarkable were not arranged without sacrifices. The characteristic weaknesses in the construction of Gothic plays have been noted before, especially in connection with *Douglas,* but here they are so conspicuous that some of them must be given comment. For example, the sensational double disclosure in the final scene, of the identities of Montgomeri and the Carmelite, are arranged by obvious manipulation. Why does not Valori, home to a "widow" who has mourned for twenty years, make himself known immediately, even before his suspicions of the minion determine him to continue in his disguise? There is no real answer to that kind of question, and perhaps it is unfair to demand one of a Gothicist. To the playwrights who aimed at effect and who wrote in a genre in which effect was positively all that mattered, achievement of that end excused all else. Quick revelation of the Carmelite's identity would have made impossible the staging of the final spectacle, and postponement of the truth made it possible; therefore, the playwright withheld the secret: such was the justification which sufficed for all Gothicists. Earlier and greater dramatists had sometimes sacrificed the probable in favor of the spectacular, also; but there is usually evidence that they cared about, and sought to patch up their motivation. Perhaps it was part of the Gothicists' creed that they should do neither. From Cumberland forth, no loss of probability was too expensive if a spectacle was gained.[7] If, rather incidentally, an effect could be motivated, well; if it could not, no matter.

VIMONDA

McDonald's *Vimonda* is another outstanding specimen of the Gothic drama that was elaborately furnished before any horrific elements were borrowed from Germany. Unlike some of the plays previously examined, it shows no compromise of Gothic with other materials. None of the numerous other dramatic tendencies of the age are apparent in it; its Gothic is unadulterated. Its end is purely mystery, gloom, and terror, and its atmosphere contains only what will serve that end.

Characteristically, the business in *Vimonda* is the unraveling of a secret. Several years before, Dundore and Barnard, as they thought, had murdered Rothsay, the heroine's father. He, however, recovered from their attack, has occupied an abandoned ruin near the castle. Often glimpsed at night, he is repeatedly mistaken for his ghost. Dundore causes Vimonda to suspect that Melville, her lover, was the assassin. The nocturnal investigations of Rothsay have led him also to suspect the hero. Finally, after the ghost legend has been played out, the father identifies himself and baldly accuses Melville of attempted murder. The play ends with Dundore slain in a fight with Melville; Melville poisoned; and Vimonda killed by shock. Rothsay will linger out his days "in the cloister." The only atypical feature of *Vimonda* as Gothic tragedy is this catastrophe which brings death to the "good" characters as well as to the villain.

Numerous earlier plays, such as *The Countess of Salisbury* and even *The Count of Narbonne,* were written without realization of the full possibilities of dramatizing Gothic materials. But the period of experimentation was past when McDonald wrote, and he began exploitation of the Gothic sources of terror immediately and continued it to the end. His first setting is elaborate: "A narrow Valley, surrounded with Romantic Rocks and Woods—in the bottom a Tower decorated with Arms and Sepulchral Figures." Entering with Melville, Vimonda strikes the tone sustained until the final curtain:

> This deep recess, on which at height of noon
> The sun scarce looks, I chose, the fittest scene
> For secret woe and awful meditation.[8]

She had built the tower in memory of her assassinated father. Though Melville urges her to leave the valley and return to cheerful life, she has resolved to remain to cry vengeance upon the murderer:

> Why do I toss each night in shuddering dream,
> And rave of bloody swords and ghostly wounds?
> 'Tis the dread phantom of my murder'd father
> That haunts yon towers, that tears my heart with terror,
> That cries Revenge! it frowns, and vanishes.
> This monument shall be my oratory;
> There shall my constant knees the marble weary;
> There will I cry for vengeance on the wretch
> Who wrought the deed accurs'd of Heaven!

When Melville asks who has seen the specter, she replies that, besides her servants, she had seen it:

> Last night,
> As at the window of my Bow'r I stood,
> What time the moon behind yon mountain's edge
> Descending, gave the vale a farewell glance,
> Close by the margin of the moat it came,
> Slow gliding; once it paus'd, and seem'd to look
> Up to the battlements. My blood ran cold.
> Frantic, I would have spoke to it; but Horror,
> With grasp convulsive, seiz'd me, choaked my breath,
> And turn'd my limbs to marble. Thus I stood
> In ecstasy of dread, till in yon grove
> Beyond the postern gate its form was lost.

Not until the end of the second act does the reader learn that the ghost is Rothsay himself. He appears before Alfreda, a servant, who at first mistakes him for a specter and registers the conventional terror. In a speech packed with Gothic terms, the apparition tells how he has long lurked in the environs of the castle:

> With an old follower, in a ruin near,
> Nightly I walk my melancholy rounds
> About the castle, or by a dark passage
> Under the moat, unknown to all but me,
> Securely enter.⁹

His nocturnal prowling has taught him only to suspect everyone—Dundore, Melville, and even his daughter.

Meanwhile Dundore, intent on usurpation, has shown Vimonda a sword, dark with congealed blood. By asserting that it is Melville's and that the blood is her father's, he has induced her to suspect her lover. She determines to test him, and her choice of a place in which to do so is typical. Melville is conducted to her father's tomb, and the melodramatic situation, the solemn language, and the dismal subterranean setting together manufacture an atmosphere conducive to the feelings which all

Gothicists purpose to arouse. Vimonda herself thrusts the bloodstained dagger before her lover's eyes:

> Lord Melville, by the faith thou owest to knighthood,
> Tell whence thou hadst this weapon![10]

The height of the spectacle is reached when the ghostly figure of Rothsay appears from the darkness of the tomb and towers over them all. Vimonda cries,

> 'Tis there! 'Tis there!
> Great God, it is my father!

After the thrill has been registered, Rothsay reveals his mortality. He then adds his accusation that Melville had been the midnight attacker.

The ruinous tomb is used again for the final scene, in which, as in the preceding, spectacle is the keynote. Dundore's henchman, Barnard, who had actually struck the blow that wounded Rothsay and who had suffered remorse past bearing, exposes the truth—too late. Dundore has induced Melville to drink poison, saying that was Vimonda's desire. Melville, having drunk, stabs Dundore before falling. Vimonda, learning her error, goes mad and dies. The remorseful Barnard kills himself, and Rothsay vows to spend his last days "in the cloister."

Vimonda presented the fullest accumulation of Gothic elements that had yet been used in a single play. Its preëminent quality, for which it is as notable a specimen of Gothic composition as the best of Mrs. Radcliffe's novels, is a sustained atmosphere of mystery, gloom, and terror. The least-Gothic feature is the villain, Dundore, whose ancestry was Elizabethan.

THE REGENT

In striking contrast to *Vimonda*, Greatheed's tragedy *The Regent*, acted six months later, is chiefly remarkable for its Gothic villain. Since other materials of this play include little not previously reviewed, we may center attention upon him. Together, this villain and the one who dominates the play next to be examined present opportunity to describe certain vital forces in the evolution of the protagonist, with whose growth and shifting function we shall become increasingly concerned as we near the time of the Byronic hero.

The Regent poses the usual opening problem. Several years before, the good Duke Ansaldo had gone to visit his uncle, King of Leon. He had left as regent his trusted friend Manuel. Ansaldo never had returned, and, as it was known that he had left his uncle's palace, was presumed dead. The gossip of servants suggests that he had been assassinated. The strange moodiness of Manuel has drawn mistrust upon him. Solerno boldly asserts:

ness:
> He's a villain, certain; is ever restless,
> Nay, even 'mid the revelry of wassail
> Sometimes black melancholy seizes on him,
> Glaring around with epilepsied eye....[11]

Solerno's logic is noteworthy: Manuel is restless and melancholy; therefore, "He's a villain, certain." Doubtless the theatergoer of 1788 was accustomed to this reasoning. The signs constituted the outward show of agony; agony meant remorse; remorse meant evil deeds past; evil deeds meant villainy. Thus agony identified itself with evil and was the distinguishing mark of the villain.

Solerno had gathered the conventionally infallible evidence against Manuel: the suspect's reaction when suddenly confronted by a particular object. The armor of Ansaldo, "that brown with gore, through which the Moorish spear yet stands infix'd," had been moved from its customary stand and placed in a gallery. Solerno had seen Manuel come upon this statue in the semidarkness.

> One stormy evening...
> I saw Don Manuel pacing too and fro
> There where Ansaldo's iron effigie
> Gleams mid the chivalry of ancestors.

> The rattling casements stream'd with heavy drops,
> And hollow blasts hurtling through peak'd vaults
> Rebellow'd down the gloomy passages,
> Making the doors to groan of this old mansion;
> In haste he went and seem'd to be disturb'd,
> More than the elements disquiet seem'd;
> While I unseen stood watching his demeanor,
> His eye upon the vacant statue fell;
> Appall'd he started back, with either hand
> Shielding his face, as though a ghost had crost him,
> Then on the figure gaz'd with folded arms
> And forehead all convuls'd, and quiv'ring lip.
> Long having stood absorbed in that profound,
> He smote his brow, and earnestly exclaim'd,
> "Oh deed accursed, would it had ne'er been done!"
> More words perchance had broke from his dark mind,
> But hearing something stir, he pry'd around,
> And much alarm'd slunk back to his apartment.[12]

Manuel's first soliloquy shows how emphasis had shifted from the villain as an object of terror to the villain as a creature of agony:

> ... Would that one stroke had done the business clean
> Which splinter'd thus lies fest'ring in my brain.
> Ansaldo's form by night, by day pursues me.
> His single name rings dreadful in my ear,
> Knots all my flesh and bristles every hair.
> Is this the happiness so dearly bought,
> Purchas'd in murder, ratified in gore?
> 'Tis beyond bearing—O, the thought distracts me!
> Hence Conscience! hence! avaunt, heart-rending fiend![13]

Here the last four lines, especially, indicate the additional function which the Gothic villain was called on to perform.

From its source in Manuel, gloom has spread over all. Solerno and Paula, fellow servants, comment on the contagious affliction:

> Sol.   The menials eye askance and grimly scowl,
> Sullen and mute they hurry to and fro,
> Seeming to ape the gloom that roosts around,
> And where the livery of the sooty sky.
> Where is the man of crimes?

Paula. E'en now I met him,
Right on he went, nor turn'd his head aside,
But seem'd to fear his footsteps would be heard.
Crossing, he glanc'd me as we'er want a toad,
Yet utter'd he no word."[14]

Though already remorseful, Manuel harasses Dianora, the imprisoned widow of Ansaldo, and threatens to stab her unless she will marry him. When she scorns the knife at her throat, he threatens to slay her son. After issuing an ultimatum, he wheels, dashes out—and as abruptly reënters to accost his victim anew. At last, in the forest at night, he comes face to face with the ghost of Ansaldo. Fear of the supernatural seizes him, but he overcomes it, returns to the castle, and desperately renews his assaults on the heroine. We learn now that Ansaldo had not been killed, but, returning from his visit, had been set upon by "fierce banditti at the entrance of a rude defile" and wounded. Recovering, he had returned to occupy a ruin near the castle. He meets Solerno, convinces him—after the usual "thrill"—that he is mortal, and the two steal into the castle by night through

> A secret sally-port, that us'd of yore
> Forth to emit thy well-accouter'd Sires...[15]

They enter Dianora's chamber as Manuel and his banditti are at her throat. A fight ensues, and Manuel falls. His dying speech bears a new note as conspicuous as that in his first soliloquy; filled with sound and fury for the actor and asserting at the same time the terrible end that awaits vice, it provided at once a tidbit for John Philip Kemble and a sop for the Lord Chamberlain's censor:

> Burst! cleave, ye vaults! Hail ruin upon all!
> Sunder the earth and yawn to swallow us!
> Thou ghostly devastation burst they chains,
> Breathe pestilence and bellow shriv'ring thunders.
> I'm lost... there, there he gnaws!
> Another champ or two, and I am sped.
> Dead, sans enjoyment, damn'd but for a dream!

> Again—oh, stop awhile—Behold, it opens!
> Seize fast—kind man—hold! hold! they snatch at me!
> One moment more ye horrible—avaunt!
> Off! off! assist me! help—oh, help me! (dies)[16]

The reversion to the tradition of the old morality play is as obvious as it is significant.

KENTISH BARONS

The most notable remaining play of the period before 1792 is Francis North's *Kentish Barons*, acted in 1791. Like *The Regent*, this tragedy is mainly of interest for its villain.

North's Mortimer is a moralizing criminal who is actually made to come downstage and preach sermons on the consequences of evil. He had contrived to get Elina, bride-to-be of Clifford, secretly by night into his castle and entirely under his power. He gloats to a servant:

> Why think'st thou, Osbert, that I brought her hither?
> Think'st thou 'twas only to enjoy her person?
> That were but poor revenge; yet I'll enjoy her,
> And quickly, too—kind, warm, and yielding to my purpose.[17]

To introduce these lines in a play of 1791 was to invite trouble with the censor. But North was bold, and his villain's intentions were elaborated even more specifically:

> No hated priest shall join our hands together,
> Whose hearts could never pair. Yet I'll deceive her.
> What! a feign'd marriage! Good, it shall be so!
> The livelong night I'll revel in her beauties,
> And in the morning tell her she's undone.

Immediately after these lines, North suddenly reversed the direction of his villain's thought. Mortimer is made to exhibit himself as an object lesson; he sinks into the black mood of remorse, shudders at his own plan, and finally comes forward:

> ... how wretched is the man
> Who builds upon deceit! Though fraud and artifice
> May for awhile support the tott'ring fabric,

> Though it seem fair and beauteous to the eye,
> Yet all is grief and wretchedness within,
> And though by nature bold, he feels a horror,
> A dread of something which he strives in vain
> To banish from his mind, that spoils the harmony
> And mars the heavenly music of the soul.
> But the plain honest man fears no detection....

We may be certain that John Larpent, the Lord Chamberlain's censor, forgave the previous voluptuous imagery when this admonishment clearly enlisted the villain in the cause of morality. To be sure, Mortimer directly thereafter makes his first assaults upon the heroine, but these, too, are immediately counteracted by a show of remorse that again proclaims the way of the transgressor rough indeed.

As might be assumed, *Kentish Barons* employs the past event, this time a disaster in which the heroine's father and infant brother had disappeared. When an audience heard the out-at-elbows servant Osbert described by Elina—

> ...Gentle youth, alas!
> I feel for him. He seems to bear a mind
> Above the meanness of his low condition;
> And had not grief and thy dear image, Clifford,
> Effac'd all lesser objects from my memory,
> I could recall some features I once lov'd
> Which much resembled his.[18]

—the initiated knew that the youth was that brother long since lost. Conclusive identification is made through the old romance method of the telltale mark on his body. Describing the lost infant, a comic servant, alcoholically inclined, says:

> He had a mark on his left arm for all the world
> Like the stain of wine on a tablecloth.[19]

Later, at the critical moment when Osbert arrives at Clifford's castle to get aid for Elina, the servant is struck by something in the ragged fellow's bearing and countenance. At first he mistakes

Osbert for the ghost of the master who had been assassinated fifteen years before. Then he demands:

> ... Have you a mark?
> Ay, a mark, your lordship, a large red mark
> On your lordship's left arm?[20]

Osbert starts violently and displays the mark. North's use of this identification was the first, but not the last, in Gothic drama. In subsequent plays the mark assumed various shapes, colors, and sizes; perhaps the height of its career was attained when, in Mary Russel Mitford's dramatization of Mrs. Radcliffe's *Gaston de Blondeville*, it was described as "like a large mulberry" which waxes and wanes, growing largest and brightest when mulberries are ripe.

THE GOTHIC VILLAIN

Two outstanding specimens of the Gothic villain have just been described in the plays *Vimonda* and *The Regent*. It is appropriate at this point to reconsider and interpret the Gothic villain and his evolution. Probably this protagonist was the most valuable contribution of Gothic literature to the romantics, and in his development the drama played a more vital part than the novel.

The villain's original function was the same in the drama and in the novel. The tyrant was the foremost accomplice, the chief henchman, so to speak, of the barbarous medieval castle, which was itself the primary source of the gloom and terror registered in the hearts of the heroines. The Gothic villain, a human object of barbarism that inhabited the architectural ruin, was the second major source. In the period between Walpole and Byron, as I have suggested earlier, certain forces acted upon this specialized villain which transformed him into a particular kind of hero. Their operation will be illustrated more fully in the plays after 1792. At present, it is possible to name these forces and to show how the drama, more than the novel, pressed the evolution and ultimately caused the transformation of the protagonist.

Three related circumstances were instrumental in effecting the change. First, the nature of the Gothic plot, which was strictly dictated by the singular purpose of exploiting mystery, gloom, and terror, required that the villain be the most forceful character. Second, the late eighteenth century saw "star" actors assume unusual prestige in the theater. Third, in this period the stage came under close moral scrutiny. Let us examine the respective bearings of these upon the nature and function of the villain.

The origin of the villain as nearly an integral part of the castle ruin made him, like it, gloomy and forbidding. His function in the plot required that his be the dominant position in the play—that he, not the hero, be the protagonist. As a principal object of terror in a work which aimed at terror, he must be allowed full sweep and advantage. The hero must not effectively rival him, lest the prime end be unattained; the hero was doomed, as we have seen, to ineffectuality, stupidity, or perpetual absence from the stage: his part was to keep out of the orbit of the most active object of terror. In the typical Gothic play, therefore, the villain's role was the actor's prize.

Here the second circumstance meshed with the first. The principal actor chose the role he desired. The distinguished players won their highest fame, of course, in the great Shakespearean roles, and in Gothic drama the nearest to these—however remote in fact—were those of the villains.[21] Without exception, then, the star actors took the villain's part when they played in a Gothic play. The consequences were inevitable: Gothic playwrights, whose bread or chance for fame might depend on the actor's decision, strove to create roles in which the impersonator could exhibit his most conspicuous talents. Thus, for instance, Boaden described Greatheed's purpose:

> ... (Greatheed) had bestowed his utmost efforts upon a tragedy called the Regent; and he very skilfully applied himself to produce a part for Kemble exactly suited to his powers.[22]

Thus playwrights coöperated to make even more striking a character whose dominance was predetermined by the nature of the Gothic plot. Under these circumstances, the villain grew in more than mere stature. Star actors usually desire and need at least an element of sympathy in their roles. In the eighteenth century, though often dictators backstage, great actors were at the mercy of the public as they had perhaps not been before and as they have not been since. Their need for sympathetic parts was imperative. They could not, or would not, play the sympathetic, but subordinate, role of the hero. The solution lay in the development of a villain who would invite sympathy.

An obvious suggestion for the direction of this development lay in the gloom which the villain had acquired at birth in a castle ruin. As actors sought sympathy in roles created by subservient playwrights, this natural gloom was intensified to agony—the password to sympathy. As it became the essential characteristic of the dramatic villain, so agony moved him surely through the degrees of villain-hero and hero-villain to Byronic hero. It became the true subject of Gothic plays near the end of the century and remained the focal center in *Manfred*.

At the same time, the third circumstance of moral solicitude operated with the others to make agony the supreme passion, and to specify the precise nature of it. Though in this period the moral concern applied to all literature, it had a particular reference to drama. It may be recalled that Dr. Johnson chided Shakespeare for missing chances to enforce a moral. Gothic tragic writers omitted no opportunities to do so. Some, like Hannah More and later Joanna Baillie, were obviously sincere; neither had any thought that the purpose of drama should be other than moral instruction. But in the works of most Gothic playwrights we sense mere apprehension that the censor might reject a play which failed to proclaim an unimpeachable morality.

An ideal mouthpiece for this proclamation was the villain—the protagonist of the play, the role enacted by the star actor. Mere punishment at the end was insufficient; playwrights who depended on a censor's approbation compelled their villains to howl in torment for their past evil deeds. After 1785 the villain in every Gothic play was a study in the agony of remorse. When at last Coleridge entitled his drama *Remorse,* before its performance at Drury Lane, he named the central characteristic not merely of his own villain but of a generation of villains.[23]

The elaborate precautions of playwrights to avoid the censor's disapproval are illustrated in the two plays just reviewed, *The Regent* and *Kentish Barons.* In these, the villains come downstage and baldly invite inspection of the ravages inflicted on them by their evil deeds; one of them, at the end, seems to become a personification of vice itself, and imagines himself snatched into Hell's mouth by fiends. Their service as horrible examples is not in the least subtle. Playwrights wished all to take note that they were on the side of morality. Thus Gothic tyrants, created first to perform a single function, came to assume an additional and quite different one.

The most far-reaching effect of moral concern was therefore an exaggeration of that agony which, for other reasons, the villain was already doomed to suffer. Ironically, the ultimate result was that moral solicitude abetted the transformation of the villain through the sympathy which his show of remorse aroused. The original gloom, magnified by the star actor's bid for sympathy and made ostentatious by the playwright's "morality," swelled to an irresistible agony that carried the protagonist across the dividing line and won him acceptance, in a flood of tears, as Byronic hero.

CHAPTER VI
ANN RADCLIFFE AND GOTHIC DRAMA

IN 1792 A. F. Tytler published the first English translation of *Die Räuber*. There is little possibility that *Sturm und Drang* had any influence upon Gothic drama in England before that date. As we have seen, English playwrights, with the help of their contemporary novelists, had developed a native drama of mystery, gloom, and terror in their own way and through their own resources. Though awareness of German literature was shown in 1788 when Henry MacKenzie read a paper at Edinburgh on German drama, English plays in the years immediately thereafter reveal no traces of foreign influence. Earlier, in 1785, Reynolds had made a loose adaptation of Goethe's *Werther,* and *The German Hotel,* translated by Marshall[1] from J. C. Brandes' *Der Gasthof,* was acted at the Covent Garden Theatre in 1790—the first German play brought to the English stage. But neither was of a kind to contribute to the Gothic genre, and since there were no further translations, adaptations, or even suggestions of outside influence before 1792, it is apparent that Gothic drama remained to that date, at least, in all respects an English product.[2]

Actually, the year 1792 can be taken only as the date at which there *might* have occurred the earliest mingling of German and English horrific materials in Gothic plays. There is no evidence of borrowing from *Die Räuber* until several years later, and the mass invasion of the stage by imported elements, with the sentimentalism of Kotzebue in the van, did not take place until the years 1798–1802. But if Gothic playwrights acquired nothing from Germany which showed immediately after 1792, they did take renewed impetus from another source—the novels of Ann Radcliffe. Her materials, methods, and motifs, which were added

---
[1] For notes to chap. vi, see pages 251–252.

before and surpassed in quantity those contributed by the Germans, conspicuously enriched the storehouse drawn upon by playwrights.

Though she wrote no plays, Mrs. Radcliffe's novels furnished numerous adaptable plots and a tremendous new impulse to Gothicize. *The Castles of Athlin and Dunbayne* (1789) was loosely adapted twice, as *Edgar, or Caledonian Feuds* (C. G. May 1806), by George Manners, and as *Halloween; or, The Castles of Athlin and Dunbayne* (publ. 1809), "A New Grand Scotch Spectacle," by J. C. Cross. *A Sicilian Romance* (1790) was very loosely adapted by Henry Siddons as *The Sicilian Romance; or, The Apparition of the Cliffs* (C. G. May 1794). From *The Romance of the Forest* (1791) came two plays, Boaden's *Fontainville Forest* (C. G. March 1794), and an anonymous melodrama, *Fontainville Abbey; or, The Phantom of the Forest* (Surrey, March 1824). *The Mysteries of Udolpho* (1794) was used in part by Miles Peter Andrews in an "opera" called *The Mysteries of the Castle* (C. G. Jan. 1795) and again inspired an unacted melodrama by John Baylis, *The Mysteries of Udolpho; or, The Phantom of the Castle* (publ. 1804). Still another adaptation of this novel was an anonymous "dramatic opera" called *The Castle of Udolpho* (publ. 1808). *The Italian* (1797) appeared as *The Italian Monk* (Hay. Aug. 1797), by Boaden. Finally, *Gaston De Blondeville* (post. 1826) was adapted under that title by Mary Russell Mitford and published unacted in 1854.[8]

The ten adaptations represent merely the direct impact of Mrs. Radcliffe's novels on the stage. It is impossible to measure the full extent of her influence. As we have found earlier, definite debts other than adaptations can rarely be established in Gothic plays. It cannot be proved, for instance, that the protagonist in a certain novel, play, or poem was borrowed directly from Mrs. Radcliffe's Montoni or Schedoni, for "Montoni" and "Schedoni," under other names, existed in Gothic drama more than a dozen years before Mrs. Radcliffe published her first novel, and they continued to appear afterwards in works which may have owed no direct debt to the novelist's dark figures. It is usually possible to find the source of an element which appears in a Gothic play for the first time, however, and both Mrs. Radcliffe and the German school can be accurately credited with introduction of certain new elements. But once something new had made a first appearance it was lost in the general pool, and later playwrights might borrow it then rather than directly from its original source.

BOADEN AND ANN RADCLIFFE

James Boaden approached with some misgivings the task of making the first adaptation of a novel by Ann Radcliffe. Would it be possible to create through settings, dialogue, and action the effects achieved by the descriptive narration which had brought the novelist immediate fame? The playwright discussed the problems involved in his undertaking:

Mr. Boaden had read the Romance of the Forest with great pleasure, and thought that he saw there the ground-work of a drama of more than usual effect. He admired, as every one else did, the singular address by which Mrs. Radcliffe contrived to impress the mind with all the terrors of the ideal world; and the sportive resolution of all that had excited terror into very common natural appearances; indebted for their false aspect to circumstances, and the overstrained feelings of the characters.

But, even in romance, it may be doubtful, whether there be not something *ungenerous* in thus playing upon poor timid human nature, and agonizing it with false terrors. The disappointment, I know, is always resented, and the laboured explanation commonly deemed the flattest and most uninteresting part of the production. Perhaps, when the attention is once secured and the reason yielded, the passion for the marvellous had better remain unchecked; and an interest selected from the olden time be entirely subjected to its gothic machinery. However this may be in respect to romance, when the doubtful of the narrative is to be exhibited in the drama, the decision is a matter of necessity. While description only fixes the inconclusive dreams of the fancy, she may partake the dubious character of her inspirer; but the pen of the dramatic poet must turn everything into shape; and bestow on these "airy nothings a local habitation and a name."[4]

Jephson's problem in 1781, as he adapted Walpole's *Castle of Otranto,* was one of eliminating the excesses of Gothic machinery. Boaden acknowledged no such difficulty in 1794; on the contrary, he determined that "an interest selected from the olden time be entirely subjected to its gothic machinery." It is to be remembered that Mrs. Radcliffe customarily hedged in her treatment of the supernatural. In her novels a great many sights, sounds, and events are described which seem explicable only as manifestations of an unearthly power; but once the utmost in terror has been wrung from these incidents, everything is explained as having proceeded from natural causes.[5] Boaden believed that "the passion for the marvellous had better remain unchecked." His decision, therefore, was to omit, not Mrs. Radcliffe's excesses, but her natural explanations of the supernatural. For the first time, a playwright undertook to out-Gothicize a novelist. The result was a play more elaborately Gothic in its furnishings than any previously acted.

FONTAINVILLE FOREST

From the prologue—"Caught from the Gothic treasures of Romance..."—to the final scene this play serves the Gothic purpose. The novelist's opening description of the flight of La Motte and his wife, with their acquisition of Adeline en route, is omitted, and the first scene takes place in "A Gothic Hall of an Abbey, the whole much dilapidated," where the fugitives have taken refuge. Dialogue and setting create an atmosphere comparable to that which Mrs. Radcliffe had achieved by long descriptions of the abandoned ruin; says Peter, a servant,

> This is a horrid place. I scarce dare crawl
> Through its low grates and narrow passages;
> And the wind's gust that whistles in the turrets

> Is as the groan of someone near his end.
> Heaven send my master back! On my old knees
> I begg'd him not explore that dismal wood!
> ...
> He went at dusk; by the same token then
> The owl shriek'd from the porch—He started back;
> But recollected, smote his forehead, and advanc'd.
> I clos'd the Abbey gate, which grated sadly.⁶

Boaden lost little by condensing the novelist's pages. The very sketchiness of the opening scene conveys a sense of the mysterious. The physical setting, kept before the very eyes, admirably replaces the lengthy accounts of mouldering ruins; and dialogue, as usual, supplements the setting through repeated mention of Gothic fixtures not represented on the stage.

La Motte at length returns from a mysterious errand, accompanied by the frightened Adeline, whom his wife conducts to a chamber. Later Madame La Motte returns and tells how, "sunk in startled sleep," the unknown girl had writhed and shrieked of her father and of ruffians. La Motte tells how he had found her, and here Boaden lavishly displayed the Gothicists' accumulated treasure:

> 'Tis horrible and strange... Listen;
> The evening being calm, I took my walk
> To ruminate at full—wrapped up in thought,
> Night stole upon me. Through the pathless wilds
> No signs could I discover that might lead
> My erring steps back to this Abbey's towers.
> The storm came sudden on; a little while
> The shading tree protected me—At length,
> A distant taper threw its trembling light
> Across the alley where I stood; I ran,
> So guided, till I reach'd a paltry cottage.⁷

In the cottage an unknown man, in the company of ruffians, had forced him to swear to take the girl away forever.

The first scene poses three mysteries: From what is the gloomy La Motte a fugitive? Who is Adeline? Why was she thrust into the hands of a total stranger? In the second scene, La Motte, desperate for money and fearful of starvation, resolves to rob some traveler in the forest. "Wild and dishevell'd," he rushes into "a dark Wood, with a ruined Abbey in the background," and accosts a marquis. He seizes money and jewelry, but the attendants surprise him, and he flees into "a darker part of the Wood." But conscience has already stung him:

> I scap'd unhurt. Unhurt! O memory,
> I'm all one wound, while I yet live to think!
> O dearly purchas'd wealth, won by the loss
> Of future peace! Up, damning baubles, up!
> Close to the heart, which you have wrung from comfort.
> Hence, Monster, hence, nor blot the beauteous day.
> Hail, cavern'd glooms, to your deep shade I fly,
> Darkness myself, to give you living horror.[8]

Meanwhile, at the abbey, Adeline tells as much as she knows of herself. Her mother dead, she had been reared in a convent. On arriving "at her majority," she was commanded by her father to "take the veil." Rebelling, she was snatched from the convent at night, presumably on her father's orders, and directly thereafter thrust into the hands of La Motte.

In Act II the inhabitants of the abbey, already frightened, are terrified when La Motte, returning "in great agitation" from the robbery, reports

> ... On entering just now,
> The outer porch, I saw a human figure,
> Gliding mysteriously along the hall.[9]

The introduction of this gliding figure, with the depiction of the terror it occasions, illustrates a species of trickery to become increasingly common in Gothic plays. Though Boaden had expressly stated his intention of dispensing with Mrs. Radcliffe's "explanations," he adopted her technique in this instance in order to provide an incidental thrill. After the momentary sensation has been achieved, its cause is brushed aside as inconspicuously as possible; here the figure "gliding mysteriously" turns out to be only Louis, son of the La Mottes, arriving for a visit. Perhaps the most lasting lesson Mrs. Radcliffe taught her fellow Gothicists was to squeeze at least a moment of excitement from each trifle.[10] It was Lewis who was later to excel in this specious art.

No sooner has Louis joined the group than Peter cries from the turret that horsemen are approaching. La Motte hastily exits through "a sliding Pannel." The marquis whom he had waylaid enters, identifies himself as owner of the abbey, and invites Madame La Motte and Adeline to remain as occupants. La Motte, hearing the conversation but not seeing the visitor, reënters, recognizes the victim of his robbery, and "starts back violently." The two talk privately, and the marquis hints darkly that their relations may be improved if La Motte will serve his designs; leering toward Adeline, he suggests that "this fair one may heal the breach between us."

Before the end of Act II the plot has five tangled problems: La Motte's plight as a fugitive from Paris; his precarious position as a known robber; the mystery of Adeline's identity; the circumstances of her strange appearance on the scene; and the menace of the marquis' designs. No Gothic dramatist, however, was overawed by any number of complications that involved mystery, and Boaden proceeded at once to introduce a new turn. Adeline is shown in her gloomy chamber. With that restlessness common to all her kind—no Gothic heroine is ever content with the multiple dangers that already threaten—she sets out to find new and greater terrors:

> The night is rough, and through these shatter'd casements
> The wind in shrilling blasts sweeps the old hangings.
> Whether the place alone puts such thoughts in me,
> I know not; but asleep, or waking, still
> Conviction haunts me, that some mystery
> Is wrapt within these chambers, which my fate

> Will have me penetrate.—The falling gust
> With feeble tone expires like dying sighs—
> The tap'stry yonder shakes, as tho' some door
> Open'd beyond it. (Takes her lamp) Ha! 'tis so! the bolt
> Tho' rusty, yields unto my hand; I'll see
> To what it leads. How, if I sink with fear,
> And so benumb'd, life freeze away in terror?
> No matter, powerful impulse drives me onwards,
> And my soul rises to the coming horror.[11]

Seeking motivation to send forth his heroine with the inevitable Radcliffean lamp in quest of terror, Boaden here expressed the soul of the Gothic urge. "A powerful impulse drives me onwards," the harassed heroine avers, "And my soul rises to the coming horror." It is an appropriate speech for a young lady transported to the barbarous time with the tacit understanding that she is to act as register of its terrors. The impulse which dispatches Adeline to seek that which will expand her soul with the ecstasy of terror was perhaps identical with that which prompted the public, experiencing vicariously her contact with the "sublime," to relish her reactions. The Gothic maiden *wanted* to be affrighted, and dramatists, aware that the age was eager to respond with shudders and joy, competed with one another in assembling a fearful machinery of objects through which a heroine might move and be accommodated. The passage, incidentally, enforces the contrast between Gothic and Elizabethan purposes. Adeline seems to echo Juliet's lines when she asks,

> ... How, if I sink with fear?
> And so benumb'd, life freeze away in horror?

Juliet says,

> How if, when I am laid into the tomb,
> I wake before the time when Romeo
> Come to redeem me? there's a fearful point!
> Shall I not then be stifled in the vault—
> ...
> And there lie strangled ere my Romeo comes?[12]

Because it reflects an essential difference between Gothic and Elizabethan purposes, the difference between Adeline's and Juliet's motivation is significant. Shakespeare's heroine had urgent business in the Capulet tomb; otherwise it would not have occurred to the dramatist to send her there. Her need is to escape her father and rejoin her husband; the horrors of the tomb are incidentals to be endured. Boaden's heroine has no purpose but to gain and transmit a thrill; the horrors of the haunted chamber which she visits are not the incidentals, but the end itself.

Adeline passes through a secret door behind the fluttering tapestries, and the scene changes to "A melancholy Apartment." She enters, trembling, to view high, grated windows and a "tattered set of hanging-tapestry":

> I must be cautious, lest the sudden blast
> Extinguish my faint guide. I'll place the lamp
> Behind this sheltering bulk. What's that I tread on?
> A dagger, all corroded by the rust!
> Prophetic soul! yes, murder has been busy!
> A chilly faintness creeps across my heart,
> And checks the blood that strives in vain to follow.[18]

The first goal of her exploration—a terror that makes her swoon—has been reached. She sits, breathless, a moment; then,

> I feel recover'd, and new strength is giv'n me!
> 'Tis destiny compels,—On to my task.
> Yon tatter'd ruin yawns to tempt inquiry.

She reaches out, touches a dark mass, and everything falls; she utters a line which deserves some special distinction in the history of dramatic verse: "What scroll thus meets me in the falling lumber?" The scroll is mouldy, partly illegible, "blurr'd all by damps"—and it is what she wants:

> ... I'll hence now;
> The morning light warns me to join my chamber.

Adeline is the typical Gothic maiden, and hers is the true Gothic spirit. Another lady, non-Gothic, would visit the gloomy chamber of grated windows and tattered ruins by strong daylight, if at all. But Adeline promptly flees at crack of dawn and impatiently endures the sunlit hours, awaiting midnight for a second visit.

During the intervening day, new events occur. The marquis lewdly bids for her favors:

> This lonely place will rather fix a gloom
> For ever on your youth, that should be led
> To happier scenes of gay, voluptuous love.[14]

The heroine's reply to the overture is that of an eighteenth-century maiden of virtue whose sense of propriety accompanied her to the past age:

> I thank you, sir, for thus at once displaying
> The glaring infamy design'd for me!
> An honourable purpose had received
> At least my gratitude ev'n in rejection;
> But this, for its mean insult, has my scorn.

The heroine, perhaps, had been reading *Evelina*.

During the day, also, La Motte explores the castle and finds "a mould'ring chest." Peter and Louis learn at the neighboring village that long ago a stranger had been brought to the castle at night, "so closely that no one ever saw him afterward." Gossip reports that the man was murdered and that his spirit haunts the ruin. It is decided that the chest "contains a body which still lies unburied in the secret chamber."

On the next scene Boaden spent his best care—and succeeded in out-Gothicizing Mrs. Radcliffe's original. The novelist's Adeline reads the scroll night after night in bed in her own room, continuing each time until some accident interrupts or faintness induced by terror prevents further reading. Boaden's Adeline—at midnight—revisits the haunted chamber, there to read. The only apparent reason for her return to this dismal place to read the scroll, which she might have read by better light in her own quarters, is that the effect of terror was thus enhanced. She seats herself in the place of her choice and expresses a Gothic maiden's satisfaction:

> A general horror creeps thro' all my limbs,
> And almost stifles curiosity.[15]

In this mood she begins to read. The scroll had been written by the Marquis of Montault, and tells that he had been brought by his brother to the gloomy ruin and long imprisoned in the chamber, doomed to perish:

Adeline. His brother! What—yon Marquis!
Phantom. (Heard within the chamber) Even he!
Adeline. Hark! Sure I heard a voice! no, 'tis the thunder
          That rolls its murmurs thro' this yawning pile. (reads on)
          Poor, wretched sufferer! Accept the tears
          Of one, like thee, pursued by fortune's frown,
          Yet less unhappy.
Phantom. O, Adeline! (faintly visible)
Adeline. Ha! Sure I'm called! No, all are at rest.
          How powerful is fancy! I'll proceed. (reads on)
          Great God of mercy! Could there none be found
          To aid thee? Then he perish'd—
Phantom. Perish'd here!
Adeline. My sense does not deceive me. Awful sounds!
          'Twas here he fell!

(The Phantom here glides across the dark part of the chamber. Adeline shrieks, and falls back. The scene closes upon her.)

The curtain rises for the next scene with the same high pitch continued: "Scene: the Hall—dark. Violent thunder and lightning. The Abbey rocks, and through the distant windows one of the turrets is seen to fall, struck by lightning. Enter the Marquis, wild and dishevelled." This setting, with its combination of spectacular sounds and action, is a striking beginning of the catastrophic pictures which, after Boaden's play, were staged with increasing violence. In *Fontainville Forest* a single turret, in the distance, is seen to fall. In some later plays whole castles and abbeys were demolished to the accompaniment of thunderclaps and lightning flashes. The eyes and the ears were assailed by sights and sounds of terrific destruction. As settings became more spectacular, so the machinery to destroy all at an instant became more elaborate. Carpenters and painters were kept busy preparing scenery that would rise, sink, fall, explode, or otherwise create startling effects. The burden borne by dialogue in earlier plays by repeated mention of vaults, aisles, turrets, galleries, and off-stage supernatural occurrences was later assumed by actual settings. Gothic drama became more and more a drama of spectacle, which gained its effects through whatever calamities invention could represent physically.

Piling Gothic elements one on the other, Boaden seems to have been determined to exceed Mrs. Radcliffe's formidable exhibition of the sources of terror. Writing so, he balked not at all at the "real" supernatural, and it is noteworthy that in 1794 a playwright demanded, the manager accepted, and the audience applauded a ghost. The phantom which glides across the stage before Adeline's eyes was Boaden's proudest accomplishment. He wrote that he had been "alarm'd at venturing within that circle which none but Shakespeare had hitherto trodden with success," but had decided to experiment and "ascertain whether the failure of others had not proceeded from defective preparation of the supernatural incident, or from its imperfect or vulgar exhibition."[16] In planning the climactic entrance of his apparition, he called to mind a painting of the ghost in *Hamlet:*

> Perhaps the sublimest effect of painting is the figure of the Royal Dane, as he appeared in the large composition of Mr. Fuseli for the Shakespeare Gallery. It has what seems person, invested in what seems to be armour; it bears the regal sceptre; its countenance is human in its lineaments, though it inspires more awe than mere humanity can excite. By recollecting some of the principles of the sublime...[17]

Boaden applied "the principles of the sublime" in dressing his specter, and, after some preliminary effects that proved ludicrous, he evidently succeeded in representing a spirit which pleased the public:

> ... I recommended a dark blue grey stuff, made in the shape of armour, and sitting close to the person; and when Follet (the actor) was thus dressed, and faintly visible behind the gauze or crape spread before the scene, the whisper of the house, as he was about to enter,—the breathless silence, while he floated along like a shadow,—proved to me, that I had achieved the great desideratum; and the often renewed plaudits, when the curtain fell, told me that the audience had enjoyed "that sacred terror, that severe delight".... for which alone it is excusable to overpass the ordinary limits of nature.[18]

Harris, then manager of the Covent Garden Theatre, accepted Boaden's play, ghost and all, on first reading it. Later, some misgivings arose at rehearsals, and there was pressure on the author to remove or "explain" the specter. Boaden remained firm, and wrote for the epilogue:

> Why should your terror lay my proudest boast?
> Madam, I *die* if I *give up* the *Ghost*.

Fontainville Forest, obviously enough, belongs in the lower depths of dramatic literature. But it is a pinnacle in the Gothic tradition. The extravagant applause which greeted its performance prompted Boaden to dramatize *The Italian* in 1797 as *The Italian Monk* (Hay. Aug. 1797). This adaptation follows its source more closely than earlier dramatizations of Gothic novels had done. Though not every turn of Mrs. Radcliffe's plot is included, the main outline is so closely pursued that no summary of the story is needed. The tragedy has neither the excesses of Gothic spectacle which characterize *Fontainville Forest* nor the cautious use of effects which earlier adapters deemed politic. Its Schedoni, patterned after the villain of the novel with only such extra flourishes as were necessary to devise a striking role for the actor (Palmer), is an outstanding Gothic villain. Its Vivaldi gave to Charles Kemble a better hero role than most Gothic plays provided, though typical marks of ineffectuality remain. To the history of Gothic drama *The Italian Monk* is most important because it added (from the novel, of course) a new and highly exploitable subject—the Inquisition.[19] Of this and of its German counterpart, the *Vehmgericht,* I shall speak later.

SIDDONS AND ANN RADCLIFFE

Two months after Boaden's venturing "within that circle which none but Shakespeare had hitherto trodden with success," Henry Siddons brought to another Covent Garden audience a spectacle that rivaled *Fontainville Forest* setting for setting and shudder for shudder. The play was *The Sicilian Romance; or, The Apparition of the Cliffs,* allegedly an adaptation of *A Sicilian Romance.* Though no ghost glided across the stage, the supernatural was clearly the dramatist's foremost preoccupation. The "idea" hovers over all scenes and is made the subject of some—but in the end Siddons followed Mrs. Radcliffe in "explaining" everything. This play requires close examination.

Except for the title and the name of one character, Siddons was not specifically indebted to Mrs. Radcliffe. His is virtually an original play. The atmosphere is reminiscent of Mrs. Radcliffe's, but of no particular novel. The plot is related to *A Sicilian Romance* only as every Gothic plot is related to every other. The machinery, too, is composed of properties common to all. Probably Siddons advertised his play as an adaptation of Mrs. Radcliffe's story in order to capitalize on the immediate popularity of *A Sicilian Romance.* It is interesting to note that the work was first submitted to the censor, two months before it was acted, under the title of *The Castle of Otranto;* that application was made by Stephen Kemble, who may have believed that the name of Walpole's novel would attract the larger audience.[20] The change of title thereafter may have been made on the same grounds, with a reversal of opinion. The fact that titles could be thus exchanged to reap the harvest of the latest infatuation among the novel-reading public indicates how little an adapter really owed to a specific source, and how much to the common property of Gothicists.

In *Fontainville Forest* Boaden had focused attention where Mrs. Radcliffe's had been—on the heroine assailed by multiple terrors. His villain received less emphasis than either Adeline or La Motte, and was in fact allowed to slip back into the original function of the Gothic villain, as merely one among several objects introduced to terrify a heroine; the marquis is little more important than the ruin, the dark chamber, the corroded knife, the scroll, the gust of wind, or the ghost. Novelists, even Mrs. Radcliffe, had lagged behind dramatists in the development of the villain, and it was therefore natural that, following the emphasis of his source, Boaden should have drawn a tyrant somewhat obsolete dramatically.

In *The Sicilian Romance,* on the contrary, Siddons restored the villain to the place of emphasis which, on the stage, he had achieved in the 1780's. His Marquis of Otranto was unmistakably designed to provide the actor with a striking and sympathetic role and at the same time, through a highly conspicuous display of remorse for past crimes, to serve as morality's mouthpiece.

The first scene shows "An ancient castle in the Gothic style," with various "atmospheric" environs visible. Two "pilgrims" approach the gate, and dialogue reveals their purpose to save Alinda from an impending marriage with the marquis. They are met by Gerbin, a familiar type of gossip who, after the earliest Gothic pieces, was used to present the initial exposition and point out the mystery to be solved.

Gerbin. Why, master, I don't like to drive the unfortunate from the gate, but my young Marquis is very strict. I can give you an apartment indeed in a tower, but then it's rather inconvenient. ...A very strange apparition has been often seen to enter it, since our poor mistress died.[21]

The pattern is quite unmistakable; reading no further, we would guess that the "very strict" marquis will in fact be gloomy, impetuous, and tormented, that the "very strange apparition" will be found as solid as flesh, and that "our poor mistress" who "died" will be returned to the living.

On his first entrance—frightened servants scattering before him—Ferrand, the marquis, exhibits the tell-tale mark of evil:

> Now every heart with glowing rapture beats
> Save mine alone, where, like a vulture, guilt,
> Continual gnawing, keeps me on the stretch.[22]

A servant approaches timidly, and he flies into a rage. Julia, his child, begs him not to marry Alinda, and he starts back "in great agitation":

> I cannot bear her eye, her every look
> Brings back the memory of—Take her away![23]

News arrives that Alinda has escaped, and he shows the fury and desperation which afflict all of his tribe in moments of crisis. Before pursuing the heroine and her saviors, he visits "A Cave in a Rock," where, behind a grated door, his wife is chained to solid stone:

> Now gloomy silence reigns thro' all the air
> Save where the wind upon the whisp'ring boughs
> Talks o'er the deeds of Lucifer and me;
> There lies the wretch who causes all my care,
> Whose wrongs forever gnaw upon my heart.[24]

Self-agonized, self-pitying, asking sympathy for the torture he earned by torturing another, Ferrand might momentarily pass for the fully developed Byronic hero of a later generation; but in the next instant he shows that in his composition villainy yet dominates:

> Why, to the wretched thing I have condemn'd
> To waste its years, shut from the cheering light,
> Death would be mercy. Ha! it shall be so!

A sudden thought, and an instant move to put it into action: such had been the conventional abruptness of his ancestors. Ferrand strides to the woman, awakens, and threatens her. A scene follows of the kind to be found once in almost every Gothic play: the spectacle of a barbarous agent of medievalism menacing an oppressed female in whose terror the enlightened age saw, projected and magnified, its own attitude toward the Dark Age. While peals of thunder shake the roof of the cave, the villain twice raises his dagger and twice fails to strike because,

> ...base coward that I am!
> My nerves unstrung refuse the horried deed!

His show of noble agony invites tears for himself rather than for the prostrate creature before him. By turns offering violence and beating his breast in pain, Ferrand is in this scene sometimes the typical tyrant with the familiar marks of the object of terror, sometimes the Byronic hero, ostentatiously self-pitying, entreating tears which he would seem to scorn. The struggle ends with the hero triumphant; Ferrand magnanimously sheathes the dagger, turns from the Lady of the Rock, and closes and bars the grated door. Then, instantly reassuming his function as villain and moralist, he recollects the flight of Alinda:

> ...how have I loitered time! now for pursuit!
> Let me not stay—this conscience teazes yet,
> And tells me if there is a hell I must expect it.

The scene shifts to a convent at which the fugitives have arrived. In their flight the carriage had broken down, and they were lost, benighted, in a forest; continuing on foot, they had seen the convent lamp "glimmering through the trees." Lindor, the hero, had left Alinda and Martin, an old man, and had returned to the woods as sentry. There he was seized by banditti and led to their cave.

At the convent, as the heroine enters, the prior speaks to an "unknown wretch" called Vincent, who lies on his face before the altar:

> Prior. Hast thou been returning thanks to that providence which directed our brothers to pass the spot where thou lay'st mangled in the wood?
> Vinc. It was a just punishment for crimes too black to name; oh, holy Father, I am the veriest wretch that e'er polluted these chaste walls—damn'd beyond all reach of mercy.[26]

Several Gothic plays include such an unknown—a man, woman, or child who bears some relation to the principal mystery, and often is the key to the past event. Frequently this unknown is shown in some holy establishment where he has found refuge. Vincent explains the cause of the marquis' mysterious conduct. He had been "minister of pleasure" to the marquis, and as such a "very wicked man." In his youth, the marquis had married an Italian lady "whose virtue might have challenged the whole world," but, having heard of Alinda, daughter of the minister of state, he had been struck with the thought of the power an alliance with her would afford and had "from that moment meditated mischief" against his wife. Vincent describes the past event:

> We bore her in the dead of night to the center of an unfrequented cliff, and chain'd her in a cave, known to myself, the Marquis, and another—the world was blinded by a pompous funeral. Soon after, the Minister of State propos'd his daughter to him—the Marquis was transported with success . . . Every night I walked the rocks and carried the wretched lady her miserable pittance for the next day—but my humanity yielded to her prayers, and I suffered her one day to look at her little daughter. The Marquis discovered it, and offered thrice to stab me. I wrested the dagger from his hand, fled the castle, but was overtaken and left for dead by the ruffians he had employed to murder me—In this situation your charitable brethren found me.[26]

Alinda identifies herself as the daughter of the minister of state and asks sanctuary. On such occasions, the holy men of Gothic drama rarely prove coöperative. The prior will grant refuge only if Alinda will take the veil. When the soldiers of the marquis begin to hammer at the gates, the harassed maiden acquiesces. The marquis enters and demands her; but Vincent's information has equipped the prior with a very forceful argument:

Prior. We have an arm above to fight our battles. Approach, my children! See, here they stand; dare but to raise your arm to wrest them from me, and I'll aloud unfold a tale—
Marq. 'Sdeath! how is this? I'll hear no more!
Order the cannon this instant to play off,
Scale up their walls!
Prior. The Rock! The Rock! The Rock!
Marq. Horror and shame!
Prior. Your wretched wife—
Marq. 'Sdeath! he has me in the toil!

To make the scene more spectacular, Vincent at this instant strikes a pose above the altar, and the villain is blasted by what he takes for a ghost:

Horror! Open the earth and swallow me! What means that ghastly spectre on the walls? Look how he glares! He thrills me to the bone! Take, take him hence!

The marquis withdraws "in great agitation" and hastens back to his castle. Meanwhile the child, Julia, seeking the oft-reported "apparition of the cliffs," finds and releases her mother. The tyrant interrupts their flight, orders ruffians to slay the child, and, when they refuse, raises his own dagger. At the critical moment the *deus ex machina* intervenes; the forces of good, represented by Don Lope, uncle of the marquis, enter. The villain's power and his mind crack simultaneously.

It was more or less inevitable that eventually a Gothic villain should be shown in a mad scene. The villain had earlier seized most of the opportunities for histrionics afforded by the kind of play, and madness gave the actor an additional chance to exhibit his talents; besides, it extended a very effective bid for sympathy, and, even more, the spectacle of one driven mad by conscience served the interests of morality. Similarly, it was to be expected that when the lunatic marquis is brought before the Lady of the Rock to hear his sentence from her lips, he should be instantly and fully pardoned. Though he had chained her to a rock and left her to starve by degrees in a dismal cave, had forbidden her to see her child, and had threatened her and her child with his dagger, the lady says to her oppressor:

> Look up, my lord; if the most tender care
> Can make my love more worthy your acceptance,
> By heaven I swear, in sickness and in health
> To prove your constant, tendrest comforter.[27]

Thus, at the end, the hero in Ferrand, not the villain, has the edge. Here the protagonist receives affectionate forgiveness from her he had persecuted. A few more years, and such a one would gain from the public not only this, but adulation and a flood of tears.

I have yet to note a second way in which Siddons' play proved momentous in Gothic history. Here, for the first time in a serious Gothic play, the hero gave indication of change from his traditional insipidity. Lindor, as we have seen, after escorting Alinda to the convent, had gone into the woods and had been captured by the banditti who invariably lurk in Radcliffean forests. His fate is not disclosed until a later, critical moment. Meanwhile, after the marquis has been frightened from the convent, the prior demands that Alinda take the veil. She had scarcely bettered her position: having fled one persecutor, the marquis, she had found another, the prior. But the Alindas of Gothic story were compelled to flee and flee again before reaching an enduring refuge. Having fled the castle by night, the heroine now flees the convent by night, via secret passage. Then, arriving in the forest, she is obliged to flee the banditti; but she is ambushed, seized, and carried to the robbers' cave. She has now been menaced in all of the favorite horror environs—castle, convent, and cavern. Dragged in mortal fear before the "Robber Captain," she makes a startling and historic discovery: the captain is Lindor, who, apparently overnight, had been accepted by his captors and elected to the distinction. A few years after *The Lady of the Rock*, audiences found the motif conventional. Karl Moor, the nobleman's-son-turned-outlaw of *Die Räuber*, had become a property of Gothic dramatists.²⁸

The naturalness of the adoption of the new motif is noteworthy. Siddons, like other Gothic playwrights, had needed a device for removing his hero so that the villain might molest Alinda, the Lady of the Rock, and the child Julia with impunity. The German motif answered his need: Lindor is captured by robbers and rendered *hors de combat* at the end of the second act. And though, as captain of a band of robbers, he now has means to oppose the villain's might, he avoids the responsibility of the champion. After his reunion with Alinda, the hero valiantly proposes, "Tomorow we will fly to some spot where neither the tyranny of your father nor the avarice of the marquis can ever molest you." Hero and heroine then vanish from the drama long before it is ended, and without offering the slightest aid to the lady who was yet chained and starving in a cave. A hero, even one equipped with power, was not yet to be permitted a hand in chastising a villain. All factors considered—including the censor—playwrights evidently found it more expedient to leave that to Heaven.

ANDREWS AND ANN RADCLIFFE

The final major adaptation of a novel by Mrs. Radcliffe which I shall examine is Miles Peter Andrews' *Mysteries of the Castle*, based remotely on *The Mysteries of Udolpho*. Twice previously Andrews had dabbled in the Gothic. He had attempted to combine the grossest elements of both *The Castle of Otranto* and

Aikin's *Sir Bertrand* to form the one-act piece entitled *The Enchanted Castle* (C. G. Dec. 1786), already mentioned, and had composed an astonishing mélange of pantomime, dialogue, and song called *The Baron of Kinkvervankotsdorsprakingatchdern* (Hay. July 1781), in which an absurd baron locks his daughter in a castle chamber, whence she escapes by piling the family pictures in a heap.

With these concoctions and others of similar quality to recommend him, Andrews could not have been expected to do justice to Mrs. Radcliffe's best novel. Such lame talents as he had lay in comic pantomime and song. Creation of the gloomy atmosphere which weighs upon the castle of Udolpho was beyond him. Had he restricted his efforts to his forte, he might have written an amusing burlesque of his original, but he erred in striving for a predominantly serious atmosphere when he was constitutionally incapable of resisting indulgence in utter nonsense. He blundered, too, in allowing his fondness for the scrambling of disparate elements to cause him to invent a fable instead of following Mrs. Radcliffe's. Boaden, who had followed his model more closely, summed up Andrews' "masterpiece":

Andrews, perhaps assisted,[29] brought out at Covent Garden what was called, erroneously, a dramatic tale of the Mysteries of the Castle. But Mysteries were very far indeed from the touch of the writers; and taking the name of Montoni from Udolpho, and the name only, they fabricated a non-descript of every sort of a absurdity; and having long debauched the public taste, succeeded perhaps beyond expectation,— and certainly beyond desert.[30]

From his source Andrews indeed took very little. Most of the play was original. The result, described by Genest as "a strange jumble of Tragedy, Comedy, and Opera," nevertheless had a highly successful first run of seventeen nights and was revived at Bath as late as 1815. It was not only the most popular adaptation of a novel by Mrs. Radcliffe, but also one of the most successful plays of the period. As such, it requires examination.

Carlos arrives at Messina to punish Count Montoni, who had kidnaped and supposedly married Julia, the hero's intended bride. Through correspondence with Constantia, Julia's sister, Carlos had learned of Montoni's treachery and of the "death" of Julia. With his friend Hilario, seeking revenge, he visits a desolate castle at night. A bell tolls, they hear screams, and Carlos breaks into a chamber in time to save the heroine from Montoni's dagger.[21] The villain flees, and Hilario escorts Julia to her home. Carlos, for a time (and for no apparent purpose), disappears from the story. At length Hilario and Julia, pursued by Julia's father, arrive by boat on the shore of Calabria, where they find the hero. Reconciliations follow. The "wedding" of Montoni and Julia is revealed to have been fraudulent. The villain—without any exertion on the hero's part—has been delivered up to justice.

Gothic settings are conspicuous throughout the play. The opening scene is typical:

(The outside of an old Castle, with large gates closed—a turret-door is visible in the interior of the castle—a hole that appears to lead to a subterraneous passage—the whole appears of great antiquity and ruin.)

Carlos and Hilario, approaching, meet Clody, foolish brother of Constantia's maid, who crawls through the "turret-door" and tells them that, inside the castle, he has heard shrieks and squeals and has seen specters and apparitions. As they talk, the inevitable Radcliffean lamp flickers at a window, and a midnight bell tolls. The curtain falls as the friends crawl through the hole into the castle. It rises again to disclose "An old room, hung with antique Tapestry." Count Montoni, "muffled in a black cloak," and Bernardo, his henchman, hasten across the room and continue through "the dark windings of this dreary mansion." They hurry to Julia's chamber, intent on murder before the tolling of the bell shall have attracted "strangers." Sighs of the imprisoned heroine are audible through the walls. Carlos and Hilario enter, the latter carrying a scroll which he has picked up and which, like the glimmering light, unfailingly appears in Mrs. Radcliffe's novels. Carlos reads:

Julia, wife of the Count of ——, was forced to this castle—hark! I'm interrupted—the marble hall, the dreary vault—oh, pity and remember.[32]

Concluding that Julia is dead, Carlos vows that he "will never quit this gloomy edifice until I discover my poor Julia's sad remains—dreadful idea!—the mangled relics of her beauteous form."

A particular device of horseplay calculated to excite nervous laughter was exploited more conspicuously in Andrews' concoction of terror and nonsense than it had been before. A comic character, suddenly confronted by a supernatural manifestation, was shown trembling with fright. Andrews, to gain the effect, sacrificed consistency in his Hilario. Primarily no comic figure, Hilario is sometimes made to appear frightened to an exaggerated degree in order to project the additional (and quite incidental) thrill. The following scene well illustrates the trick which was to become a prominent feature a few years later, especially in the plays of "Monk" Lewis:

Carlos. Mark me! observe that window. Do you not see a light?
Hilario. A li—ght? (Light is seen to pass)
Carlos. It points me out the way—brightens and animates the darken'd scene. (Thunder and lightning flashes through the old walls) Heaven is in our cause—something is to be done—come! (He runs out)
Hilario. (alone) Follow! I'm numb'd—I'm petrified, I have not a limb to stand on—Soft—let me try. (advances one foot) Yes, I have put my right foot forward. No, let me take it back again! (retreats a little) What, shall I leave my friend in the lurch? Let him grapple with old Ebony by himself? for shame, Hilario! (Goes towards the two doors, opens one on right of that where Carlos had entered, which discovers a coffin standing on a bier, with a lamp on it.) Wheugh! I'm dead and buried. A coffin! (shuts door) And I dare say the Sexton will

be here before I can say my prayers. (Bernardo enters, mistakes Hilario for Montoni, and gives him a dagger, then exits. Montoni enters, mistakes Hilario for Bernardo, snatches the dagger, and exits. Thunder, lightning, and groans. Hilario shakes, steels himself, and exits through door taken by Carlos.)[33]

The fate of Mrs. Radcliffe's solemn, unrelieved Gothic mood in Andrews' hands is evident enough here. Yet the blundering playwright had hit upon effectiveness of another sort, and his combination of comedy and terror pointed out a new direction for Gothic drama, a direction which would widen the distance between it and the Gothic novel. Not all playwrights followed it, certainly; the mood of the species remained predominantly somber through the time of Maturin's *Bertram* and Byron's *Manfred*. Nevertheless, several writers quickly came out with similar mixings of effects that sometimes won great popular success. In the field of nervous laughter the playwrights seemingly could surpass the novelists. Bound by conventions which restrained Walpole in *The Mysterious Mother* and Jephson in *The Count of Narbonne*, dramatists moved cautiously at first, whereas novelists exploited horrific materials much more freely. But drama showed itself at last highly flexible, and even capable of initiating treatments in advance of the novel. Generally the Gothic novelists avoided any mingling of supernatural thrills and comedy.[34] In Lewis's *Monk*, for example, gloom and terror are unrelieved; but in his *Castle Spectre* it was the combination of thrills and comedy which earned the loudest applause.

Perhaps something of value was sacrificed with the injection of comedy into the dramatic treatment of Gothic materials. The novelists, virtually without exception, conducted their action strictly in the spirit of "high seriousness." Dramatists took increasing liberty with the Gothic mood. Regardless of what may have been sacrificed, however, it is a fact that Gothic plays became increasingly popular during the decade in which they included more and more horseplay; and *The Castle Spectre,* especially notable for its mixture of chills and laughter, was the most successful Gothic play and one of the most popular of any kind for a period of about thirty years. Perhaps it was the untalented and absurd Andrews who really started the new and highly remunerative fashion.

CHAPTER VII

GOTHIC AND GERMAN DRAMA

IN HENRY SIDDONS' adaptation of *A Sicilian Romance*, the hero vanishes temporarily from the scene and reappears as an elected captain of robbers. For perhaps the very first time a Gothic dramatist had reached beyond the native stockpile, built up since *The Castle of Otranto*, to draw an element from *Sturm und Drang*.

The date of the first borrowing is significant. By 1794 English playwrights had written at least thirty-five Gothic plays. For ten years the Gothic play had been a full-grown and well-established kind. Such pieces as *Vimonda, The Regent, The Kentish Barons*, and *Fontainville Forest* were as distinctly Gothic and also as clearly independent of foreign direction as Walpole's novel. After 1794, then, imported elements could be added only externally to the Gothic nucleus and the materials which, since *Otranto* in 1764, had already been built up around it. A few new elements from Germany, thrown upon the Gothic stockpile, could not change the whole accumulation to German, nor could they obliterate the essential distinguishing marks of the species which flourished before the first foreign element was added.[1]

Nevertheless, the epithet "German" did become attached to the species, and partly for that reason the identity of Gothic drama had been obscured. Yet the term is obviously inappropriate for the plays written in England before the first element was borrowed from Germany, and it is hardly less so for those written thereafter, since Gothicists continued in the traditional exploitation of the purposes, patterns, themes, moods, techniques, and characters which had characterized the native species since 1768. I shall attempt in this chapter to untangle the confused relationships of "Gothic" and "German" as these affect drama.

[1] For notes to chap. vii, see page 252.

I begin with a statement from Coleridge:

But to understand the true nature of the *Robbers,* and of the countless imitations which were its spawn, I must inform you, or at least call to your recollection, that, about that time, and for some years before it, three of the most popular books in the German language were, the translations of Young's *Night Thoughts,* Hervey's *Meditations,* and Richardson's *Clarissa Harlow.* Now we have only to combine the bloated style and peculiar rhythm of Hervey, which is poetic only on account of its utter unfitness for prose, and might as appropriately be called prosaic, from its utter unfitness for poetry; we have only, I repeat, to combine these Herveyisms with the strained thoughts, the figurative metaphysics and solemn epigrams of Young on the one hand; and with the loaded sensibility, the minute detail, the morbid consciousness of every thought and feeling in the whole flux and reflux of the mind, in short the self-involution and dreamlike continuity of Richardson on the other hand; and then to add the horrific incidents, and mysterious villains, (geniuses of supernatural intellect, if you will take the authors' words for it, but on a level with the meanest ruffians of the condemned cells, if we are to judge by their actions and contrivances)—to add the ruined castles, the dungeons, the trapdoors, the skeletons, the flesh-and-blood ghosts, and the perpetual moonshine of a modern author, themselves the literary brood of the *Castle of Otranto,* the translations of which, with the imitations and improvements aforesaid, were about that time beginning to make as much noise in Germany as their originals were making in England,)—and as the compound of these ingredients duly mixed, you will recognize the so-called *German drama.*

... The so-called *German* drama, therefore, is *English* in its *origin, English* in its *materials,* and *English* by re-adoption; and till we can prove that Kotzebue, or any of the whole breed of Kotzebues, whether dramatists or romantic writers, or writers of romantic dramas, were ever admitted to any other shelf in the libraries of well-educated Germans than were occupied by their originals, and apes' apes in their mother country, we should submit to carry our own brat on our own shoulders; or rather consider it as a lack-grace returned from transportation with such improvements only in growth and manners as young transported convicts usually come home with.[2]

Coleridge's statement, written in his angry review of Maturin's *Bertram,* which had been accepted over his own play[3] by the Drury Lane management, is an extreme one, for it denies even that the drama of the horrific kind written *in Germany* after *Die Räuber* was really German. Clearly, much of that drama was greatly influenced by English works; yet there appears to be a fallacy in Coleridge's argument. Had the so-called German drama written in Germany consisted *merely* of ingredients transported earlier to that country in such works as *The Castle of Otranto,* then it could have brought back nothing new to the English horrific school when it began returning to England via translation and adaptation. But it *did* bring certain new ingredients to mix in the Gothic cauldron, as we have seen in the Karl Moor motif of Siddons, and as we shall see again in later plays. Indeed, Coleridge himself admits as much, when he says "or rather consider it (i.e., the German drama in England) as a lack-grace returned... with such improvements... as young transported convicts usually come home with."

To resolve the tangle of Gothic and German elements, the horrific school in Germany must be briefly investigated. We know that English materials invaded Germany and that when these came home they had accumulated additional ones. It is necessary then, to discover what happened to the Gothic in Germany between the time it arrived there and the time it returned to England cloaked as German.

What took place in Germany was an accretion of machinery, characters, and motifs similar to that which came about in English Gothic fiction and drama after Walpole. This accretion of elements was observed in English drama in the period from 1768 to 1795. It would be ridiculous to imagine that in two countries over a period of a generation the Gothic nucleus would have accumulated precisely the same elements. Out of past and contemporary literary, social, and political materials and conditions, German writers like Veit Weber, Benedicte Naubert, and Heinrich Zschokke added to the original Walpolian concoction certain ingredients which Clara Reeve, Ann Radcliffe, and the many

English playwrights—writers in another country, with another heritage and another contemporary society—did not come upon in their pursuit of mystery, gloom, and terror. Given a common impulse, each country developed its own horrors in its own way. Thus when the paraphernalia of turrets, trapdoors, haunted chambers, castles, convents, and caverns which had gone to Germany via the Gothic novel returned to England as German drama, it brought with it Karl Moor, secret tribunals, and a diablerie which included blue flames and decaying witch beauties. In short, as Coleridge noted, the principle returned, with interest.

TYPES OF GERMAN SUBLITERARY FICTION

In Germany after Walpole horrific compositions took shape and grew in three genres, each with distinguishing characteristics but with many common elements that had been supplied by the English Gothicists. The fathers of these genres—the *Ritter-*, *Räuber-*, and *Schauerromane*—were Goethe and Schiller; it was *Götz von Berlichingen* that started the vogue enjoyed by the romance of chivalry. A study of German subliterary materials by Agnes Murphy describes this genre:

These chivalric romances were novels with medieval settings and had valiant knights as heroes. The awakening interest in the Middle Ages... and chiefly Goethe's *Götz von Berlichingen* (1773), started the vogue of these chivalric romances. Veit Weber and Benedicte Naubert were the outstanding writers of the historical romance of chivalry. There were several varieties of the chivalric romance: the historical narrative based on actual facts but with imaginary characters as heroes, the narrative with real historical persons; and finally, the chivalric romance containing motifs borrowed from the tale of terror, in which passion, rather than chivalry, predominated.[4]

Though Goethe's *Götz,* with its legitimate medievalism and its secret tribunal (the *Vehmgericht* of the later Middle Ages), gave the initial impulse, the later romances in Germany acquired the accumulated machinery of the Gothic school in England. What the chivalric romance came to be like after Goethe and the English Gothic were united (by 1790) can be judged from Miss Murphy's summary:

> Even if an author has no accurate historical knowledge, he can include enough crusades, tournaments, and tribunals to make his story satisfy the demand for historical fiction. If, in addition to such medieval motifs, the author can include elements arousing fear and suspense, he is assured of success. Many times simple mechanical devices are used to arouse fear. The knights are constantly falling through trap-doors and finding themselves imprisoned in horrible dungeons. Secret societies have ingenious methods of terrifying knights desiring membership.... There are castles equipped with secret passages and hidden doors. Strange characters, whose identity remains mysterious until late in the story, have secret hiding places in or about a castle...In most instances, seemingly supernatural apparitions are eventually explained....[5]

The debt to the Gothic school is conspicuous in this account, but equally obvious is the fact that the German writers thought of elements and motifs of terror which did not occur to Walpole, Clara Reeve, or Ann Radcliffe.

The second German type, the robber novel, grew from *Die Räuber* (1781). Schiller's was a social drama. It demanded justice for the oppressed, freedom from any established social order, and the right of man to mold his own fate. Miss Murphy summarizes its influence on the writers of subliterary fiction:

> Twelve years after the appearance of Schiller's drama, a flood of robber-novels appeared in the loan libraries. The heroes were all Karl Moors; that is, they were of noble birth, had been maltreated by society, and were fired with a desire for revenge. Mere wealth had no appeal for them. They were determined to fight for the good of humanity, and the only way they could do this, so they thought, was to destroy all persons possessing money or power.[6]

Zschokke's *Aballino, der grosse Bandit* (1793), which we shall see later in an English dramatization, was the first of the robber novels to pick up the motif initiated by Schiller. Second to it in fame was Christian Vulpius' *Rinaldo Rinaldini, der Räuberhauptmann,* also often adapted by English playwrights. In novels of this type an accumulation of machinery developed that was as remote from *Die Räuber* as was the accumulation in the later chivalric romances from *Götz.* The similarity of this accumulation to that of the English Gothicists is obvious:

> Headquarters (i.e., for the robber band) are usually in an old castle which people believe to be haunted. The Gothic architecture gives the ruins a sinister appearance and many a poor traveller meets with an unhappy fate for daring to take refuge in the castle during a storm. The castles are equipped with secret passages, hidden doors, and old tapestries and pictures. Trapdoors suddenly give way and the explorer finds himself in a dank dungeon. There are hidden rooms, some of which contain skeletons and rusty instruments of torture. If no castles are available, the robbers tunnel caves in the sides of cliffs or deep in the forests....[7]

The summary might almost pass as a description of the works of Walpole and Mrs. Radcliffe, or of a Gothic play. But there are some very specific differences. For example, neither fiction nor drama in England had any tradition of explorers falling through trapdoors—a motif conspicuous in all three of the German genres. In addition, Gothic fiction and drama lacked any tradition of travelers meeting disaster after having taken lodging in a castle during a storm. Perhaps this latter motif was adapted from Smollett, who in *Ferdinand, Count Fathom* depicted a nighttime attack on a guest in a lonely house; the motif perhaps attracted imitators in Germany, though not in England. These two differences between the German and the English traditions appear trifling; yet multiply them many times, and the extent of variation in the horrific devices of the two countries is manifest.

The third German genre was the *Schauerroman* itself. It was of later development than the other two, and with its appearance all three became more or less merged in their use of machinery, motifs, characters, and atmosphere. "The tale of terror," writes

Miss Murphy, "was different from any previous literary mode, for it was written with the sole purpose of satisfying the public love of the horrible and the supernatural.'" By this purpose it is distinguishable from the other two kinds even in the period in which all used common elements, for the robber novel retained centrally the robber-captain motif and continued to press its social theme, whereas the chivalric romance retained its essential medievalism, with the secret tribunal as the central motif. Miss Murphy credits Walpole with inspiring the German tale of terror: "The first sensational tale of terror—an English product, Horace Walpole's *Castle of Otranto* (1764)—served as a model for many similar works in England and was ultimately the inspiration of the German genre.'" It was Schiller's *Geisterseher* (1789), however, which really initiated the type in Germany.

In England, as we have seen, later Gothicists elaborated the original machinery of Walpole. So, in Germany, the writers of tales of terror added new elements to the same machinery. But the English and the Germans did not contribute identical elements. The following is a summary of *Schauerroman* characteristics:

The basic motifs ... were ghosts,—real or manufactured,—the devil, evil spirits, Gothic castles, tempests, imprisoned heroines, kind hermits, birthmarks, wicked monks, secret societies, magic mirrors, swords, enchanted wands, and all the other paraphernalia associated with black magic.... There was always the lovely blond heroine, who, at some time ... suffered imprisonment in a haunted castle or among corpses in a dank dungeon. The hero was the valiant youth of obscure birth and was eventually revealed as the lost child of a noble family. There was at least one villainous monk, and sometimes there were as many as three.... Secret societies were an important motif ... Conjuration of spirits and pacts with the devil were motifs inspired by the current interest in cabbalism. An effect of supernatural awe was built up by the use of desolate scenery, tempests, screeching owls, and hovering bats. Exciting events invariably occurred in haunted castles, burial vaults, or dark, windswept moors.... Ghosts stalked through corridors, clothed in flowing white robes or in black armour, dragging chains or carrying flickering candles. In the earlier narratives, the ghosts were real spectres, but after 1800 the tale of terror in which supernatural events were explained became the vogue. People, long believed dead, appeared as phantoms to haunt their persecutors or murderers. These pseudo-spirits used mechanical devices to increase the terror which they wished to arouse. A phosphorescent glow, clanking chains, or tinkling bells announced their prescence. Suspense attained by supernatural mystery was a requisite of a good tale of terror. Even in novels where supernatural events were explained away, the denouement was supposed to contain astounding discoveries, which would partially repay the reader for the suspense he had endured. Mysterious manuscripts, letters of warning, inexplicable music, dismal groans, and suddenly disappearing lights were some of the motifs used to create an atmosphere of expectation and dread.[10]

The over-all pattern is identical with that followed by writers in the Gothic school; it is only in details that there are differences. The description here is of the German species around 1800, and we have seen many of these elements in English plays before 1790. The flickering candles, glimmering and disappearing lights, haunted chambers, mysterious manuscripts, obscure heroes, and various other properties we have met repeatedly. But we have not met the devils, the black magic, the tribunal, the evil monk, the enchanted wands, the phosphorescent glow, and the magic mirrors. When these began appearing in English plays (most notably in those of Lewis), they made up that "improvement" of which Coleridge wrote.

In summary, what happened to Walpole's Gothic nucleus in the two countries was as follows. In Germany the borrowed machinery joined the materials of German movements initiated by Goethe and Schiller and, in addition, inspired the third genre. By 1789, in England, the Gothic in fiction and drama had attained elaborate development, but had scarcely begun to grow in Germany. On the whole, Germany lagged about ten years behind England throughout the period of development. (Note that the supernatural came to be explained away in Germany only after 1800, whereas Ann Radcliffe had introduced this device in England in 1789.) Up to 1798 the stream of influence flowed from England to Germany rather than from Germany to England. When the flood then turned, it brought both the substance originally lent and several additions from a foreign heritage. It arrived in England with such a rush of dramatic adaptations, translations, and borrowings that the English origins of Gothic drama were forgotten.

That the rush obliterated the identity of the Gothic play but not, unless very temporarily, that of the novel is understandable. Walpole had specifically labeled his novel "Gothic," and the term stuck to prose fiction. Futhermore, when the loan to Germany was returned, it came chiefly in dramatic form; hence it was the native drama, not the novel, which was most completely buried. It is interesting to note that Lewis' *Monk* has regularly been classified among Gothic works, but the same author's *Castle Spectre* has generally been called German. Yet in his novel Lewis used far more German materials than in his play, so that if German is to be applied to either, it should be applied to the novel.

BOADEN AND A GERMAN MOTIF

A year after Siddons enriched the native drama by introducing the nobleman-turned-outlaw motif, a second major addition arrived from Germany. "On the 3d of June," wrote James Boaden, "a second tragedy from the pen of Mr. Boaden was acted, with applause, at Covent Garden Theatre."

It was called the Secret Tribunal, and founded on the romance by Professor Kramer, called Herman of Unna. A critic of that time was pleased to write of it, that "the successive scenes were awful and impressive"; that "the characters were drawn with a bold and spirited hand, and the general effect such as the author certainly intended." I can hardly be expected to dispute so favorable a sentence; and yet, if the author of it be living, which I cannot know, I shall amuse him by saying, that I now think I ought to have done more with the subject; chiefly in the way of preparing a strange and unheard of institution. The author of the romance had three volumes to work out his interest, and unfold his terrors. I had occupied but 70 pages in conducting my play to its catastrophe.[11]

Despite Boaden's assertion that the romance was by "Professor Kramer," it was actually one of the works of Benedicte Naubert, a romance of chivalry entitled *Herman von Unna*.[12] The play follows the original only distantly, as Siddons' had followed Mrs. Radcliffe's *Sicilian Romance*. *The Secret Tribunal* was indebted to its source chiefly for the principal characters and, of course, for the institution it introduced to the English stage—the secret tribunal.

For more than one reason, the *Vehmgericht* was an important addition to the Gothic pile of horrors. It gave opportunity for striking settings, and it expanded the power of the villain. Such a device of terror fitted naturally into the Gothic pattern. After Boaden's play, the villain was frequently a member or a judge of the tribunal.[13] By his association with that body, his stature as an evil force was greatly heightened. The meeting place of the tribunal, an underground vault, secret and awful, necessitated minor alterations in the familiar Gothic setting. The spectacular and mysterious summons of accused persons, usually at midnight, accorded well with Gothic methods, moods, and purposes. The hooded, secret judges and the dark figures who glided through the night on mysterious errands for the court were additions of a kind which blended readily with the traditional background. As a whole, the new motif indicated expansion, not change, of the Gothicists' paraphernalia.

Boaden's initial problem was to acquaint the English audience with the new source of terror. His prologue explained the institution which was to serve as his central motif:

> What time the policy of German rule,
> Fetter'd the native freedom of the soul;
> When superstition held her sanguine state,
> And dealt at will the rapid blow of fate.

> The world beheld all pledge of safety gone,
> And even monarchs trembled on the throne.
> Judges, with functions unconfin'd and free,
> Waited to register their dark decree.
> The culprit once condemn'd, a num'rous band
> Of secret agents hunt him thro' the land,
> Nor age, nor character, nor kin have force
> To stay their barbarous, unrelenting course.
> Bound by an oath th' avenging steel to draw,
> Guilt became piety, and murder, law.

Very characteristic of the drama of the time are the lines which follow, Boaden having seized opportunity to applaud the liberty of his own country:

> Britain, rejoice! The envied power is thine
> To punish malice and to thwart design.
> Open as day our courts judicial move,
> And rich or poor their equal influence prove.
> Rejoice! your upright juries make you free!

But in the epilogue this very circumspect playwright made certain that his intentions should not be misinterpreted. He apprehended, perhaps, that the public or the licenser might conclude that, in his opinion, since secret tribunals were now extinct, a man might enjoy freedom to execute whatever crimes he chose. The epilogue reasserts bluntly what the action of the play exemplifies, that the tortures of remorse are visited on the guilty, that the monitor of the conscience has effectively replaced the "avenging steel" of the secret tribunal:

> Such the dread scenes of a benighted age,
> Which, heav'n be prais'd, now stain alone the page,
> Thence by our poet drawn, but to display
> Old English justice in unclouded day.
> But is this institution quite destroy'd?
> Secret tribunals! are none now employ'd?
> Thousands! yes, while we sink in soft repose,
> Our judges' eyes no gentle slumbers close.
> The Heart is the tribunal which we fear,

> Forever hid, and yet forever near.
> Its agents are the senses, and they gain
> Intelligence for that shrewd judge, the Brain.
> The awful trial, carefully conceal'd,
> Until the doom is fix'd, lies unreveal'd.

It is clear that, to Boaden, who was in perhaps as good position to judge as anyone, absorption of even a major German motif effected no essential change in the kind of drama he was accustomed to write. Emphasis on the principal characteristic of the Gothic protagonist—his brooding agony of remorse—was to continue.

A brief summary of the plot of *The Secret Tribunal* seems necessary in order to show the mixture of Gothic and German. Herman, a prince, loves Ida Munster; Ratibor, Herman's uncle and brother of the Duke of Wirtemberg, is evilly attracted to her. Ambitious as well as debauched, Ratibor covets his brother's title and resolves to use his power in the secret tribunal to get it. As the duke traverses a dark wood, Ratibor's thugs assault him. Herman combats the unknown assailants, and in the melee exchanges swords with one of them. Later he notices that the weapon bears the legend, "Regiment of Ratibor." Arrested with the bloody sword, however, he is himself mistaken for one of those he had helped to repel, and is thrown into prison to await trial before the tribunal. Ratibor, foreseeing the possibility of damning evidence, moves to prevent Herman's appearance at court. He forges a tribunal order for the execution of the hero and intends to give it to the jailer. Ida, anticipating danger, visits Herman and urges him to escape to her father's house. He flees, but Ida is now in difficulties, for Ratibor had conspired to poison his brother's wife with a cup given by Ida's hand. Confused, however, he had given to the jailer, not the order for Herman's death, but a letter exposing his own guilt in the poisoning. Ida's father, as a member of the tribunal, is required to summon her to court. In the trial scene at the underground meeting place, Herman appears at the critical instant, and his evidence blasts the villain.

We note that for the first time a hero is instrumental in overthrowing a villain. Yet Herman retains the marked incompetence which had always characterized the type he represents. Like all heroes since Walpole's Theodore, he is clapped into a dungeon early and kept out of the action through the many scenes in which the villain ranges unchallenged. The ultimate exposure and overthrow of Ratibor comes not through the hero's personal intelligence, energy, and valor, but through the confusion and error of the villain, whom remorse has brought to the verge of breakdown. Evidence is thrust into Herman's hand, and, thanks to Ida's prompting, he has the wit to use it.

As the epilogue makes plain, introduction of the new motif did not remove the emphasis from the villain's remorse. Ratibor bears the marks which had deepened rather than multiplied since the first Gothic villain. He does evil, and conscience smites him:

> ... a cold
> And aguish tremor shakes my very flesh,
> And my heart heaves at every joy around me.
> When the alarm subsides, a chilly dew
> Bathes all my limbs.[14]

Suddenly confronted by a statue of Herman's father, he is as appalled as tyrants had always been by comparable objects:

> Behold! the frowning front of Herman's father!
> How solemn and majestic! how severe!
> On me he bends the gaze—of senseless stone!
> I'll look no more.[15]

He is similarly shaken when he sees the phantom of the duchess:

> Hah! what sea of blood rises before me!
> While thro' the crimson waves a phantom glides
> In threat'ning horror—Lo, it is my sister!
> O shield me, Ulric, from her frown! hide, hide me![16]

He moves abruptly, mentally and physically; he instantly resolves and instantly moves to execute. He bursts upon the scene with an ultimatum, rushes out again, and returns with a new one. Though membership in an all-powerful secret organization has added new twists to his schemes and increased his power to terrify, he remains essentially a typical Gothic villain who yet bears the marks of his function as accessory to the medieval ruin.

Similarly, the conventional machinery, techniques, and settings have been supplemented, not changed, by the new acquisition. Boaden contrived to include a secret passage, the tolling of a bell at midnight, a "Gothic chapel in ruined and decay'd condition," two dark forest scenes, a dungeon with Radcliffean "grated windows," and a "spacious, vaulted court of justice underground." A bell tolls incessantly during the trial scene, and the setting, the hooded figures, and the mystery enveloping the tribunal conspire to manufacture the truly sensational. Especially striking is the manner in which Ida Munster is summoned to appear before the court. She is alone in her chamber at night when her father, under order, enters and fixes to the door a great sheet bearing the words, "Ida Munster, Traitress! Appear Before the Secret Avengers of the Eternal!" He falls swooning after performing the task imposed upon him as a member of the secret body. Later, the dismayed Ida asks how to reach the place of the tribunal; her father replies,

> ... All accus'd
> When the first quarter after midnight tolls,
> Go to the center of the market place.
> Thence they are led before the secret judges.
> If guilty, they are never heard of more.[17]

The next scene shows Ida alone in the market place. A bell tolls midnight. A "dark, gigantic form" approaches silently, identifies himself as the "Minister of Vengeance," and leads her away.

There is perhaps as much reason to call *The Secret Tribunal* German as there is so to describe any other horrific play of the period. The new motif does indeed occupy a central place in it. Yet when the work is viewed against the plays so far examined it is seen to be firmly rooted in the Gothic tradition. The new motif has not made another species of drama; it has been absorbed by the old.

THE REAL GERMAN DRAMA IN ENGLAND

Though German is inaccurate as applied to plays like *The Secret Tribunal*, which bear the marks of native Gothic tradition, it is accurate as applied to one kind of dramatic importation—the Kotzebuean sentimental drama. Beginning in 1797—precisely when the Gothic plays were enjoying their greatest popularity— Kotzebue's plays made up far the largest part of the subliterary materials which invaded the English stage. There were no fewer than sixty-five translations and adaptations of Kotzebue's works between 1797 and 1802, the peak year being 1799.[18] Many of these were made by Agnes Plumptre, Benjamin Thompson, and Charlotte Smith—writers little known today—whose versions were not brought to the stage. But authors better known also translated or adapted. Sheridan, Mrs. Inchbald, and Cumberland were especially instrumental in familiarizing the reading and theatergoing public with the "sickly German tragedy" of the prolific social-sentimental dramatist. *Das Kind der Liebe, Die Spanier in Peru,* and *Menschenhass und Reue,* each of which was translated or "altered" five or six times, were the most popular; as *Pizarro, The Stranger,* and *Lovers' Vows,* versions by Sheridan and Mrs. Inchbald, they were the most successful representations of Kotzebue, and continued to hold the stage through much of the nineteenth century. The celebrated burlesque by Canning and Frere, *The Rovers,* published in the *Anti-Jacobin* in 1798, though it deflated the popularity of the species, did not eliminate it.[19]

Coleridge, as we have seen, denied that German should be attached even to Kotzebue, since, he stated, Kotzebuean drama was concocted out of Richardson, Hervey, and Young. To that extreme position my study brings little support. There seems no good reason to deny the epithet to the original plays; neither is there reason for denying it to Kotzebue translated into English. The sentimental play with a social message was primarily a German development, however much it may have inherited from Richardson, Hervey, and Young. When it came to England in translation, it came as a "new" kind of drama which was only remotely connected with the Gothic. It added little, if indeed anything, to the Gothic school which the English playwrights and novelists had developed, and was in fact composed of materials different in kind from the horrific importations which arrived at the same time and were seized on by Gothicists.

Yet the invasion by this species had one effect which requires mention in this account of an essentially different species. Though Kotzebue's plays contributed virtually nothing to Gothicists, they added to the confusion in which the Gothic genesis was obscured, for they came in large numbers at the very time Gothic playwrights began to use motifs from the *Ritter-, Räuber-,* and *Schauerromane*. The impact of foreign importations was thus heavily increased, and the whole popular drama, whether horrific or sentimental, acquired the name German. Even Gothic plays by writers who specifically disclaimed interest in or knowledge of German sources were so branded. The only real bearing of Kotzebuean drama upon Gothic drama, then, is that it helped to bury the identity of the latter.

CHAPTER VIII

LEWIS AND GOTHIC DRAMA

THE NAME of Matthew Gregory Lewis is perhaps the most important in the history of Gothic drama. Lewis wrote many plays which exploited the familiar paraphernalia, added new tricks to the art of terrifying, and reached a wide audience over a period of many years. He reached maturity precisely in time to inherit the combined properties of English and German subliterary materials, and to use the so-called new melodrama introduced from France. Better than any other, he represents the juncture of the native and foreign streams. Further, his influence on Byron and Shelley was more immediate than that of any other confirmed Gothicist, and that fact contributes much to his significance.

By 1791 Lewis, then sixteen, had begun a prose romance which, he wrote his mother, was "in the style of the *Castle of Otranto.*" He laid the work aside, traveled in Germany for eight months, and imbibed profusely of German horrors. He then returned to England and read *The Mysteries of Udolpho,* which he pronounced "one of the most interesting books ever published." Inspired anew, he set to work again at his unfinished romance, but again laid it aside when he conceived the idea of *The Monk*. Early in 1797 he again picked up the romance and this time dramatized the finished chapters. Thus what had begun as a Gothic novel took final shape as a Gothic play, inspired respectively by Walpole, Mrs. Radcliffe, and the horrors supped in Germany. The finished piece, which he called *The Castle Spectre* (D. L. Dec. 1797), is one of the most remarkable Gothic plays. In it Lewis exploited the combined materials of his predecessors and contemporaries, English and German, and out-Gothicized them all. As the best evidence of the state of Gothic drama after almost thirty years of development, the play requires close analysis.

The Castle Spectre

Acted forty-seven times, *The Castle Spectre* was the most successful play of its time. Genest quotes Cooke, the actor, on its popularity: "I hope it will not hereafter be believed, that the Castle Spectre could attract crowded houses, when the most sublime productions of the immortal Shakespeare would be played to empty benches."[1] Obviously, theatricality, not literary merit, was responsible for the success.[2] Consistency of character, probability of action, and forward movement of plot are sacrificed throughout to immediate sensational effect. When opportunity arrives for a spectacle, forward action is abruptly halted, and an irrelevant, unmotivated, but thrilling scene is staged. When the episodic scene has been emptied of chills, the action is resumed until there is a new chance for spectacle. Previous chapters have shown that from the earliest time Gothic drama was devoted to "effect"; *The Castle Spectre* makes even *Fontainville Forest* and *The Sicilian Romance* appear only half-heartedly given to sensationalism.

A statement by Lewis in the preface to the first edition illuminates the nature of the species and reëmphasizes all that has been said of the willingness of Gothic playwrights to sacrifice even the fundamental principles in order to achieve effect. As attendants on his villain, the author included four monstrous "blacks," whose only function was to enhance the terror of the setting; they are, indeed, elements of setting rather than characters. Told that these blacks were anachronistic, Lewis replied:

That Osmond is attended by Negroes is an anachronism, I allow; but from the great applause which Mr. Dowton constantly received in Hassan ... I am inclined to think that the audience was not greatly offended at the impropriety. For my own part, I by no means repent the introduction of my Africans; I thought I could give a pleasing variety to the characters and dresses, if I made my servants black; *and could I have produced the same effect by making my heroine blue, blue I should have made her.*

[1] For notes to chap. viii, see page 253.

I have italicized what seems to me an extraordinarily frank and revealing description of the essential nature of Gothic drama and the Gothic purpose. Lewis' fellow Gothicists knew precisely what he meant and accepted his remark with perfect seriousness.

The play opens in "a Grove," with a comic scene between Motley, the fool, and Father Philip, who seems to be a combination of Falstaff and Juliet's nurse made into a friar. Scenes like this had grown common since about 1792, earlier plays having generally omitted all that did not help create a gloomy atmosphere. Usually they came at the beginning and were made to disclose the initial situation, to suggest the mystery, and to prepare for the entrance of the villain. As Father Philip leaves, Percy reveals himself to Motley, who had been his servant, and tells how, disguised as "Edwy the low-born and the poor," he had wooed and won a peasant girl, Angela. This morning, however, he had learned that she had been removed from her cottage by "the unknown, who sixteen years before had confided her" to the care of a cottager. Having investigated, Percy had found this unknown to be Kenric, a henchman of Lord Osmond. Intending to demand the release of Angela, the hero requests admission to the castle. Motley's reply echoes, in a much more humorous vein, the refusals of all servants since the old gatekeeper in *The Mysterious Mother:*

Oh! that will never do; for, in the first place, you'll not be able to get a sight of Osmond. I've now lived with him five long years; and, till Angela's arrival, never witnessed a guest in the castle. O! 'tis the most melancholy mansion. And, as to the Earl, he's the very antidote of mirth. None dare approach him, except Kenric and his four blacks; all others are ordered to avoid him; and whenever he quits his room, ding dong! goes a great bell, and away run the servants like so many scared rabbits.'

"Strange," muses Percy, prompting the audience to the usual question, "and what reasons can he have for—"

Oh, reasons in plenty. You must know there's an ugly story respecting the last owners of this castle. Osmond's brother, his wife, and infant daughter were murdered by banditti, as it was said; unluckily, the only servant who escaped the slaughter deposed, that he recognized among the assassins a black still in the service of Earl Osmond. The truth of this assertion was never known, for the servant was found dead in his bed the next morning.

Thus, characteristically, *The Castle Spectre* begins by introducing a twofold mystery: What ails Earl Osmond? What is the truth about the past event?

The first of many thrills based on deliberate trickery occurs in the second scene. Father Philip talks with Alice, a gossip, and their dialogue invites fear of the supernatural and intensifies the atmosphere of gloom and terror which envelops the castle. Alice has heard "unearthly music" which seemed to emanate from a "haunted" and uninhabited room. She is stating her conviction that it was played by the ghost of her deceased lady, Evelina, when suddenly she is interrupted by what is made to appear a supernatural visitation:

Alice. (screaming) Oh, Lord bless us!
Father. Eh! what,—oh, dear!
Alice. Look, look!—A figure in white!—it comes from the haunted chamber![5]

After a moment of strained suspense, the apparition is revealed to be merely Angela, who is wandering through the castle like a Radcliffean maiden. This kind of willful deception, in which Lewis specialized and excelled, was imitated widely by his contemporaries.

The author's reading of *Udolpho* is apparent in his heroine's first speech:

I am weary of wandering from room to room; in vain do I change the scene, discontent is everywhere. There was a time, when music could delight my ear, and nature could charm my eye—when I could pour forth a prayer of gratitude, and thank my good angels for a day unclouded by sorrow. Now, all is gone, all lost, all faded.[6]

Alice repeats Motley's story of the mysterious event of sixteen years before. At the end of the first act, Angela realizes that her situation is desperate, for she has seen on Osmond's brow the infallible mark of villainy:

(musing) Osmond was his brother's heir. His strange demeanour! Yes, in that gloomy brow is written a volume of villainy.—Heavenly powers! an assassin then is master of my fate! An assassin too, who—I dare not bend my thoughts that way! Oh! would that I had never entered these castle walls!⁷

Act II brings the tyrant on the stage for the first time, but not before an elaborate "atmospheric" preparation has been made. The first scene represents "An Armoury," where suits of mail with names of the former owners are arranged on each side. Motley guides Percy in and advises him to hide in the armor of the late Earl Reginald. The dialogue overflows with the stuff which makes mystery, gloom, and terror.

Motley. You must make up your mind to play a statue for an hour or two.
Percy. How?
Motley. Nay, 'tis absolutely necessary. The late Earl's servants are fully persuaded that his ghost wanders every night through the long galleries, and parades the old towers and dreary halls which abound in this melancholy mansion. He is supposed to be dressed in complete armour ... Now hear my plan. The Earl prepares to hold a conference with lady Angela; here, placed upon a pedestal, you may listen to their discourse unobserved, and thus form a proper judgment both of your mistress and her guardian ...⁸

Percy has barely donned the armor when, after long preparation, the audience is granted a first spectacular view of Osmond and his blacks:

(The folding doors are thrown open; Saib, Hassan, Muley, and Alaric enter, preceding Earl Osmond, who walks with his arms folded, and his eyes bent on the ground. Saib advances to a sofa onto which, after making a few turns around the room, Osmond throws himself. He motions to the attendants, and they withdraw. He appears lost in thought; then suddenly rises, and again traverses the room with disordered steps.)

Osm. I will not sacrifice my happiness to hers! No, Angela, you ask of me too much. Since the moment when I pierced her heart, deprived of whom, life became odious; since my soul was stained with his blood who loved me; with hers whom I loved; no form has been grateful to my eye, no voice spoken pleasure to my soul, save Angela's, save only Angela's!—Mine she shall be, though Reginald's bleeding ghost flit before me, and thunder in my ear—"Hold!" Peace, stormy heart! She comes!

The anguish of Osmond seems peculiarly excruciating, and he displays it even more ostentatiously than had any previous villain. Though his crime had been especially vicious, it was prompted by love, and as the play continues it is perfectly plain that despite Osmond's evil acts Lewis intended him to invite sympathy. He possesses a high degree of attractiveness and some truly admirable qualities. In him the blend of the haughty, the cruel, the pitiable, and the grand was calculated to gratify the actor, the censor, and the public.

In an early scene, and at first with a show of magnificence, Osmond woos the heroine. It is impossible not to notice that Angela betrays less revulsion at his advances than, for example, Isabella expresses for those of Manfred in *Otranto*. Romantic grandeur and gloom had already begun to render the medieval tyrant, originally conceived only as a monster to frighten maidens, less odious to their eyes. But the traditional relationship is restored after Angela repels Osmond with "Never, so help me Heaven!" He seizes her as roughly as Manfred might have, and cries out, "Your fate then is decided!" She shrieks, and the voice of Percy comes hollowly from the armor of Earl Reginald, commanding "Hold!"

Osm. (Gazing upon the armor) It came from hence! From Reginald! Was it not a delusion? Did indeed his spirit—Well, be it so! Though his ghost should rush between us, thus would I clasp her!—horror!

What sight is this? (At the moment he again seizes Angela, Percy extends his truncheon with a menacing gesture, and descends from his pedestal. Osmond releases Angela, who rushes from the chamber, while Percy advances a few paces and remains gazing on the Earl steadfastly.) I know that shield!—that helmet! Speak to me, dreadful vision! Tax me with my crimes! Tell me that you come—Stay! Speak! (Following Percy, who when he reaches the door turns and signs to him with his hand. Osmond starts back in terror.) He forbids my following! He leaves me! The door closes! (In a burst of passion and drawing his sword) Hell! Fiends! I'll follow him, though lightnings blast me! (He rushes from the chamber.)⁹

The striking courage of Osmond is more heroic than any quality Gothic heroes had ever evinced. Though certain that he is pursuing an apparition, he does not hesitate—and the very next scene finds Percy his prisoner. Thus, as usual, the hero is removed from the action and from the view of the audience during the crucial events that follow. Actors who played heroes, as we have seen, could expect to languish in a dungeon, out of sight of their public, during two or three of the usual five acts.

It is Father Philip, not Percy, who offers to lead Angela to freedom. He is a comic type, and Lewis, through the speeches and reactions of this fat friar, reveals the tongue-in-cheek attitude toward the familiar Gothic properties that is conspicuous in most of his works, even *The Monk*. The manner of Lewis is thus generally distinguished from that of Walpole, Mrs. Radcliffe, and Maturin, the other principal figures in Gothic literature, all of whom seem to become absorbed in their own painting of unrelieved gloom and terror; it is always obvious that Lewis relished his profession and his reputation as terrifier. Thus, with what seems almost the touch of burlesque, he makes Father Philip describe his plan to free the heroine:

Observe this picture: it conceals a spring; whose secret is unknown to all in the castle except myself. Upon touching it, the panel slides back, and a winding passage opens into the marble hall. Thence we must proceed to the vaulted vestibule; a door is there concealed similar to this: and, after threading the mazes of a subterranean labyrinth, we shall find ourselves in safety on the outside of the castle walls.[10]

Earlier, Lewis had clearly relished the account of the castle which he had given through Motley:

Had I minded all the strange things related of this castle, I should have died of fright in the first half hour. Why, they say, that Earl Hubert rides every night round the castle on a white horse; that the ghost of Lady Bertha haunts the west pinnacle of the chapel tower; and that Lord Hildebrand who was condemned for treason some sixty years ago, may be seen in the great hall, regularly at midnight, walking about without his head. Above all, they say, that the spirit of the late Countess sits nightly in her oratory, and sings her baby to sleep....[11]

Exaggeration marks both of these assemblages of Gothic properties. The Gothic had been ridiculed on the stage before, but never by one who so obviously took an abnormal joy in playing with objects of gloom and terror.

The play continues with Kenric's enlistment on Angela's side, for this henchman had learned that his master planned to poison him. He visits Angela's room, and only then, half through the fourth act, do we learn that Reginald, supposedly assassinated sixteen years before, yet lives. Kenric confesses,

I was the last to quit the bloody spot; sadly was I retiring, when a faint groan struck my ear. I sprang from my horse; I placed my hand on Reginald's heart; it beat beneath the pressure... Having plunged the other bodies in the Conway's flood, I placed the bleeding Earl's on my horse, and conveyed him, still insensible, to a retreat to all, except myself, a secret. There I tended his wounds, and succeeded in preserving his life. Lady, Reginald still lives.[12]

This past event varies only slightly from the typical one; usually it is the villain who has secretly imprisoned some victim, but here, unknown to the villain, the prisoner is held by another. Kenric divulges another secret: Angela is not a peasant, but the daughter of Reginald. She was that infant over whose throat the dagger of Osmond had passed, and she "still wears that mark." Osmond, having slipped into the room and overheard the conversation, turns Kenric over to the blacks, and "after pacing the floor with a furious air, while Angela eyes him with terror," demands that she instantly wed him or see her father die. He approaches to seize her, but Angela "starts from the ground suddenly, and draws her dagger with a distracted look." Osmond attempts to grasp the dagger, but "his eyes rest upon the hilt, and he starts back with horror."

Osm. By hell! the very dagger which—
Ang. Ha! hast thou found me, villain? Villain, dost thou know this weapon? Know'st thou whose blood incrusts the point? Murderer! It flowed from the bosom of my mother![13]

The sight is overwhelming; Osmond falls senseless into the arms of the blacks, who carry him from the chamber. As Angela stands alone, the castle bell strikes one, and she hears the sound of "unearthly music." A remote voice sings a cradle song. Then an elaborate scene unfolds:

(The folding doors unclose, and the oratory is seen illuminated. In its centre, stands a tall female figure, her white and flowing garments spotted with blood; her veil is thrown back, and discovers a pale and melancholy countenance; her eyes are lifted upwards, her arms extended towards heaven, and a large wound appears upon her bosom. Angela sinks upon her knees, with her eyes riveted upon the figure, which, for some moments, remains motionless. At length, the spectre advances slowly to a soft and plaintive strain; she stops opposite Reginald's picture, and gazes upon it in silence. She then turns, approaches Angela, seems to invoke a blessing upon her, points to the picture, and retires to the oratory. The music ceases, Angela rises with a wild look, and follows the vision, extending her arms towards it. The spectre waves her hand, as bidding her farewell. Instantly the organ's swell is heard; a full chorus of female voices chaunts, "Jubilate!" a blaze of light flashes through the oratory, and the folding doors close with a loud noise.)[14]

The spectacular appearance of the "real" supernatural, heightened by the organ's swell and the chorus of voices, the illumination and the mechanical movement of fixtures, was one of Lewis' specialties. He had been urged to "leave the ghost in the green room," and Genest remarks that introduction of the supernatural "rendered the play contemptible."[15] Yet it was reported that "the situation in which the Ghost first appears in the oratory to her daughter riveted the audience," and that "the Spectre was as well treated before the curtain as she had been ill-used behind it."[16]

The opening of the last act shows "A view of Conway Castle by moonlight." Percy, who has escaped from the dungeon, and Motley, with followers, debate whether to assault the castle or await the arrival of Father Philip and Angela through the secret exit. Since one is a fool and the other a typical Gothic hero, they decide to wait. The scene shifts to "A vaulted Chamber," through which the fat friar and the heroine approach. Father Philip touches a secret spring, a door flies open, they go out, and the door closes as Osmond and Hassan reach the chamber. They, too, find the secret spring and continue the pursuit. The next scene presents another elaborate spectacle:

(A gloomy subterraneous Dungeon, wide and lofty; the upper part of it has, in several places, fallen in and left large chasms. On one side, are various passages leading to other caverns; on the other, is an iron door with steps leading to it, and a wicket in the middle. Reginald, pale and emaciated, in coarse garments, his hair hanging wildly about his face, and a chain bound round his body, lies sleeping upon a bed of straw. A lamp, a small basket, and a pitcher are placed near him. After a few moments he wakes and extends his arms.)[17]

The fugitives enter through "one of the chasms above." The friar sees what to him is the ghost of Earl Reginald approaching with a lamp; he turns to flee, stumbles, and extinguishes the torch in his haste. Angela, in mortal terror, is left to face the "Unknown":

Hark! 'twas the clank of chains! A light too! It comes yet nearer! I cannot find the door! Save me, ye powers! What dreadful form! 'Tis here! I faint with terror! (sinks almost lifeless against the dungeon's side.)

Reginald approaches, sees Angela, and mistakes her for the spirit of his deceased wife. He, too, faints. Angela revives first, and each at last realizes the other's identity. As they are about to embrace, Osmond and his blacks enter. The villain demands that his brother compel Angela to marry him, but Reginald refuses. "Drag him to yonder cavern!" commands the tyrant; "Let me not see him die!" Reginald seizes a sword to defend himself, but the blacks overpower him, and Osmond approaches to strike the deathblow. At this crisis, Lewis once more boldly introduced the supernatural:

(Osmond draws his sword and rushes upon Reginald, who is disarmed and beaten to his knees; when, at the moment that Osmond lifts his arm to stab him, Evelina's Ghost throws herself between them. Osmond starts back, and drops his sword. Angela, disengaging herself from Hassan, springs suddenly forward, and plunges her dagger into Osmond, who falls with a loud groan. The Ghost vanishes.)[18]

At this instant, Percy enters. The hero, as usual, has played no part in the main action. The evil course of the tyrant has been halted by a fat friar, a girl, an emaciated old man, and a ghost. Yet the hero asserts a hero's prerogative; he abruptly asks Reginald for his daughter's hand. Reginald replies with a rebuke long overdue to all such heroes:

Percy, this is no time to talk of love. Let me hasten to my expiring brother, and soften with forgiveness the pangs of death.

Percy next asks whether Reginald can so far forget his own past sufferings as to forgive the villain who caused them. The answer once more focuses attention upon the agony, and the shifting attitude toward it, which transformed the Gothic villain into the Byronic hero:

Ah! youth; has he had none? Oh! in his stately chambers, far greater must have been his pangs than mine in this gloomy dungeon; for what gave comfort to me was his terror, what gave me hope was his despair.

The moral note is apparent here, and is very emphatic in the closing lines, as Reginald addresses Osmond:

> And, oh, thou wretch! whom hopeless woes oppress,
> Whose days no joys, whose nights no slumbers bless,
> When pale Despair alarms thy phrensied eye,
> Screams in thine ear, and bids thee heaven deny,
> Court thou Religion! strive thy faith to save;
> Bend thy fix'd glance on bliss beyond the grave;
> Hush, guilty murmurs! Banish dark mistrust!
> Think, there's a Power above, nor doubt that Power is just!

From this lengthy summary it may be possible to judge the extent to which Gothic machinery had grown by 1797. Lewis' boldness in his treatment of the supernatural, for instance, is far beyond that of James Boaden three years before. Boaden, it will be remembered, took the greatest pains to prepare his phantom, and then permitted only a fleeting glimpse of it gliding across a darkened corner of the stage; Lewis brought his specter twice upon the stage, in illuminated scenes, and involved it in such action that it could not have avoided being conspicuous. Similar excesses are apparent in the "Monk's" treatment of other properties.

With *The Castle Spectre* Gothic drama assumed a popular position not below that of the Gothic novel. Besides having a very long and eminently successful first run, this concoction went through seven printed editions in 1798 and eleven by 1803. Still popular in 1829, it was turned into a prose romance by Sarah Wilkinson—perhaps the only Gothic play involved in a reversal of the usual novel-dramatic adaptation relationship. Its fame came to equal and perhaps to surpass that of *The Monk;* in the fourth edition of that novel (1798) was the advertisement "by M. G. Lewis, Esq. M.P. Author of The Castle Spectre." Though the novel had been written first, the publisher used the play to recommend it.

One important aspect of *The Castle Spectre* remains to be discussed. From the early nineteenth century to the present, the play has passed as a notorious specimen of German drama. Undeniably there is as much reason to call it German as there is so to describe any other Gothic play. But let us examine the facts to see just how strong this reason is.

The main character types—villain, hero, heroine, and unknown—, the atmosphere, the techniques, the motifs, the settings, and the machinery, when viewed against a background of Gothic tradition, blend with that background and are indistinguishable from it. I have earlier shown that this tradition was well established in England before any subliterary materials were borrowed from Germany. Furthermore, English sources are indicated in the facts that Lewis began work on the prose romance which later became *The Castle Spectre* after reading *Otranto* and before he visited Germany, and that he resumed work on his subject after reading *Udolpho*. The influences of Walpole and Mrs. Radcliffe predominate in the completed play.

This is not to say that there are no German elements in it. There are several, but they are limited to a single passage, and they are readily distinguished from the native materials with which we have become familiar. In the scene which follows—one of several which are irrelevantly staged for sensational effect—Osmond describes a dream induced by his diseased conscience—and by Lewis' travels in Germany:

Methought I wandered through the low browed caverns, where repose the reliques of my ancestors. My eye dwelt with awe on their tombs, with disgust on mortality's surrounding emblems. Suddenly a female form glided along the vault; it was Angela! She smiled upon me, and beckoned me to advance. I flew towards her; my arms were already unclosed to clasp her, when, suddenly, her figure changed, her face grew pale, a stream of blood gushed from her bosom! 'twas Evelina!— such as when she sank at my feet expiring, while my hand grasped the dagger still crimsoned with her blood. "We meet again this night," murmured her hollow voice. "Now rush to my arms; but first see what

you have made me, my bridegroom. We must never part again."
While speaking, her form withered away; the flesh fell from her bones;
her eyes burst from their sockets; a skeleton, loathsome and meagre,
clasped me in her mouldering arms ... Her infected breath was mingled with mine; her rotting fingers pressed my hand, and my face was
covered with her kisses ... And then blue dismal flames gleamed along
the walls ... the tombs were rent asunder ... bands of fierce spectres
rushed round me in frantic dance; furiously they gnashed their teeth
while they gazed upon me, and shrieked in loud yell,—"Welcome, thou
fratricide! Welcome, thou lost forever!" Horror burst the bands of
sleep; distracted, I flew hither."[19]

The single passage contains the only motif and all of the specific
properties that had not previously belonged to the Gothic tradition. The beautiful, disintegrating woman, the blue flames, and
the "fierce spectres" were plainly borrowed from the horrific German tales. But these are introduced in a dream, in an irrelevant
episode. It would require the actor about two minutes to tell them
over. They constituted a considerable addition to the Gothic paraphernalia; but they afford insecure ground indeed on which to
affirm that *The Castle Spectre* is German.

OTHER PLAYS BY LEWIS

The success of *The Castle Spectre* filled the coffers of Drury
Lane. During the next dozen years Lewis supplied both Covent Garden and Drury Lane with Gothic spectacles, of which
all require naming and some require examination in an account
of Gothic drama. In chronological order these plays follow:
Adelmorn, the Outlaw (D. L. May 1801); *Alfonso* (C. G. Jan.
1802); *The Harper's Daughter* (C. G. May 1803); *Rugantino; or
The Bravo of Venice* (C. G. Oct. 1805); *The Wood Daemon;
or The Clock Has Struck* (D. L. April. 1807); *Adelgitha; or The
Fruits of a Single Error* (D. L. April 1807); *Venoni; or The
Novice of St. Mark's* (D. L. Dec. 1808); *Raymond and Agnes*
(Norwich, Nov. 1809); *Timour the Tartar* (C. G. April 1811);
and *One O'Clock; or The Knight and the Wood Daemon* (Ly-

ceum Aug. 1811), a revision of *The Wood Daemon* as a "Grand Musical Romance." In addition to these plays directly from his pen, Lewis must be credited as the source of two adaptations of *The Monk: Don Raymond; or, The Castle of Lindenburgh* (C. G. March 1797), a "ballet pantomime" by Farley (?); and *Aurelio and Miranda* (D. L. Dec. 1798), by Boaden.

On the whole, these plays illustrate at once the continuation of the familiar Gothic trappings which had accumulated since Walpole, and the introduction of new excesses which tended to obscure the Gothic origins. Castles, convents, and caverns, agonized tyrants and persecuted maidens, sliding panels and underground passages, midnight bells and supernatural manifestations, and the past event—all these abound, along with an admixture of new elements which, whether they emanated from Lewis' own mind or from German tales, were brought firmly into line with the traditional Gothic purpose. I shall examine those plays which, for one reason or another, are most noteworthy.

ADELMORN, THE OUTLAW

Adelmorn, an amazing collection of claptrap, shows as well as any play upon what evil days drama had fallen. It is nevertheless important in the history of Gothic drama and in the history of English literature. It is a link—and a particularly valuable one—between the crude and monstrous elements of the Gothic school and the finer romantic ones, for example, of Shelley's *Prometheus Unbound* and Byron's *Manfred.* It is the kind of vital link that studies in the Gothic novel have failed to reveal.

In this "dramatic romance," Baron Ulric had stabbed Count Roderic and had so contrived the deed that everyone, including Adelmorn himself, believed Adelmorn guilty. Duke Sigismund had sworn never to pardon the assassin, and Adelmorn, after receiving the death sentence, had escaped to Britain, where he married Princess Innogen, daughter of Sigismund. When the play opens, Adelmorn, goaded by a supernatural voice, has returned to Germany to avenge his uncle's death. He occupies a cottage in the woods near the castle. Spies of Ulric, now Count of Bergen, find and imprison him in the castle dungeon, but not before he had saved Duke Sigismund from a wolf in the forest. Innogen pleads for her husband's pardon, but her father, though moved, refuses to break his oath. Lodowic, Adelmorn's foolish servant, also cast into a dungeon, discovers Father Cyprian, whom Ulric had imprisoned for two years. As Adelmorn is led to execution, Lodowic enters with evidence of Ulric's guilt. But this proves insufficient, and it remains for Roderic's ghost to rise and blast the assassin.

In this play, as in *The Castle Spectre,* Lewis contrived to exhibit virtually the whole contents of the Gothic treasury. The usual castle, convent, and cavern settings abound, and there are dungeons with grated windows, winding staircases, galleries, vaults, underground passages, bells, forests by moonlight, sliding panels, and violent scenes of nature in thunder, lightning, and rain. But these seem overshadowed by the spectacular arrangements for the three appearances of the ghost.

The first "real" manifestation of the supernatural occurs when Adelmorn, chained in a gloomy dungeon to await execution, falls asleep. Whether or not what follows is to represent a dream the author leaves unexplained. The dungeon, with its grated windows, chains, and flickering light, might have been a sufficient source of terror for any earlier playwright, but not for Lewis. As Adelmorn sleeps, there is a "Chorus of Invisible Spirits," and then the following elaborate and amazing spectacle is pictured. The scene deserves to be quoted in its entirety:

(Part of the wall opens, and discovers [in vision] a blasted heath by moonlight—the figure of an old man, a wound on his bosom, and his garments stained with gore, is seen holding a bloody dagger towards Heaven)

Chorus: Clouds around the phantom lour;
Vengeance, 'tis thy fated hour,
Pealing thunders speak it near.

(The moon turns red—a burst of thunder is heard, and Ulric appears held by two demons)

Chorus: Lo, 'tis come! the victim's here!

(The old man plunges his dagger in Ulric's bosom, who sinks into the arms of the daemons, and is carried off by them)

Chorus: See, he struggles! vain endeavor!
See, he dies, he's lost forever:
Mortals, view his fate and fear!

(The heath vanishes—a glory appears, into which the old man is seen ascending upon brilliant clouds)

Chorus: Now from earth his flight addressing,
Upwards see his spirit move;
Youth, receive his parting blessing,
Pledge of pardon, pledge of love.
Sweet his angel accents swell:
Adelmorn, farewell, farewell!

(The wall closes—Adelmorn, who during the vision expresses the various emotions produced by it upon his mind, starts suddenly from his couch)

Adel. Stay, oh stay!
Chorus. (At a distance) Farewell!"[20]

The scene is crude and creaking, lurid with blood, daggers, and a red moon; yet we have not found a Gothic spectacle quite like it before. The very process of transmutation is exposed in its blending of Gothic monstrosities and the ethereal machinery of high romanticism. It shows that groping beyond and above the baser materials of castles, convents, and caverns by which dramatists, not novelists, opened the way to Byron and Shelley. The walls that here draw apart to disclose a blasted heath and a red moon needed but to be changed to clouds that would roll back to show Alpine or Earth spirits, or other creations of a higher poetic conception than Lewis' two "daemons" who pinion the arms of Ulric. Surely, to knock the rough edges off this Gothic spectacle was to discover the "romantic" scenes of *Manfred* and even the sublimer ones of *Prometheus Unbound*. Nothing so mysterious as a sea change was required to complete the transformation. Needed were a refining by more delicate hands than those of the vulgar Lewis, a shaping by a more subtle chisel, and a raising by a rarer poetic spirit.

This scene from *Adelmorn* was an inevitable result of the process of accumulation which had begun a generation earlier around a nucleus of a medieval ruin. We have seen the paraphernalia grow outward from the castle ruin to the convent and the cavern; from the cavern to forests and "romantic rocks"; from these to moonlight and precipices: eventually the stretching for materials was certain to touch and finally to embrace the metaphysical world, where the possibilities for exploitation of demons and airy spirits were unlimited. The Gothic urge, requiring ever greater applications of ever more potent kind, compelled an expansion beyond the ordinary properties and forces of earth. We have seen the original tyrant, a gross object of terror equipped with personal physical authority, grow in stature and in power; as a member of the Secret Tribunal or the Inquisition, he became more formidable than he had been; as a magician, and then as one who could call up devils, he was to become mightier still. Thus, through extension into another world, both the machinery and the protagonist of crude dramatists mounted toward such a creation as *Manfred*.

The evolution of the hero in this play is as significant as that of the machinery. Adelmorn is composed in part of qualities which had earlier characterized the villain. He is therefore more impressive than the hero had been in any earlier Gothic play.

Because he believes himself the assassin of his uncle, Adelmorn endures a villain's agony of remorse. His conscience is stung by the scorpions that had earlier tormented villains alone. It is the hero, for the first time, whose sense of guilt causes him to hear the supernatural voice of the murdered man and to endure an unearthly vision. It is he who fears the darkness of lonely places and who moralizes upon evil:

'Tis late and cold—hark! how the bleak wind sighs through the forest; methinks this is my way, but the night's gloom. No moon, no stars. All dark and comfortless, like the murderer's bosom. What, if as I wander thus alone, my uncle's spirit should glide before me?—what, if while his icy hand grasped mine—oh, no, no, no! let it not be so! let not my senses quite forsake me! I would pray to thee, all-merciful, that it may not be so; but the murderer must not, dares not pray!— Hark! 'twas the thunder, as yet it rolls at a distance, but I doubt the storm will be heavy. Already, too, blue lightnings quiver along the glen . . . Ha! what was that? 'twas but the bat which flitted by me! 'twas but the owl which shrieked from yonder tree! While your heart was unconscious of guilt, Adelmorn, and your hand unstained by blood, you were not used thus to tremble; but now, fool that I am, I shudder at the falling leaf.—Guilt, guilt! oh, what a coward thou hast made of me.[21]

For the first time, a Gothic hero was attractive. Adelmorn escapes the insipidness of his forbears by assuming a villain's pain.

THE WOOD DAEMON; OR, ONE O'CLOCK

The Wood Daemon further illustrates Lewis' tendency to expand the Gothic paraphernalia to include properties of another world. Like *The Castle Spectre,* it had a highly successful first run, followed by many revivals. As late as 1871 the preface in Lacy's edition states:

We delight in dramatic devilry like the Wood Daemon, that invites attention and detains it by supernatural incident, grand stage effect, appropriate music, and splendid scenery. It is written by a man of genius. Why this melodrama has been shelved at the Metropolitan for twenty years we cannot divine. Its *worst* parts are as good as the *best* of some modern melodramatic favorites, and the *best,* need we say how much better? . . . Its present revival does credit to the taste of the manager.[22]

The plot, founded partly on a novel called *The Three Brothers*, from which Byron's *The Deformed Transformed* was also drawn, is as follows.[23] Hardyknute, a deformed peasant, had made a compact with the wood demon, the terms of which were that he should become invulnerable in battle and strikingly handsome, and that in return he should sacrifice a human victim to the wood demon annually on the seventh of August before one o'clock. Several years before the play begins, the infant Leolyn, heir of Holstein, had been stolen by gypsies, and has since been secretly protected in a peasant's cottage. As the play opens, he comes with other children to the castle of Holstein, now ruled by the usurper Hardyknute. Una, the villain's intended bride, recognizes by the "bloody arrow" on the child's arm that he is the true heir. The children present a "phantasy" before Hardyknute, who watches with pleasure until Leolyn enters; he then "starts violently," seizes the child, and stares at the arm. Meanwhile Una, in a vision, learns that she must save Leolyn. The wood demon reminds the usurper that he must sacrifice a victim before one o'clock or yield himself to furies. He accordingly forces Leolyn to a sacrificial altar in an underground chamber. But by the combined efforts of Una and the child he is at last foiled, the clock strikes, and furies seize him.

The bare summary exposes elements both old and new. In the cast, besides the wood demon, are other supernatural or preternatural creatures: wood spirits, a giant, zephyrs, and furies. No such figures had ever before appeared in a Gothic play. But in the hands of so confirmed a Gothicist as Lewis, they served to expand, not to erase or even to distort, the conventional pattern. The basic purpose to arouse mystery, gloom, and terror remained just as it was in Walpole, Jephson, Boaden, and the rest. The settings, too, emphatically assert the heritage and denote the essential kind of play that *The Wood Daemon* is: "A Gothic Hall, with large painted window"; "A marble staircase winding up towards two doors above"; "A Cavern, with a burning lamp. In the background is a grated door, with steps; above is a gallery, etc." Various elements of the elaborate machinery can be set in motion. There is a bed, for instance, which sinks through the floor when a secret spring is touched; by leaping on this bed and touching the spring, Hardyknute carries Leolyn to the cavern. In another scene the animated portrait of Walpole's novel is startlingly revived, with another portrait added for good measure. Characteristically, Lewis "improved" on Walpole's use of the portraits; on one occasion, becoming suddenly illuminated by blue flames, they advance, kneel, and beg Una to save Leolyn.

Thus settings and machinery are predominantly traditional, but certain magic properties have been added. Similarly, Hardyknute is essentially a Gothic villain, whose stature as an object of terror has been heightened through his acquisition of magic powers. Like earlier tyrants, he stalks through the castle and the dungeons, one moment sunk in gloom, the next exhilarated by a sudden thought of evil. Remorse gnaws him, and he, like others, is made to speak a speech for morality:

Ages of agony crowd before me. No, no; there's no retreating... Away, then! O Leolyn, Leolyn! the dagger aimed at your bosom most gladly would I plunge into my own, could I but sink into the grave as pure from guilt as thou wilt![24]

Entirely in Hardyknute's power, Una is the persecuted maiden harassed since Walpole. Balked in his attempt to sacrifice the child, the villain points his dagger at her as a substitute offering. The scene in the "necromantic Cavern" recalls many in which tyrants have menaced trembling maidens. Hardyknute had brought Leolyn there to slay him, but Una enters, and the boy conceals himself. Foiled, the villain blames the heroine:

Har. Gone! escaped! traitress!
    (Leolyn comes from his lurking-place, and takes Una by the hand, as if to tell her something.)

Una. Still here! I am safe, then. My lord, my lord, Leolyn is—(Leolyn kneels, implores her silence, and hides himself within the pedestal.)
Har. Speak! Leolyn is—
Una. (After a moment's hesitation) He is—he is—he is safe within the castle.
Har. You have pronounced your doom! (seizing her)[25]

Una begs a moment in which to "pray for you." As she prays, Leolyn crawls from the pedestal and mounts the clock to push the hand ahead. Outside, the voice of the impatient wood demon calls for her victim, and Hardyknute interrupts Una's prayers:

> Har. I'm summoned; come!
> Una. But one moment—
> Har. You plead in vain—
> Una. Mercy, mercy!
> Har. None! none! (dragging her to the altar)

With a desperate effort, Leolyn advances the hand, the clock strikes, and instantly an amazing machinery is set in operation:

(Enter the Wood-Daemon, rushing from behind the rock. She stabs Hardyknute. He falls into the arms of four Fiends, who come from behind the altar, to which they bear him. The snakes twist themselves around him, and they all sink into the earth. The statue and the rocks disappear. The cavern vanishes, and Leolyn and Una find themselves in the great hall of the castle, which is illuminated.)

What has happened here is apparent: to the conventional Gothic machinery, settings, character types, and theme of persecution, Lewis grafted a good deal that may perhaps be described best as necromancy. His villain retains the usual marks, but has acquired new powers: he carries an enchanted key and waves a magic wand; Una is under his magic spell. The Gothic settings are familiar, but they are moved by a new machinery of enchantment. The castle is typically Gothic, but zephyrs and wood spirits—creatures of quite another world than that which had originally surrounded the medieval ruin—fly about it. Perhaps, in concluding, a single striking incident will serve to characterize the entire mixing of familiar and alien materials: on this occasion, the wood demon flies through an open Gothic window in "a car, surrounded by four dragons."

Lesser Plays

I have examined in considerable detail the more significant of Lewis's Gothic plays. Others may be dealt with more briefly.

The "tragedy" of *Alfonso,* unquestionably the best play Lewis wrote, is the least Gothic. Devoid of the claptrap of *Adelmorn* and *The Castle Spectre,* it has a restraint rare in Lewis. In blank verse, it is his only dignified play. The author himself feared, not without reason, that it was too good to succeed on the contemporary stage:

> I have great doubts, whether even an excellent tragedy, if written in blank verse, would succeed on the stage at the present time; of course I do not flatter myself that mine will; and, after the cold reception of De Monfort, I am not vain enough to expect that Alfonso will meet with a kind one. I am not vain enough to expect my work to excell that. I therefore rather wish this production to be considered as a dramatic poem, or (if that be too lofty a character for it) as a short novel in dialogue, divided into acts, instead of chapters. In writing it, I have spared no pains. I now give it to the public, not as a good play, but as the best that I can produce: very possibly nobody could write a worse Tragedy; but it is a melancholy truth, that I cannot write a better.[20]

A significant point is suggested by the mention of Joanna Baillie's *De Monfort* and by the expressed desire to have *Alfonso* regarded as a "dramatic poem." Lewis seems to have realized that a split had occurred between theatrical and literary plays. His and Joanna Baillie's "tragedies" stand at the beginning of this split, which was to widen as the romantic generation developed. The Gothic was to continue, refined, elevated to the mystical, in the poetic drama, and debased by newly added spectacular scenes in the melodrama.

Venoni and *Raymond and Agnes* represent a continuation of Gothic tradition with less intrusion of foreign material than we have found in Lewis's other plays. *The Harper's Daughter,* an adaptation of Schiller's *Kabale und Liebe,* is a story of violent sentimentalism rather than violent terror, and is one of the less Gothic plays by Lewis. Gothic elements are included, but it is they which appear out of place, and obviously they entered the non-Gothic subject only because the author was so steeped in Gothic dye that he could not handle other materials without staining them. *Rugantino* is a version of a popular German and French tale of "Aballino," a figure who started a vogue which compared with that of Karl Moor.

Adelgitha is for one particular reason such a remarkable specimen of Gothic tragedy at the turn of the century that it requires brief individual attention. The scene is laid at Otranto in 1080. Lewis named Gibbon as the source, and the preface to the printed edition makes clear how much history meant to Gothicists whose chief aim was to dispense thrills. The author here describes his approach to the subject and recommends that he should not be censured for failure to follow Gibbon closely:

...nothing was farther from my thoughts in writing it ·(*Adelgitha*) than to compose an historical play. The fact is that having finally arranged the incidents of my plot and sketched the outline of my characters, I thought, that by giving my personages "a local habitation and a name," I should add to the interest of my drama; accordingly, I looked about for some historical niche in which I might place my gentlemen and ladies; and a very slight resemblance between their situations was quite sufficient to make me identify Robert Guiscard with the hero of my play.[27]

Gothic dramatists, unlike Shakespeare, did not merely alter history to fit dramatic need: they designed a plot and a set of characters, and then sought a place in history for them.[28] In *Adelgitha* are materials which in earlier plays are to be found associated indiscriminately with Italy, Greece, France, Spain, Germany, and England, and with times ranging from the eighth to the eighteenth century. Obviously more suggestive than Gibbon in the genesis of the play were Walpole, Greatheed, and Mrs. Radcliffe. As in *The Mysterious Mother,* the protagonist is a woman who has long borne the burden of secret sin. As in *The Regent,* the villain had been granted refuge after banishment from his own country, and repays his benefactor, absent on business to aid the fugitive, with treachery. As in Mrs. Radcliffe's novels, the Gothic effect is achieved by emphasizing the function of background. Two settings will illustrate the latter: "A Grove, with the Chapel and Shrine of St. Hilda. In the latter, Lamps are burning and the grated doors are closed. In the background is a convent situated on a Rock. The Convent bell tolls, and nuns are seen descending the rock." The second is perhaps the most elaborate cavern scene in Gothic drama: "A Cavern; through a natural Arch in the center of the back scene the sea is visible, with the moon shining on it. On one side of the arch is a rough-hewn staircase, conducting to an upper gallery, and on the same side is the mouth of an inner cave, partly overgrown with ivy and other tangling weeds; it is ornamented with a cross, an image, a skull, and crossbones, etc. On the opposite side is the great arched entrance to the cavern."

It is the action conducted in this second setting which, with its consequence, sharply illustrates one of the characteristics of Gothic drama and makes *Adelgitha* noteworthy. The heroine, pursued by the murderous usurper Michael, rushes into the cavern. The villain discovers, curses, threatens, and finally assails her. Frenzied, Adelgitha at last turns on the merciless oppressor of her husband, her son, and herself, and stabs him. Then, stricken with horror, she flees to her "Gothic Apartment" (Lewis specified even that the chairs should be Gothic), where, in the next scene, she sits with "her hair dishevelled, in an attitude of fixed despair," crying out, "Oh! murdered, murdered Michael!"

When her husband and her son, both long persecuted by the villain, learn of her crime, they are as horrified as she; the former, the valiant Robert Guiscard, swoons like one of Mrs. Radcliffe's maidens at his wife's confession. But this is not all; as though Adelgitha's, her husband's, and her son's remorse might not be sufficient evidence of his disapproval of the murder, Lewis took a further precaution through an emphatic footnote in his printed edition:

> ...but above all, I must request *that no one will mistake Adelgitha for a heroine*. I mean to represent in her ... (etc.)[29]

We have seen that Gothic villains were made to endure remorse for their crimes, partly to convince censor and public that playwrights were morally "right." Good characters were never allowed to stain their hands even with the blood of the wickedest. When at last Adelgitha revolts from the convention which has bound heroines and made heroes look impotent, she is made to apologize for her act by shrieks of remorse; her family are made to share in the horror of her fallen condition; and at last the author, to place himself beyond a suspicion of complicity, disowns his heroine.[30] Well represented by *Adelgitha* in 1807, Gothic drama (even by the author of *The Monk*) remained at that date strictly—sometimes incredibly—moral.

The epilogue to *Adelgitha* critically surveys the theatrical fare and the taste of the times, and sheds light on the widening gap between literary and acting plays:

> When all is full around—above—below,
> And eager crowds sit jammed in every row,
> Ask for what cause they crowd and push and stew.
> For Shakespeare? Otway? no! the play is *new!*
> ...
> But oh! too oft does Otway's lute complain
> And Shakespeare wave his magic wand in vain.
> While Young or Congreve, Sheridan or Rowe
> Scarce at one house attract a decent show.

> Too oft some *novelty*, all glaze and pother,
> With gaping gazers deluges the other.
> Too oft does Romeo feel his deepest woes
> Spring not from Juliet's death—but vacant rows.
> . . .
> Yet why blame novelty? Where ere mine eyes
> I turn, fresh tokens of her powers arise!
> 'Tis her command makes Lydia Languish stop
> Daily her sky-blue coach at Hookham's shop.
> Some strange hob-goblin story meets her view,
> She's seized with rapture! why? the book is *new!*
> In vain Cecilia's leaves their charms unfold.
> "Cecilia"—lisps the nymph—"That book is *old!*
> The characters are drawn from life, 'tis said.
> Give me a work which draws them from the dead!"
> So cramm'd with mysteries that the more it has on't,
> The less the reader makes, or tails or heads on't.
> With ghosts, and tapers, and robbers so alarming,
> One's *terrified to death*—and then that's *charming!*

This account of a dismal chapter in the history of English taste by the foremost purveyor of theatrical monstrosities and "new" claptrap perhaps explains the success of such a play as *Timour the Tartar*, one of Lewis' most excessive spectacles. It was written, said the author, "merely to oblige Mr. Harris, who prest me very earnestly to give him a spectacle in which Horses might be introduced." Perhaps it was *Timour* which initiated a series of animal plays. Horses soon appeared in other plays, and not only horses, but dogs and magpies. Magpies assumed roles of greater consequence than had customarily been given heroes in Gothic plays.

The craze for novelty tolerated no limitation of excesses, and in these excesses the conventional Gothic elements, somewhat "old" and relatively dignified, were often overwhelmed. In 1795 it had been remarkable that, as a catastrophe, a fragment of a ruin was shown falling. In the early nineteenth century, lightning struck castles and caverns, demolishing everything except hero and heroine. The pursuit of the novel often led to spectacles which bore no apparent relation to the Gothic quest for objects of mystery, gloom, and terror, though actually it had been that quest which started the exploitation of objects and events ever farther afield from the conventional castles, convents, and caverns. It grew "old" to blow up a castle: A burning forest, a rampaging flood, or a falling bridge provided the "new" sensation. Searching for the spectacular, some playwrights themselves forgot the Gothic Revival which had long ago given the impulse toward this very search.

The adaptations of *The Monk,* previously named, complete the certain impact of Lewis on the Gothic drama of his time. The ballet pantomime of *Don Raymond* is a hodgepodge which does for Lewis's celebrated novel about what Andrews' *The Enchanted Castle* had done for *The Castle of Otranto*. It stages for scenic effect, without attention to either characterization or plot, and episode (that of the "bleeding nun") of the novel. Boaden's *Aurelio and Miranda* was a very complete bowdlerization of *The Monk,* and is significant for that reason. I have earlier stated that though other forms of literature were also subjected to moral scrutiny, the drama was singled out for extraordinary attention. Boaden's adaptation of *The Monk* illustrates this fact strikingly. Boaden originally entitled his dramatization *The Monk;* but in the Larpent manuscript a line has been drawn through this title, and the new *Aurelio and Miranda* substituted. Nor is this all. Boaden's chief characters, like Lewis', were Ambrosio and Matilda, the evil monk and the she demon. Throughout the manuscript, these names have been scratched out, and, everywhere that they had appeared, "Aurelio" and "Miranda" written in. Boaden leaned backward to avoid the remotest possibility of censure; he stated in the prologue:

> But though his subject such, no virgin ear
> Shall startle at one loose expression here.

To live up to that promise in adapting *The Monk* could mean only one thing: that nothing of *The Monk* should remain in the adaptation. Therefore not only the names, but also the relationship of the two principal characters with each other has been changed. "Matilda," the female voluptuary of the novel, is in the new "Miranda" a woman of virtue. Before the play is done, wedding bells have pealed for the pair. But at the first performance all of Boaden's and the censor's care proved to have been in vain. Kelly reported that "it was no sooner found out that Miranda was a virtuous woman, instead of a demon, than many in the pit and galleries evinced dissatisfaction."[31] The play ran only six nights.

THE PLACE OF LEWIS

Lewis's claim to a place of first importance in the history of the Gothic novel is contested by Walpole, Mrs. Radcliffe, and Maturin. His preëminence in Gothic drama is almost uncontested.[32] The number of Gothic plays from his pen equals that of any other playwright, and his novel was adapted several times. His influence upon his contemporaries and successors, both greater and lesser' than himself, perhaps exceeded even that of Mrs. Radcliffe. Furthermore, he stood between the two centuries and was most instrumental in passing the Gothic collection over to the romantics.[33] His plays represent better than any others a composite of the traditional, native materials and the foreign and new ones. He wrote at the time that theatrical and literary plays parted company, and such a piece as *Adelmorn* pointed the direction in which each kind was to go. In addition, *The Monk* was translated into German before the flood of German materials reached England, so that the German deluge which came had already received the contribution of Lewis. *The Monk* was also adapted several times for the French stage, and thus when translations and alterations of Pixérécourt began to appear on the English stage, they brought back materials borrowed from Lewis in the first place. Actually, then, Lewis did more than utilize the two foreign sources that were added to the native tradition. He contributed to the English tradition, lent materials to German and French writers for development in their respective countries, and finally capitalized on the results of the international circulation when native and foreign elements were reunited in England.

CHAPTER IX

GOTHIC DRAMA AND MELODRAMA

PERHAPS the most confused period in the history of the English stage is around the year 1800. New impulses were coming and going in every direction. To show the fate of the Gothic in such a time is not easy. Drama had split into theatrical and literary plays, and Gothic elements and motifs continued to appear in both. The arrival of German plays of horrific and sentimental varieties complicated the scene. Besides, a new source of confusion had arisen with the importation of the melodrama from France.

The term "melodrama" has done nearly as much as "German" to bury the identity of the Gothic species. When English horrific plays have not been called the one name, they have been called the other. Under either label—and sometimes under both at once, "German melodrama"—their true origins have remained hidden.

On November 13, 1802, Thomas Holcroft's *A Tale of Mystery* appeared at the Covent Garden Theatre. On the title page of the manuscript is affixed the description—"a melodrama." It was the first time this designation was applied to an English play. But examination of the work shows it to be concocted of the very elements which we have found in the Gothic plays acted in England during the last thirty years of the eighteenth century.

A brief summary of the development of melodrama up to the appropriation of the term by Holcroft as a label for a conventional Gothic play seems necessary.

With regard to the word *mélodrame*, there were the following changes in meaning; when first introduced into France from Italy the word was used as a synonym for opera in general; in 1781, at Du-Bois' suggestion it acquired the meaning of a *scène lyrique* and during the Revolution began to be applied to pantomime with dialogue.[1]

---

[1] For notes to chap. ix, see pages 253–254.

From about 1779 to 1791 the *Comédie Française* held a monopoly on legitimate dramatic productions in France. Only pantomime and puppet shows were allowed the other theaters, but various means were employed to circumvent the paralyzing restrictions of the *Comédie Française*. An enterprising manager named Arnould dropped historical fantasy and began to dramatize recent events in pantomimic form with musical accompaniment. In 1791 the National Assembly freed the theaters from the restrictions imposed by the *Comédie Française*, and the popular drama received a great impetus. The form which Arnould had developed progressed toward a definite dramatic species in the hands of producers who sought to give audiences the theatrical fare they desired in that violent age:

> But it is to Guilbert de Pixérécourt that we look for the establishment as a distinct dramatic type... What had been a hybrid form of entertainment—an exaggerated story interspersed with music and dances and acrobatics—he made into a distinct type, with as many rules and conventions as had heretofore cluttered up the distinctly classical drama of the *Théâtre Française*. Pixérécourt's early plays from about 1791 are largely experimental, *but with Coelina, ou l'enfant du mystère, he arrived at the complete formula for the mélodrame.* This form has been little changed by his successors.[2]

Coelina, adapted, became Holcroft's *A Tale of Mystery*, which is thoroughly in the Gothic tradition—as well it might be, for Pixérécourt's *Coelina* was obviously influenced strongly by Gothic writers from Walpole through Ann Radcliffe.

To the *scène lyrique* and the pantomimic entertainment with musical accompaniment, Pixérécourt added something which resulted in "the complete formula for the *mélodrame*." What was this vital something? We find the clue in the fact that directly before he wrote *Coelina* this French playwright wrote a play called *Le Château des Appennins; ou Le Fantôme vivant*. The principal characters of this work are Montoni and Emilie; its plot, like these, is drawn from *The Mysteries of Udolpho*.

The something which, added to the *scène lyrique* and the pantomimic entertainment, resulted in "the complete formula," then, was neither more nor less than the mood, manner, and material of the English Gothic school. In completing the formula, Pixérécourt merely continued to exploit the elements he had used in his adaptation of Mrs. Radcliffe's novel. After *Coelina* he continued to deal with the same properties; he was, in fact, something of a French "Monk" Lewis, who adapted, among other works, Heinrich Zschokke's *Aböllino, der grosse Bandit,* the German robber novel concocted out of Schiller's materials in part, but in greater part from the English horrific school.

English Gothicists, then, were the principal forces in the evolution of the *mélodrame:* Pixérécourt adapted English materials under a French label; Holcroft and other English playwrights took over the label and attached it to plays of a kind which had existed more than thirty years, and which, carried piecemeal to France, had evolved the *mélodrame* to "the complete formula." We have seen the same circle in examining the Gothic-German relationship. Gothic materials went to Germany and returned to overwhelm their own sources under German; just so, they went to France and returned to bury them under melodrama.

Indeed, the general nature of French influence on the course of Gothic drama is comparable to the German. We have seen how English materials developed in Germany under various forces peculiar to that country and returned, with interest accrued, to England. Similarly, in France, works of the Gothicists were quickly received, developed under such forces as Rousseauism and the Revolution, and came back to England in adaptations of Pixérécourt and others. By the end of the first decade of the new century, French, German, and English materials had become international baggage, and some works were battered from much travel. For instance, Elliston's *The Venetian Outlaw,* acted in 1805, was adapted from Pixérécourt's *L'homme à trois visages,* which in its turn was adapted from Zschokke's *Aballino*—a tale that had been inspired by English Gothicists in the first place. By such a route went other works, and it is usually reasonable to assume that when a play shows the characteristics described in previous chapters, then, whether the particular adaptation came through the French or the German, and whether it went by the name melodrama or the name German, it was a Gothic piece that had merely completed an extensive trip.

GOTHIC MELODRAMAS

Not every early nineteenth-century melodrama after Holcroft shows the distinguishing marks of Gothic drama. The plays by Hook and Pocock, for instance, reveal only negligible acquaintance with or interest in the conventional materials. Of real preoccupation with castle, convent, and cavern there seems to be none in their plays. Still other pieces under the name melodrama show Gothic traces, but these, overwhelmed by the new devices of sensationalism, are barely discernible. In general, the plays by popular melodramatists like Thomas Dibdin, Thomas Lynch, and Fredric Reynolds betray somewhat incidentally the fact that the new pursuit of the sensational was really an extension of the Gothic quest. But in a third group of plays designated melodrama the traditional elements continued to flourish. Though all of these introduced some materials previously unknown to Gothicists, the basic preoccupation of the authors stamps the works as predominantly Gothic. In this group belong several plays by Lewis which have already been discussed; his melodramas are *Rugantino, The Wood Daemon, Venoni,* and *Raymond and Agnes.* As we have seen, all are in the Gothic tradition, with certain foreign additions. They do not differ in any way from Lewis' earlier plays, written before the new label was introduced by Holcroft.

Besides the plays of Lewis, others typical of this third group are *The Foundling of the Forest* (Hay. July 1809), by William Dimond, and *The Woodman's Hut* (D. L. April 1814), by Samuel James Arnold.[3] Examination of these will illustrate the treatment of the traditional materials under the new label.

THE FOUNDLING OF THE FOREST

William Dimond was author of some thirty plays between 1806 and 1837, twelve of which were specifically designated melodrama. In all twelve, Gothic interests are apparent; in half of these, they predominate.[4]

The Foundling of the Forest conforms to pattern in that the action is based on a mysterious past event. Twenty years before, Count de Valmont had returned home to find his castle burned and sacked, and, as he supposed, his wife, Eugenia, and his child destroyed in the flames. For twenty years he has lived in "an attitude of fixed melancholy." Two children have grown up in his castle—Geraldine, his niece, and Florian, whom he had found and adopted. The opening scene, in "A Hall in the Chateau de Valmont," depicts Longueville commanding Bertrand, his creature, to assassinate Florian and so leave the way clear for himself to marry Geraldine and claim the uncle's title. The relation of Longueville to a Gothic ancestry is at once apparent, for he is described as "ever in some sullen mood, with scowling brows, or else in a cross-armed fit of melancholy ... with wildness in his looks and words."[5] Any doubt about his villainy is dispelled when Bertrand, objecting to the commands, hints at the nature of the disaster which had occurred twenty years before:

Fatal avarice! Already have we bartered for those cursed estates our everlasting peace—for those did midnight flames surprise the sleep of innocence—for those did the sacrificed Eugenia with her shrieking babe—[6]

Longueville forbids further remarks and gives specific directions for further crime:

This night Florian returns triumphant from his campaign. Two of my trusty bloodhounds watch the road to give me timely note of his approach. One only follower attends the youth. In the thick woods, 'twixt the chateau and Hunningen, an ambush, safely laid, may end my rival and my fears for ever. In the west avenue, at sunset, I command your presence. Mark me! I command you, by your oath!

The play continues with the ambush scene: "Night—a wood—very dark—thunder and lightning." Bertrand and Baron Longueville appear, disguised, following Florian's trail. Next appears "Another part of the forest, darker, more entangled and intricate. The tempest becomes violent. Alternate lightning, and utter darkness." Florian enters on foot, his horse having thrown him; he is lost; he sees the figures of two thugs who have accompanied Bertrand and Longueville, guesses their purpose, and hides in a hollow tree, regretting what heroes of Gothic plays have invariably regretted—that he has left his weapons elsewhere. When opportunity permits, he leaves his hiding place and spies a light among the trees. The scene shifts to a cottage, where a candle burns in the window. Here lives a crippled old lady and "an Unknown Female, wildly dressed," apparently mute, who is addressed as "Silence." Florian dashes in: "The Unknown opens the door, but on seeing Florian, recoils with trepidation—he catches her hand, and forcibly detains her. The Unknown shrieks violently—she covers her eyes with both hands for an instant, and then, with the look and action of sudden insanity, darts away into the thickest of the wood."⁷

Sixteen years before, her form "meagre and wasted," the unknown had been found wandering in the forest. The old lady had taken her under her protection, but had never solved the mystery of her origin or the reason for her conduct: "She is accustomed to wander in the woods by night when anything disturbs her mind. She'll return to me anon, calm and passive as before. I have known it with her often thus." Florian remains to share the humble food, and as he is preparing to depart at last, Bertrand and the two "Bravoes" (characters who ten years before would have been called "banditti" in Mrs. Radcliffe's fashion, but are now called by a name popularized by Lewis' *Rugantino* and other "Bravo" plays, all ultimately from *Aballino*) break in. Weaponless, of course, like any other hero, Florian is being dragged outside to death when—

(Enter the Unknown Female from the wood—she pauses opposite to Bertrand—His advanced arm falls back nerveless by his side, his limbs shake with strong convulsion, and he reels backward.)

Bert. Support me—ha! or I die!

(The Bravoes release Florian and fly towards Bertrand, who sinks in their arms—the Unknown, with a light and rapid step, crosses in front of the group to where Florian remains kneeling—she spreads her wild drapery between him and the ruffians in an attitude of protection).[8]

Bertrand stares at her "deliriously" and cries,

Look! Look! She rises from the grave! she blasts me with her frown! Away! away! heaven itself forbids the deed!

Though we have seen unknowns in earlier plays, lurking as apparitions about their usurped castles, "Silence" is the first of her sex to return and affright a villain. Very likely the Haymarket audience in 1809 realized even before Bertrand's "Look! Look! She rises from the grave!" that what seemed a specter was really the Countess Eugenia, lost twenty years before.

In a following scene Bertrand's conscience, no longer endurable, drives him to return to the cottage and beg forgiveness. He tells that even on the night of the fire he had attempted to save Eugenia, but had been unsuccessful because "a falling turret crossed my path." Eugenia describes her escape to the woods through "a hidden passage dug beneath the rampart." In the forest, as the madness of her distress overcame her, she had momentarily put down the infant she carried, wandered a few steps away in "the mazes of the wood," and so had lost him. It was this infant whom the count had found.

The closing scenes show sensationalism at its wildest. Eugenia flees from the cottage to the castle, the villain pursues at her heels, the castle bell tolls, and muffled bravoes glide stealthily about— all in a setting of "Moonlight. A rugged cliff overhanging the river." Bertrand saves both Eugenia and Florian, the count recovers from his twenty-year melancholy, and Longueville is borne off captive. Exposure of a "sanguine cross" which "indelibly remained" on his hand where Longueville's dagger had scarred it identifies Florian as the child of the count and Eugenia, and general rejoicing follows the family reunion.

THE WOODMAN'S HUT

The Foundling of the Forest represents that melodrama in which Gothic conventions, though mixed with new elements, continued to predominate. Arnold's *Woodman's Hut,* acted five years later, represents a melodrama in which other elements have more nearly submerged the traditional properties, yet in which a sufficient number survive to indicate the ancestry of the play.

For twenty years Baron Hernhausen and the Count of Conenburg had waged war on each other. As the price of peace, the baron had demanded Amelia, the count's daughter. Seven months before the play opens, the old count had died and Amelia had mysteriously vanished; presumably she had been abducted by the baron. In the conventional first scene servants, gossiping about the situation, "point up" the usual mystery:

Laura. The question is, why the young Lord Ferdinand, nephew of our late master, the Count of Conenburg, has taken possession of this castle and estate?

Moritz. Well, about five years ago our powerful and terrible neighbor, the Baron Hernhausen....

Laura. Ay—the great Baron who lives yonder, on the other side of the river, in the Black Castle, as it is called...."[9]

The scene shifts to the Black Castle of the gloomy baron. Here Wolfender and another of the baron's creatures are instructed to surprise Conenburg and kidnap the young count. The two devise their scheme, heavily involving Gothic fixtures:

Wolf. You remember the grotto in the garden of the castle?
Kaunitz. We have good reason to remember it, for it was from that very place we carried off the girl. At the end of the grotto is a subterranean passage, which leads without the walls, through which we conveyed her.
Wolf. That subterranean passage will again answer our purpose....[10]

The young count, who is unhappy because "a beautiful peasant girl" whom he had met in the forest has disappeared, is enticed to the grotto; a cloak is thrown over his head, and he is hurried along a secret path "that leads through vaulted passages beneath the moat." The carriage which was to bear them to the baron's castle breaks down in a Radcliffean forest, and captors and captive proceed on foot to a cottage. Here lives Amelia, who, with her nurse, had earlier escaped the baron's clutches.

To this point—about half through the play—*The Woodman's Hut* is a typical Gothic play. The castles, the subterranean passage, the past event, the escape of the heroine, the breakdown of the carriage in the forest, and the sight of a "glimmering lamp" in the cottage window were parts of a paraphernalia more than forty years old. But suddenly the pursuit of terror turns away from tradition. The sensational is sought in objects and incidents of a new kind. If we were to read only the latter half of the play, close scrutiny might fail to establish direct connection with the Gothic school.

Unrecognized by the ruffians, Amelia pretends to offer such comforts as her dwelling affords. She induces them to drink wine in which she has placed an opiate. They fall asleep, and Amelia, her nurse, and the count flee. The act ends with a spectacle:

(Lightning and thunder—the walls of the cottage are struck by a thunderbolt, and fall with a loud noise—the river is seen through the opening, very much agitated—the storm is at the height—a boat, in which are the Count, Amelia, and the nurse, is seen by the lightning, violently tossed upon the river—the Count and Amelia make great exertions against the furious waves—Maria, her hair dishevelled, her hands raised up to Heaven, and on her knees—this scene is shown by the repetition of the lightning.)[11]

The scene illustrates the search for novel effects in which the Gothic origin of this very search was obliterated. The final act buries that origin even deeper beneath an avalanche of the new. Fleeing into the forest, the fugitives become separated. The count and the nurse are given refuge in a woodcutter's cabin, where soon Amelia arrives, the pursuers at her heels. The count fires a blunderbuss from an upper window, then leaps down, sword in hand, to meet the attack. The woodcutter brings his fellows, and a general battle ensues. Suddenly a red glow appears on the horizon. The forest is on fire, and all are apparently trapped. The last scene shows Amelia, the count, the nurse, and their allies crossing a burning bridge, a section of which falls blazing into the river just as they reach the farther shore. The baron's henchmen are doomed as the fire swoops toward them, and Wolfender cries, "They have escaped! Just Heaven! We are caught in our own snarl!" The play ends with the count and his party "expressing joy and gratitude" on the safe side of the river, while Wolfender, Kaunitz, and the others are on their knees "in an attitude of despair."[12]

Perhaps no play could be found which would better illustrate the gradual change of the Gothic species into the later melodrama of the nineteenth century. In the first half of this piece the familiar settings and properties dominate; in the second, the new has flooded in. The action has passed from the traditional castle to the cottage—"the woodman's hut."[13] The hero fires a blunderbuss. There is a hazardous river crossing by boat, and another by a burning bridge. There is a forest fire. Very plainly, the Gothic quest was overreaching itself, losing all contact with its origins in the Revival, and so producing quite another dramatic kind. In this later kind, in which eventually heroines were to be tied to railroad tracks and to carriages approaching the whirling teeth of saws, to be pursued across frozen rivers by bloodhounds, and in which old people were to be cheated out of their meager holdings by scheming mortgagors, every evidence of the distant origin in the Gothic Revival was to disappear.[14]

The question is not whether the ultimate origin of this later kind was in that Revival, but, rather, just at what time the Gothic species should be said to have become another kind of drama. We have followed the Gothic quest for new elements. We have seen how a Gothic ruin—the nucleus of the machinery of gloom and terror—attracted to itself, first, elements legitimately Gothic, as the various parts of castles and convents, then others less immediately related to medievalism, as forests, caves, banditti, and precipices. The expansion, always directed by the impulse to Gothicize, continued from Walpole through Mrs. Radcliffe and Lewis, and the accumulated paraphernalia grew enormous. During the same period, the villain acquired new terror resources. He became a member of the Inquisition or the Secret Tribunal. He was surrounded, in *The Castle Spectre,* by four towering blacks who multiplied his personal force as a creature of evil. He acquired magic powers, and assumed superhuman capacities by leaguing himself with the preternatural. Yet through all this time he remained the same gloomy usurper, essentially, bent on persecution, though tortured by remorse for his past deeds.

In many plays of the early nineteenth century the surge of new elements, induced by the taste for novelty which Lewis reprimanded (and fed) came to obliterate the original impulse which had set the whole process going. With the Gothic nucleus gone, Gothic drama certainly became another kind. But at what possible earlier stage did it become another kind? Was it when precipices were added to castles and caverns? When four blacks supplemented the villain? When a blunderbuss was fired from a window? When a forest fire was introduced as the catastrophe? Or did it become another species only when the last vestige of the Gothic origin was obliterated—the whole familiar Gothic machinery sloughed off in the gradual evolution of the new materials and motifs?

The precise dividing line between Gothic drama and that later kind of melodrama which betrays no Gothic origins is difficult to fix. Perhaps, however, it is less important to fix it than to interpret the change, to show the process by which a new species was evolved out of the old.

Burlesque Gothic Melodrama

In the first years of the nineteenth century, the Gothic which survived under the label "melodrama" became associated with claptrap and spectacle that made it increasingly preposterous. One consequence was the appearance of some burlesques. The first of these was Thomas John Dibdin's *Boniface and Bridgetina* (C. G. March 1808), a "burlesque melodrama"; a second was Dennis Lawler's *The Earls of Hammersmith; or, The Cellar Spectre* (Olympic, Jan. 1813). These, by showing up the absurdities of the Gothic school, prove that as late as 1808 and 1813, at least, the new effects of melodrama had not entirely stolen the spotlight from the methods and materials of conventional Gothic drama. Dibdin and Lawler directed their fun especially at those properties which had been conspicuous since 1768.

Dibdin's burlesque, presented as *The Knight of the Hermitage* follows the tradition of great burlesques from Beaumont to Sheridan in having a play within a play. It hits many of the characteristics with which audiences were familiar. The play-within-the-play opens with a brooding "stranger" sitting outside a "romantic hermitage." A foolish passerby pauses to talk:

Nicholas. Now what can such a jolly soul as you have to trouble you?
Stranger. Trouble! A-a-h! I'd near betrayed my secret (aside) Good youth, I have no troubles, none. Therefore I pray thee do not ask further for them.
Nicholas. Nay, for my part, I never ax'd at all.
Stranger. For know, good youth, my secret shall die with me.
Nicholas. The sooner the better. (Going)
Stranger. Stay! on second thought I'll yield to thy entreaties, for I need consolation, and my griefs will narrow by expansion. Let's see that no one overhears us.
Nicholas. Mercy on us! what in the name of wonder will he tell me?[15]

What is the secret? That had been the traditional problem for nearly half a century. Immediately after Nicholas's last line above, music strikes up the tune, "Oh dear, what can the matter be?" The scene continues with another stroke, this time at the spectacular manner in which "unknowns" customarily identify themselves at last as barons, counts, or dukes long believed lost but really alive and residing humbly near their usurped estates:

Nich. But father Solomon, how comes it that, today, after keeping silent for three years—
Str. Son of old Nick the Sexton, part of my secret is—that I am not Solomon!
Nich. Why, bless your reverence, that never was no secret at all.
Str. Then thou hast heard of one *Sir* Hildebrand?
Nich. Can't say I ever did.
Str. Then learn to thy great astonishment, that warrior stands before thee!
Nich. Where? (looking about)
Str. Here! (throws off his hermit's gown and shows brilliant armour) Art not amaz'd?
(Music: "Don't you see by my hunch, sir?")
Nich. Why, yes, I am indeed, to think how the deuce you contrive to wear so many clothes atop of one another in this warm weather. And who can have kept them so neat and tidy for you?

After these jests, the play proceeds to poke fun at the familiar past event. Sir Hildebrand describes at length how "three years ago" his castle, daughter, nephew, and all were wrested from him by "the villain in the castle yonder." Next, the Gothic machinery of ghosts, secret panels, and subterranean passages becomes the target. The haunted chamber of Mrs. Radcliffe is here a haunted windmill tower. Finally, the nobleman-turned-outlaw motif is deftly struck. One robber remarks to his associates, "But talking of our *captain*, I begin to think it time, my comrades, that we should try to find out who he is." Another replies, "Why, e'ent it enough to know he's a fine mysterious fellow, who comes and goes nobody knows whence, how, nor where, and as for finding out who he is, he is so devilish close that I believe he hardly knows that himself." The piece concludes with an elaborate catastrophe which shames the final scene of the new popular kind, for the windmill is on fire, the castle is blazing, and banditti are attacking from all sides.

Though its ridicule is not so inclusive, *The Earls of Hammersmith* is scarcely less clever. It strikes several Gothic salients, often with hilarious effect. Lord Bluster is a tyrant usurper. His first entrance, in the striking, mystery-enveloped manner of the typical villain, turns out amiss: "Enter Lord Bluster, lost in thought, Calipash and Calipee bow to him—he does not see them—but with a tragic gesture of his hand knocks one of their hats off." Bluster thus states the perennial problem:

(To himself) My rest is disturbed by Goblin, Ghost, and Fairy. No!
I will rid me of these nightly fears. (To Calipash and Calipee)
Grave counsellors and pillars of the state—
A vault there is beneath the castle, here,
A vault in which I keep my ale and beer.
That vault is haunted![16]

Sir Walter Wisehead, hero, offers to sleep in the vault to win the hand of Lady Margaret Marrowbones. He is shown at night, waiting, with "a candle, a bottle, glass, blunderbuss. Clock strikes one—thunder. Ghost of a footman rises and presents a note to Sir Walter." Sir Walter reads aloud: "The ghost of the Dowager Countess of Hammersmith presents her compliments." The ghost of the dowager enters, with the ghost of Betty, her maid, holding her train. The footman presents a scroll, and Sir Walter reads: "Wed not Lady Margaret Marrowbones! She is your grandmother!" The footman offers yet another scroll: "Your father is imprisoned in the castle: yon secret door leads to his dungeon." The ghosts sink, but before Sir Walter can enter the dungeon he is joined by Lady Simple, whom he had discovered earlier to be his mother. They go via secret passage to find Lord Simple. In the dungeon they come upon him, laden with chains and bearing several years' growth of beard. Lady Simple, after briefly embracing her husband, draws back abruptly:

There, that will do, now go and get shaved."

The final stroke is at the Karl Moor motif. Sir Walter joins a band of robbers, and with their help succeeds in overthrowing the tyrannical Bluster.

CHAPTER X

GOTHIC ACTING DRAMA, 1801–1816

By 1800 English dramatic works had split into "acting" and "literary" pieces. That the dividing line between these was often thin is indeed indisputable. Similarly, often only the label attached by the author distinguishes a melodrama from another kind of acting drama. On the whole, however, the division is useful and for purposes of the present chapter is found particularly helpful.

Early in the century Gothic materials continued to abound in all dramatic classifications. In melodrama they sometimes predominated, sometimes were secondary, and sometimes were buried beneath the avalanche of new devices. In all melodrama, the Gothic was ever more cheapened; its path was downward. We need read only a few of the works of Dimond and Arnold to sense that, by comparison, the Gothic tragedies of Jephson, Greatheed, and even Boaden preserved at least a show of dignity; these writers, who believed that Gothic terror and the sublime were virtually synonymous, handled even the grossest absurdities with a kind of awe. At the other extreme from melodrama, in the literary drama, the Gothic path was upward. In the hands of greater poets—if worse playwrights—crude elements were elevated and refined. Thus at both extremes the tendency was toward obscuration of the Gothic origins and identity—in the one by burial amidst claptrap thrills and the cheapest sensationalism; in the other by transmutation. During the same period, however, in numerous acting plays not labeled melodrama, the Gothic continued surely in the line it had followed since Walpole. In this "middle" drama, conventional materials and purposes continued to dominate. An examination of the most representative works of this latter kind will be made in this chapter. Many others, some of which might have served as well, are listed in the Appendix.

ANALYSIS OF FOUR GOTHIC ACTING PLAYS

Outstanding specimens of Gothic acting drama between 1801 and 1816 include *Julian and Agnes* (D. L. April 1801), by William Sotheby; *The Towers of Urbandine* (York, 1805), by George Charles Carr; *The Curfew* (D. L. Feb. 1807), by John Tobin; and Bertram; or *The Castle of St. Aldobrand* (D. L. May 1816), by Charles Robert Maturin.[1] Analysis of these will illustrate the continuation of Gothic development in the heart of the period of high romanticism.

JULIAN AND AGNES

Sotheby's *Julian and Agnes* is the strangest and perhaps the best Gothic play. It is at once conventional—in its settings, atmosphere, and characters—and unique, in its intensity, which often resembles that in *Manfred* and approaches that in *Wuthering Heights* when Heathcliff wanders in desolation. It is further remarkable because its hero-villain is an early and startlingly vivid portrait of the Byronic hero. It is difficult to remember, as we read this play, that the poet whose name was given to that particular kind of hero was but thirteen years old when it was acted.

Until the middle of Act III of *Julian and Agnes*, dark mystery enshrouds two apparently unrelated sets of characters and two separate actions. First, there is a wanderer called Alfonso, who has come, from where and for what reason none knows, to the Convent of St. Bernard in the Alps. He is consumed by a nameless agony which at irregular intervals sends him out to wander wildly through blizzards by day or night, across hazardous ravines and naked crags. Occasionally in these mad excursions, on nights when violent storms have deterred the monks, though oath-bound to venture, from leaving the convent walls, he has come upon and rescued blinded, snow-bound travelers. Second,

---

[1] For notes to chap. x, see pages 254–255.

there is a woman called Agnes, seemingly in an agony comparable to Alfonso's, who is forcing her way over the Alpine summit. With her, on a sleigh, against which Agnes pushes with her own hands, is a beautiful, half-mad, and dying woman addressed as Ellen. It is for Ellen's sake—but no further clue is at once given—that she is seeking a certain dell on the other side of the mountains. Guides vainly urge her to turn back, to take refuge from the blizzard in the Convent of St. Bernard; she continues upward.

While Agnes struggles up the mountain slope, the provost reaches the convent and endeavors to extract from Alfonso the secret which had baffled the monks. He promises that ease will follow confession:

> Prov. Know, too, our holy church
> Has pray'rs and penances of power to cleanse
> The soul from all infections.
> Alf. This to me!
> Who commun'd with his soul and talk'd with guilt
> Lonely on unknown heights, where none ere gaz'd.
> Penance to me! who watchful of the sound
> Heard the night tempest call, and walk'd abroad
> When nought but Heaven's avenging ministers,
> The lightning of wing'd whirlwind mov'd on earth!
> Talk not to me of penance.'

A new ring is very apparent in this utterance. The dark gloom of the old Gothic villain has turned to the high, piercing anguish of the Byronic hero, and has here received a finer expression than ever before.

Alfonso's fear is that the provost will compel him to return to "that strange world below"—the world of society in the valley. He is at last induced to divulge the truth of the "past event" when the provost has allayed this fear. Ten years before, Alfonso, really Julian, Count of Tortona, had married the beautiful and virtuous Lady Agnes. After a short period of happiness, he had gone to war. He and a youthful banneret had been wounded, and the latter, apparently dying, had asked the nobleman to find and protect his sister, "an orphan, who has but me." Both had fainted from their injuries, and Alfonso, reviving after being removed to safety, assumed that the banneret was dead. Faithful to his promise, he had sought the sister, Ellen, and, his senses lost to her beauty and virtue, had married her. Years passed; he lived sometimes with one wife, sometimes with the other. Then, one day, he had encountered the banneret whom he had supposed dead. He was greeted with "Traitor!" and struck by the youthful avenger. In sudden wrath, he had slain the banneret. Then he had spread the rumor of his own death and ascended the Alps to lose himself from men.

On concluding his story, Alfonso is stricken with renewed agony. The monks strive to hold him, and he cries:

> You shall not hold me here, unseen by men!
> No, I will stalk commission'd o'er the world
> Like Heaven's enquiring spirit—Guilt shall shake
> At my approach, and youth turn grey before me.[8]

Breaking the grasp of the monks, he rushes forth to seek relief in the blizzard without. He is next shown on the Alpine slope, climbing upward against a setting that anticipates the Jungfrau scenes of *Manfred:* "Mountain peaks, cover'd with snow, surrounding the pass on the north side of the Convent. Alfonso climbing upward over rocks and precipices." On a snowy height, he turns and gazes down:

> What! force me back?
> Roof me in cloister'd cells where never sun
> Glanc'd on the face of man! Must they explore
> Which way I tread, and track me to my haunts,
> Like a lone beast that makes his viewless lair
> In the unfrequented wilderness?
> What am I?
> A wretch, moon-stricken, to be ey'd and bound,
> Unfit to hide where man makes residence.
> Would that I were not what indeed I am,
> Or being what I am, in form of man,

> That heaven had cast me in the idiot mould
> Of those that in the valley gasp in the sun
> With disproportion'd throats and uncouth limbs
> That know not their own use.[4]

Cries of those in peril reach him, and he leaps from the rock:

> Lo! the avenger here!
> Wash off, kind Heaven, the murder on this blade
> By the assassins' blood—I have in battle cop'd
> With mighty men, and foil'd proud warriors.

Robber assassins, attacking Agnes and her party, have slain or driven off the guards. The moaning of Ellen ceases, and the robbers, thinking her dead, carry her off for burial in the snow. As an assassin moves to strike Agnes, Alfonso leaps from above and slays him. Another wounds Alfonso mortally, but is himself cut down. Lying in the snow, Alfonso recognizes Agnes and makes himself known to her:

> ...I have thrown
> In the smooth vale of innocence and peace
> Rank baleful seed: and I have pluck'd the fruit
> That leaves a scar and blister on the soul,
> When all of earth sinks to its native dust.
> You know me now.

Monks arrive to carry the dying Ellen and Alfonso to the convent. There, Ellen returns to consciousness long enough to forgive her betrayer. The two die, and Agnes, whose efforts to carry Ellen across the Alps to her birthplace had resulted in tragedy, survives to grieve, though cheered by knowledge that she had brought the two together and gained forgiveness for Alfonso. Noteworthy is the fact that both women, though wronged, bear only affection and keen sympathy for Alfonso.

In *Julian and Agnes* Sotheby combined villain and hero in a single figure. He was not the first to do so in a Gothic play. Thomas Whalley in *The Castle of Montval* (D. L. April 1799) and Joanna Baillie in *De Monfort* (D. L. April 1800) had similarly blended them. Furthermore, Lewis' *Adelmorn,* with its agonized hero, appeared at the Drury Lane only a month after *Julian and Agnes.* Thus, in the space of two years, four dramatists transformed villain into hero. The nearly simultaneous evolution of the protagonist in four different minds came neither by chance nor by collusion. It was the inevitable result of the development of the Gothic villain on the stage. The gloom of the old tyrant, persecutor and ravager of women, object of terror second only to the architectural ruin, was intensified by actors' interpretations and by moral solicitude which exacted painful remorse. The consequence of this agony, emphasized more heavily than the crimes that brought it, was an invitation to such sympathy as could be accorded only to a hero. Hence the villain, in the eyes of the heroine, the dramatist, and the public, became a hero, but one of an especial kind on whom indelibly remained the marks of criminal ancestors.

THE TOWERS OF URBANDINE

One of two Gothic plays[5] by Carr, comedian of the Theatres Royal, Hull and York, *The Towers of Urbandine* requires examination for distinctions of its own: its inclusion of an enormous number of Gothic elements, its clear revelation of the original sources of these, and its elaborate development of the familiar persecution theme.

Carr apparently attempted to stuff into a single play the contents of the whole Gothic tradition, and did manage to include nearly all of the elements which had appeared in all earlier Gothic works together. If the mood were not so deadly serious throughout, we would suspect that the playwright intended a burlesque, for conventional properties are piled up to absurd proportions. The play uses no fewer than six secret doors and subterranean passages. Instead of the usual persecution plot which involves one persecutor and one or two victims, here are four persecutors, four victims, and six persecution plots. All of the major Gothic settings appear: a ruined abbey, a castle, a convent, a cavern, and a dark forest. Precipices and "blasted crags" are lacking, but terror from natural sources is represented by thunder and lightning. Both "haunted-chamber" and "nobleman-turned-outlaw" motifs appear, and there is evidence of specific debts to Walpole, Mrs. Radcliffe, and Lewis.

At the opening of the play Rosaline and her father occupy an ancient abbey in a forest. The first scene, in "A desolated Gothic chamber," shows the daughter asking the cause of the melancholy which for eight years has afflicted the father. After "excessive agony," he prevents further question because "solemn vows forbid what you require." A servant narrates to Rosaline an event of the past, and here, evidently, Carr was indebted to *The Romance of the Forest:*

'Tis now eight years since Sir Alfred roused us in the middle of the night at Malcolm Castle and with yourself, attended by only Owen and me, traveled with the utmost speed to this dreary old Abbey here in the midst of the Forest of St. Oswythe.⁸

Residence in the abbey ends abruptly. A servant, gasping, reports that as she looked from the "western turret" she had seen a man "galloping most furiously from the thickest part of the forest towards this old Abbey of ours, mounted on horseback and muffled up in a large red cloak." Having had no company for eight years, all become frightened. The father, "starting violently," at length descends to talk with the stranger. Soon he returns, "greatly agitated," to inform Rosaline that he must leave and that she is to go at once to the Castle of Urbandine.

At Urbandine her trials begin. Rosaline no sooner arrives than she is assailed by Gondemar, son of Baron Otho of Urbandine. Baron Otho halts his son's first attempts on the heroine, and Gondemar resolves to quit the castle and find other means of possessing her. His henchman darkly advises of a cavern, "secret, unknown to all," whither she may be enticed. Paulina, fearful that Rosaline may steal the affections of Constantine, the baron's stepson, openly menaces the heroine. Baron Otho, as debauched as his son, threatens her honor. His actions are further motivated by a mysterious ambition for Constantine to marry Paulina, and he therefore stands between hero and heroine. At the end of the first act, therefore, the dangers to Rosaline are multiple: she is subject to the unknown fate that hangs over herself and her father, and she is threatened by Gondemar, Paulina, and Baron Otho. Shortly a new source of terror is added. At breakfast after her first night in the castle, she describes an experience which seemingly involved the supernatural:

> As at the casement for some hours I sat,
> When as my eyes were bent towards the Tow'r
> That forms this noble castle's eastern wing,
> I was surprised by a pale glimmering light
> Which plainly showed a tall and fearful form.
> It much astonish'd and alarm'd me too,
> Since you yourself, my Lady, said last night
> That wing was closely locked.[7]

The vague answers do not allay her fears:

Otho. That Tow'r contains somewhat
      Of mystery we cannot reach.
Baroness. In my late father's lifetime I well know
      Those chambers were kept shut—the cause assign'd
      Was that in days of yore a sovereign prince
      Had in those very chambers been confin'd
      And slain.

Constantine resolves to spend a night in the chambers. Alone with Rosaline, he urges that they be married secretly, to forestall opposition. The baroness, overhearing, approves, and the hero—as though deliberately inviting disaster—instructs Rosaline to meet him

> Just at the tolling of the midnight bell
> Within the chapel...[8]

Approaching the chapel at midnight, Rosaline is seized by Gondemar and dragged to "A rocky Cavern, illuminated by a pendent lamp." With the threat, "The present moment gives you to my arms," the villain forces a shriek from her that brings Constantine. Gondemar stalks away with the final threat, "Remember me and tremble!" Heroine and hero leave the cavern, make their way to the chapel, and approach the altar. As they are pronouncing their vows, Otho enters, orders Rosaline "instantly conveyed to her chambers," and demands that Constantine as instantly marry Paulina or "suffer my eternal curse." Constantine refuses and departs.

Curiously, the intervening events had not altered the hero's resolution to occupy the haunted chamber. Again the author seems to have borrowed from *The Romance of the Forest*, with the variation that it is the hero, not the heroine who, with lamp in hand, goes exploring. Constantine's speech as he enters the "Eastern Tower" reads like a catalogue of Gothic wares:

> ... as the grating hinge
> Proclaim'd my entrance in this dreary tow'r,
> A sudden chill assail'd my heart, the quick
> Pulsation in my veins began to cease;
> And lo! a voice, most audibly me thought,
> Exclaim'd, "Rash youth, forbear!"—but hence
> With superstition! Never let me yield
> To idle apprehensions—Yet the still
> Solemnity that reigns within these walls
> Excites reflections awful to the mind—
> Whilst the huge statues starting from the gloom
> Seem to proclaim the place foul murder's seat.
> The tatter'd remnants of yon stately bed,
> Once richly splendid, glittering in pride,
> Presents a picture of the fate of man,—
> Hark! what was that? methought
> Echo proclaiming to my certain sense
> The closing of a door; as if it came
> From the apartments underneath—yet 'twas

> But fancy, or perhaps the hollow wind;—
> Within yon cabinet I found this scroll;
> Somewhat perhaps 'tis possible to learn
> From its contents.—Do thou rest there, my sword.[9]

Like any other Gothic hero, he lays his weapon aside. As he sits reading by his flickering lamp, Gondemar enters through a secret opening behind a tapestry, takes the sword, and thrusts it against his brother's breast. A henchman brings Rosaline in, for she has again been captured. In her presence Gondemar stabs Constantine. Immediately remorse strikes the villain: "Why thus does pale horror stiffen all my joints?" Because he had struck his brother to secure Rosaline, she is now odious in his sight, and, his hand at her throat, he forces her to swear never to reveal his crime. He then orders the henchman to return her to her chamber "by the secret pass by which thou broughtest her hither."

In her room once more, Rosaline, "in great agitation," nearly betrays to the baroness the secret she had sworn to keep. Immediately a voice cries "Beware!" and the women survey the room in terror. The baroness flees, and Rosaline cowers on the bed. Slowly the tapestry on a wall moves aside, and Gondemar emerges from a secret passage. He is poised to strike Rosaline when suddenly he "becames agitated, and staggers back, appalled":

> What horrid groan was that
> Which struck upon my ear? And see, behold!
> Look where that pale and bloody form appears—
> 'Tis Constantine! oh, fatal vision, speak!—
> Thine eyeballs glare with anger! and thou pointest
> The way for my departure! Lo! I come!
> I fly the fatal deed! hence! hence! Ye fiends!
> And spare this hell of torment I endure![10]
>   (rushes out)

As the fourth act begins, Rosaline, the most harassed of Gothic heroines, is menaced from a new direction. Baron Otho—perhaps imitating the policy long ago laid down by Manfred in *Otranto*—

has resolved to divorce the baroness, and announces, "—her barren throne is destin'd for—thyself!" His command to the heroine is abrupt:

> ... Therefore prepare
> Within this very hour to yield to me
> Thy willing vows; or to the altar's foot
> I'll have thee dragg'd. So now no more—away![11]

Rosaline flees to Paulina, who, eager to settle accounts, guarantees protection and dispatches the heroine, with a servant—and through yet another secret passage—to a place "at the North Cliff." But Rosaline's lot has not been improved. She learns, too late, that Paulina, with the help of a hardened creature named Agnes, in whose custody the heroine now finds herself, designs her murder. But at last the mystery which, from the opening scene, has lain forgotten in the tumult of events is clarified by Paulina. Paulina's and Rosaline's fathers are brothers; the strange melancholy which had haunted Sir Alfred during the period of his eight-year residence in a ruined abbey was occasioned by the usurpation of his estate by Paulina's father, who had besides

> ... by deadly oaths
> Bound him never to reveal
> That he existed—nor ever after to disclose
> The means by which his brother did extort
> These oaths. In close confinement were himself
> And wife, with thee, their smiling infant, kept,
> From hope, from comfort, and the cheering sun—
> Thy mother's tender frame not long could bear
> Such rigours; and her better part soon sped
> Its way to heaven.[12]

Given "Till thou hear'st the bell toll twelve" to prepare for death, Rosaline escapes through a "secret chasm" discovered by moving aside a trunk in her chamber. In boy's clothes supplied from this trunk, she finds herself in "a dark wood," where rain, thunder, and lightning, as we would expect, immediately join the conspiracy against her. But after Mrs. Radcliffe a heroine who fled to the woods inevitably encountered greater menaces than these. Rosaline finds soon that the forest is infested by banditti, two of whom quickly seize and carry her to their cave for their captain; en route, one remarks significantly that this captain "is quite unknown to all of us." When Rosaline is placed before him, the mysterious figure "starts violently," throws off his mask, and reveals the face of Gondemar. Here, then, the nobleman-turned-outlaw motif has been used with a variation, for the villain rather than the hero has turned robber. Though he threatens Rosaline, the terrors of conscience so smite Gondemar that he cannot murder her. He moves repeatedly to strike her, but each time believes himself confronted by his brother's ghost. In desperation after several failures, he at last promises Rosaline security, but not freedom:

> Beyond the gloomy confines of this cave
> Never expect to pass.[13]

Two scenes now close the play. The first shows a convent to which the baroness has retired. The former henchman of Gondemar arrives and discloses that Constantine yet lives, "for on the fatal night remorse seiz'd me." He had taken the wounded hero "to a remote spot beneath the vaults." Constantine's followers have ousted Otho from the castle, and the baroness departs to find her son. The final scene shows the attack of Constantine's men upon the cave of the banditti. The hero confronts his evil brother, who is again terrified by what he takes for a ghost. At length satisfied of Constantine's mortality, he tears off his robber's mask, and then, though Constantine offers forgiveness, stabs himself. The hero stands solicitously above him:

> Say, would that look confess
> Repentance of thy crimes? It does! it does!
> And freely from my soul do I forgive thee!
> (Gondemar groans and dies)[14]

The play ends with all the criminals dead or imprisoned and all the erstwhile victims happily reunited.

THE CURFEW

Although it does not pile up the quantity of Gothic materials and motifs which makes *The Towers of Urbandine* an outstanding specimen of Gothic drama, *The Curfew* requires attention for an especially important reason. Though students of drama have given Tobin's play greater space for discussion than most of the plays I have examined, they seem to have placed it in the wrong dramatic descent. Genest, a contemporary who should have known better, stated that "it is a very happy imitation of the old dramatic writers"[15]—that is, of the Elizabethans. A hundred years after Genest, Professor Nicoll commented, "Tobin shows the wholehearted acceptance of Elizabethan standards, with the occasional acceptance of elements borrowed from Kotzebue and Schiller."[16] Finally, a doctoral dissertation on Elizabethan influence in this age places *The Curfew* unreservedly among Elizabethan imitations.[17]

That this play is indebted to Shakespeare and his immediate successors is obvious. But its debt is hardly greater than that of any other Gothic play between *The Mysterious Mother* and *The Cenci*. That is to say, there is in *The Curfew* no deeper Shakesperean influence than that which shows superficially in turns of phrase and echoes of the master's lines. For example, when Florence is to wear a man's clothes, Bertrand tells her how easy it will be to play a man's part:

> 'Tis but to strut, and swell, and knit your brow,
> Tell twenty lies in a breath, and round them off
> With twice as many oaths; to wear a sword
> Longer than other men's, and clap your hand
> Upon the hilt, when the wind stirs, to shew
> How quick the sense of valour beats within you.[18]

The speech echoes passages in both *As You Like It* and *The Merchant of Venice*. Again, the agonized baron, speaking to the robber whom he takes for a friar come to ease his conscience, says,

> ... You can blow out from the distracted brain
> The memory of guilt, and chase away
> The frightful apparition of foul deeds...[19]

Here the source is obvious. Again, a single line spoken by Fitzharding illustrates the "imitation"—theft, rather—". . . which being done, You are a man again."

This kind of superficial echo could be pointed to in virtually every play so far examined, and if such evidence were sufficient, it would be possible to call every play an "Elizabethan imitation." Merely in the passages I have cited in earlier chapters, though they were chosen for other reasons, it would be possible to show imitation, borrowing, and plain pillage. Gothic playwrights snatched from everyone to make up their plays. They took whatever served their purpose from the English sentimental novel and from graveyard poetry, from France and Germany, from heroic and sentimental drama; indeed, they took from the Greeks and Romans, from old English ballads, from Ossian, and from Richard Brinsley Sheridan. And, especially, they took from the great Elizabethan. But, always, what they seized was turned to their peculiar purpose of arousing mystery, gloom, and terror. Their kind of drama, directed by this purpose and eternally revolving around the primary Gothic fixtures—castle, convent, and cavern—did not become a sentimental kind by random borrowing from Richardson, a heroic kind by including a phrase of Almanzor's rant in the hero's speech, or German by having a nobleman turn outlaw. Neither did it become Elizabethan by seizing from *Macbeth* or *Hamlet* a striking phrase which handily filled the momentary need. For these external trappings were distinct from the essential preoccupations which led Gothic dramatists to develop a species of drama different from any other.

The marks which show the true preoccupations of Tobin in *The Curfew*—which show, indeed, what the play is *about*—are the settings—gloomy castle chambers, "a dark part of the forest," "a chapel," in the midst of which is a tomb, "a cavern," and "a desolate heath"; the motifs—a haunted-chamber motif, a persecution motif, and a nobleman-turned outlaw motif; the principal characters—an agonized villain, an insipid hero who spends most of the play in a dungeon, and a harassed female; a technique which involves the usual past event; and the atmosphere, thoroughly Gothic, dominated by the bell which has no business in the play except that of providing a thrill: it rings always and only when the stage is darkest, when trees wave in the breeze, when robbers loom up suddenly to affright an already-frightened heroine, and when the chapel and tomb form a background of terror.

The plot of *The Curfew* is itself quite in the Gothic tradition. Twenty years before, Baron de Tracy, abused by false letters, had stabbed his wife as unfaithful. Wounded, she had fled with their infant son. Since that time, the baron had suffered remorse, and Matilda, the wife, had secretly occupied a small cottage on the heath. Her son has grown up and joined a band of robbers. Matilda, suspected of witchcraft, is brought to trial before her husband. Florence, daughter of the baron, falls into the hands of robbers, and, after harrowing experiences, is restored to the arms of the hero. But the combined efforts of Matilda and the son-turned-robber, all is finally righted.

Though more restrained, the tendency of *The Castle of Urbandine* to pile up Gothic materials is repeated in *The Curfew*. First, the familiar device by which heroes are ultimately recognized and restored to rank is here multiplied: *three* characters are so identified, one by a bloody arrow, one by a scar on the cheek, another by a scar on the hand. Second, the agony which had long been the special prerogative of the villain is here liberally bestowed upon three figures—villain, hero, and robber-chieftain. It is the latter, Fitzharding, who is most striking. To Baron de Tracy's offer of friendship, this outlaw, who, though vicious, has been made attractive by the addition of some specific qualities, retorts:

> Never! whilst I can die thine enemy!
> What you have made me, still expect to find me:
> A man, struck from the common roll of men;
> Exil'd from all society, stamp'd like Cain
> To wander savage and forlorn....
> For till you can divorce me from myself,
> Or put another soul into this body,
> You may as soon enthrone the fires of heav'n,
> Or shake the rooted earth from its foundation,
> As alter me. Your friendship I disdain;
> Despise your power. My life I value not.[20]

The defiant mood of Fitzharding, in a play of 1807, was close to that of the Byronic hero. It was ten years later that Lord Byron exiled himself, to spend the rest of his life uttering essentially the same defiance, and sometimes in nearly the same idiom.

BERTRAM; OR THE CASTLE OF ST. ALDOBRAND

Montague Summers has written of Charles Robert Maturin that "even his Sermons must be recorded" in a Gothic bibliography.[21] Most famous for *Melmoth*,[22] Maturin has a high place among the major writers of Gothic fiction. As the author of three outstanding Gothic plays,[23] he is also eminent among Gothic playwrights. His literary career began in 1807 with a Radcliffean romance, *The Fatal Revenge*. Sir Walter Scott, ploughing through numerous "flat imitations of the Castle of Udolpho," read his work and reviewed it favorably.[24] The young Irish clergyman addressed a grateful letter, and thus commenced a correspondence which lasted until Maturin's death in 1824. In 1808 Maturin published *The Wild Irish Boy,* and in 1812 *The Milesian Chief,* a novel from which Scott took suggestions for *The Bride of Lammermoor*. From the start to the end of his career Maturin was devoted to the Gothic. A remark in his preface to *The Milesian Chief* delineates the principle on which he worked:

> If I possess any talent, it is that of darkening the gloomy, and of deepening the sad; of painting life in extremes; and representing those struggles of passion when the soul trembles on the verge of the unlawful and the unhallowed.

This analysis of his own talent might have served as motto for *The Castle of Otranto, The Mysteries of Udolpho, The Monk, Manfred,* or *The Cenci.*

Richard Lalor Sheil, another Irishman, had been successful at the Crow Street Theatre in Dublin with a first play, *Adelaide.*[28] In 1813 Maturin tried his hand at drama. Before the end of that year he had completed and sent to Dublin the manuscript of *Bertram.* It was promptly rejected and returned, to lie among the author's papers for more than a year. In 1814, happening upon it, Maturin decided to offer it to some other theater. But if the Crow Street manager would not accept it, who would? He remembered Scott, who had already proved a benefactor, and wrote for advice. The great romancer answered that he would receive the manuscript "upon this slender chance of my getting Kemble to review it."[29] Scott read *Bertram,* gave it to Daniel Terry (the "Terry-fier" who turned several of Scott's novels into melodramas) for alterations, and recommended it to Kemble. Despite all, Kemble refused the play, and for another year it remained among Maturin's papers.

In 1815 the procurement of plays for the Drury Lane Theatre was in the hands of Lord Byron. Supplied with five hundred new plays—including Coleridge's *Fall of Robespierre* and *Zapolya*— not one of which he "could think of accepting," Byron requested Scott to offer a play. Instead, Scott recommended *Bertram.* Byron was immediately "delighted" with it, and his fellow manager,

George Lamb, "could not go to bed without finishing it."[27] Byron sent Maturin an acceptance and fifty guineas.

In May, 1816, the play was acted with Kean as Bertram. An account of the first performance reads,

... it will be observed that the part of Bertram is peculiarly adapted to the powers of Mr. Kean, by whom it is represented with extraordinary energy and effect. He is a mixture of ambition, pride and revenge; a character ashamed of the feelings of ordinary men, who has little in common with them but his passion for a lovely woman, and in whose sorrows ordinary men of course cannot sympathize.[28]

Though he did not use the name, it is apparent that the reviewer was here describing the Byronic hero. Another reviewer went further; he stated that the leading character was made up of

that same mischievous compound of attractiveness and turpitude, of love and crime, of chivalry and brutality, which in the poems of Lord Byron and his imitators has been too long successful in captivating weak fancies and outraging moral truth.[29]

Goethe read the play in 1817, and he too recognized the Byronic:

Das neuste englische Publikum ist in Hass und Liebe von den Dichtungen des Lord Byron durchdrungen, und so kann denn auch ein *Bertram* Wurzel fassen, der Gleichfalls Menschenhass und Rachegeist, Pflicht und Schwachheit, Umsicht, Plan, Zufälligkeiten und Zerstörung mit Furienbesen durcheinander peitscht und eine, genau besehen, emphatische Pose zur Würde eines tragischen Gedichtes erhebt.[30]

Further testimony to the identification of the character Bertram and the play *Bertram* with the Byronic is needless. Byron's own age immediately observed that both were Byronic, and present examination sustains the observation. But—and here is the point that gives significance to the statements quoted above—a view of both the character and the play against the background of the dramatic tradition which we have followed since *The Mysterious Mother* in 1768 makes it apparent that their origins preceded Byron's birth; for both character and play are thoroughly in the

Gothic tradition. To identify them with the Byronic is therefore to identify the typical Gothic protagonist and the dramatic type he dominated with the Byronic.

A number of years before the opening of the play, Bertram, a nobleman distinguished for valor and other qualities, had been banished as result of St. Aldobrand's machinations and had become a robber captain. Imogine, his intended bride, had then married St. Aldobrand to save her father from ruin. As the play begins, Bertram and his banditti are shipwrecked near the castle of St. Aldobrand and the monastery of St. Anselm. They get ashore safely, and Bertram meets Imogine. Learning of her marriage, he becomes inhumanly cruel. At intervals his harshness is softened by his love and by the presence of her young child. He persuades her to meet him secretly before he exiles himself forever; the meeting occurs, and the consequence is mutual remorse. Bertram learns that St. Aldobrand is returning home with the king's commission to hunt down and kill him. His bitterness overmasters him, and he decides not to leave, but seeks out his enemy and slays him. Imogine goes mad and dies, and Bertram stabs himself.

The bare summary exposes a past event, banditti, castle and convent, a persecuted heroine, and a central figure characterized by mingled cruelty, grandeur, and remorse. The settings are also typical of those used for nearly half a century in Gothic plays. Act I, scene 1, presents "Night. A Gallery in the Convent of St. Anselm. Thunder, lightning, rain and wind." The second scene has "The sea shore. The Convent illuminated in the background. A storm—thunder and lightning. The bell tolls at intervals. A group of Monks discovered on the rocks with torches." Various scenes occur in the halls and the "Gothic chambers" of the castle. The doors themselves are specified as "Gothic." There are spectacular exterior views of the castle: "A terraced rampart of the Castle of St. Aldobrand—a part of the castle is seen, the rest concealed by woods.—Moonlight." Act V, scene 1, has "The Chapel in the Convent of St. Anselm, the shrine illuminated splendidly and decorated." The last scene of the play includes the lone favorite not represented in preceding scenes: "A dark Wood—a Cavern—Rocks and Precipices above."

If the quoted testimonies of the age identify the play positively with the Byronic, assuredly the sketch of plot and settings identifies it as positively with the Gothic. In no materials or purposes does *Bertram* differ from the Gothic drama of the preceding half-century.

Just as the whole play is Gothic, so is its protagonist a Gothic villain transformed to a hero who retains the conventional marks of villainy. Bertram is consumed by an inexplicable torment; the prior describes him:

> ... ever in the pauses of his speech
> His lip doth work with inward mutterings,
> And his fixed eye is riveted fearfully
> On something that no other sight can spy.[31]

Again,

> He sleeps—if it be sleep; this starting trance,
> Whose feverish tossings and deep-mutter'd groans
> Do prove the soul shares not the body's rest.
> How the lip works! how the bare teeth do grind,
> And beaded drops course down his writhen brow!
> I will wake him from this horried trance;
> This is no natural sleep.[32]

What ails this Bertram whom contemporaries identified as Byronic? His villainous ancestors in past decades suffered for three reasons: because, born of a castle ruin, they were afflicted with its gloom; because star actors interpreted the villain's role, and agony was at once opportunity for histrionics and invitation to public sympathy; and because they had committed crime for which conscience—and the censor—demanded a show of remorse.

It was through this suffering that the villain became a hero; consequently, as hero, he continued to suffer. The trait which transformed him naturally remained dominant—even though he no longer had a personal cause, or sometimes even a reasonable excuse for possessing it.

Bertram is an excellent exemplification of this fact. In the early scenes of the play, when the prior describes his "feverish tossings and deep-mutter'd groans," there is no source for his agony except his inheritance from his dramatic ancestry. The remorse of these villainous ancestors was at least ostensibly rooted in the dark crimes they had committed. But Bertram, before the early scenes which show him tormented, had committed no crime; and at the time his agony is most intense he does not even know that Imogine, from whom he had been separated, had married: his torture therefore cannot be ascribed to that cause. Bertram, then, if the foolish truth must be stated, suffers because he is the kind of hero who suffers.

The spectacle of a hero suffering remorse when he has committed no crime to cause it was an inevitable result of the transformation of villain to hero. As "villain," the character could be supposed to have committed foul crimes, and, because he had committed them, his most violent show of agony could be excused. As "hero," his reputation could no longer be blackened by crimes of such magnitude as would motivate that very agony which, by rendering him attractive, had made him a hero. *Bertram* shows little effort by Maturin to solve this vital riddle. Bertram suffers only because he was created in the tradition of the agonized protagonist.

Dark, grand, mysterious, lonely, defiant, and tormented, Bertram is the hero of the flashing eye, the proud nature, and the splendid physique. The attractive qualities of the old villains are assembled to make his bid for admiration, forgiveness, and tears.

He and his shipwrecked robbers, after reaching the castle, are seen by Imogine, who remarks to her attendant:

> Their wild and vulgar mirth doth startle me.
> But as I passed the latticed gallery
> One stood alone. I marked him where he stood.
> His face was veiled; faintly a light fell on him;
> But through soiled weeds his muffled form did show
> A wild and terrible grandeur.[33]

The attendant—also female—replies:

> I marked him, too. He mixed not with the rest.
> But o'er his wild mates held a stern control;
> Their rudest burst of riotous merriment
> Beneath his dark eye's stilling energy
> Was hushed to silence.

Later the heroine confesses:

> A form like that hath broken on my dreams,
> So darkly wild, so proudly stern.[34]

In these lines is final proof that the transformation has been completed. The villain has changed sides and here receives the seal of feminine approval. It is perhaps not impertinent to repeat that the type of Bertram had been created as an object of terror; from Walpole's Isabella down through five and a half decades young ladies like Imogine and her attendant had fled in panic through haunted galleries and subterranean vaults, pursued by men like Bertram. Now the women confess an instant and utter fascination: the admiration for dark eyes and proud physique and the magnetic attraction of a great soul agonized have overcome all, and terror of the Gothic villain has become worship of the Byronic hero.

"In *Bertram* there is nothing of the 18:th century," asserts the modern biographer of Maturin, who suggests that the Gothicist's debt extended only to Byron.[35] It is manifestly unfair to lay this judgment upon the head of one biographer, who but repeats the error of Maturin's contemporaries and reflects the usual modern opinion formed in unawareness of the Gothic tradition in drama."

Mere failure to relate *Bertram* to that large share of the eighteenth century represented by the Gothic tradition would perhaps not in itself be a grave matter. But this failure illustrates a general misconception which is important. To misjudge the relation of *Bertram* to the Gothic tradition is to misjudge the relation of the Byronic in general to that tradition. It is to suppose that the Byronic came into existence in 1812 with publication of *Childe Harold* and by 1816 had had only four years of expression in *The Giaour, The Bride of Abydos, The Corsair,* and *Lara*. As a matter of fact, these years and these poems were consummations, not beginnings.

CHAPTER XI

JOANNA BAILLIE AND GOTHIC DRAMA

THE PLAYS of Joanna Baillie clearly need revaluation.[1] They should be considered in relation not only to Gothic drama, but to the age, and especially to the poems, plays, and novels of Scott and the poems and plays of Byron. Author of twenty-six plays—fourteen tragedies, eight comedies, three dramas, and one musical drama—all of which are well above the general level and some of which are among the best dramatic works between 1750 and 1850, Miss Baillie seems not to have received her rightful place in the history of English drama. Here it is possible to study her only as a Gothic dramatist, and even in this respect it will scarcely be feasible to attempt full descriptions of her plays, so numerous are the marks of the school.[2]

Of the twenty-six dramatic works, ten may be classified as predominantly Gothic, and all reveal conspicuous marks of the tradition. The ten, written between 1795 and 1805, carried the familiar materials and motifs to a higher level than they had usually attained. When both the quantity and the quality of her contributions are considered, Joanna Baillie must be placed among the foremost Gothic dramatists. She was as prolific as Lewis, and her work is consistently better than his. Not one of her plays degenerates to the insincerity of *The Castle Spectre* and *Rugantino,* and some of them lift the conventional elements to new heights.

Most of her Gothic plays are included in the series "in which it is attempted to delineate the stronger passions of the mind." These "Plays on the Passions," numbering thirteen in all, were published in three groups, in 1798, 1802, and 1812.[3] Their plan and purpose are well known, and a single statement from Jo-

---
[1] For notes to chap. xi, see pages 255–256.

anna's biographer will provide such a basis as is required in the present task:

> The chief object of Joanna in these plays was to delineate passion in its progress, to trace it from its early beginning, and to show the fearful gulf towards which it hastens, if not checked in the earlier portions of its career. She has thus a high moral purpose in her design; which, if the drama can warn and save, will not altogether have been defeated.... The sole difference between her design and the usual practice of dramatic composers is, that while they have in most instances selected a story for the striking nature of its details, which rendered the prominence of one master passion necessary, she proposed to render her plots subservient to her main end, the development of one predominant and overruling passion.⁴

To elaborate the subjects of hatred, fear, jealousy, and remorse in dramatic form, however, required the use of settings, characters, action, and plot. In another age, the choices of these might well have been otherwise, but Miss Baillie, writing when Gothic plays were popular and when Mrs. Radcliffe's novels were in high favor, chose to "body forth" her themes of passion through Gothic settings and machinery, character types, and techniques. In showing the destructive passion of her central figures, she followed, consciously or unconsciously, the traditional treatment of the Gothic villain. It is a striking fact that, regardless of the particular passion she had isolated for study in a given play, the manifestations are those of the villain tortured by remorse.

The ten tragedies which belong to Gothic drama are *Orra, The Dream, Henriquez, Romiero, Ethwald* (in two parts), *De Monfort, Rayner, The Family Legend, The Separation,* and *Witchcraft.* Full analysis of these individually would require a volume. Group examination must therefore suffice, with broad attention given to characteristic settings, machinery, and protagonists. *Orra,* which seems best to illustrate Miss Baillie's "Gothicity," will be discussed separately.

General Characteristics of Joanna Baillie's Plays

The settings of these plays include castles, convents, caverns, chapels, forests, and precipices, all of which are employed not as mere places to hold the action, but as sources of mystery, gloom, and terror. All Gothic playwrights were fond of darkness; Joanna's scenes are darkest of all. Gothic settings, especially after 1790, were highly elaborate; Joanna Baillie's vie in this respect with the spectacles of Lewis. The author's specifications for her settings may be chosen almost at random to illustrate the preponderance of the Gothic. *De Monfort* has "Moonlight. A wild path in a dark wood, shaded with trees"; "The inside of a Convent of old Gothic architecture, almost dark; two torches only are seen at a distance, burning over a newly covered grave. Lightning is seen flashing through the pointed windows, and thunder heard, with the sound of wind beating against the building"; and "A large room in the convent, very dark." *Ethwald,* though its scene is laid in Saxon times, presents "A forest: the view of an Abbey with its spires in the background"; "A wide-arched cave, seen by sombre light"; "A dark, narrow gallery in an abbey"; "A gloomy apartment in an old castle, with grated windows high from the ground"; "A small dark passage. Enter Ethwald with a lamp"; "A dark, gloomy, vaulted apartment in an old castle. Enter Edward from a dark recess." *The Dream,* the general scene of which is "the monastery of St. Moritz in Switzerland; a castle near it," presents "An open space before the gate of the Monastery, with a view of the building on one side, while rocks and mountains, wildly grand, appear in every other direction"; "A burying-vault, almost totally dark; the monuments and gravestones being seen very dimly by the light of a single torch, placed by the side of an open grave"; "Wood with the castle spires seen in the background; the stage quite dark." *Romiero* shows "Night. A grove near the walls of the castle, which is seen in the background, the moon appearing behind it"; "The inner porch of a ruined Chapel"; "An old Gothic Chapel." *Henriquez* is unusually dark and gloomy, with "The burying-vault of the castle, with monuments of the dead; and near the front of the stage, a newly covered grave, seen by the light of a lamp placed on a neighboring tomb, the stage being otherwise dark." *Rayner* has many forests and caverns, and darkness is emphatically demanded: "A wood: dark night with a pale gleam of distant lightning seen once or twice on the edge of the horizon. Advancing by the bottom of the stage, a few moving lights, as if from dark lanterns are seen. . . . *It is particularly requested if this play should ever be acted, that no light may be permitted upon the stage but that which proceeds from the lanterns only.*" *The Family Legend* emphasizes caves, "craggy rocks," and wild wastes, but does not omit Gothic chambers, halls, and galleries. *The Separation* has "arched gateways," all dark and gloomy, vaults, and a "rustic hermitage." *Witchcraft* includes "A wild moor, skirted on one side by a thick, tangled wood—the stage darkened to represent faint moonlight through heavy gathering clouds. Thunder and lightning"; "A half-formed Cave, partly roofed with rock and partly open to the sky . . . a burn or brook crossing the mouth of it, banked by precipitous rocks." No scene of any one of the ten plays lacks the predominating influence of the long, pointed Gothic shadows, the symbols of mystery, gloom, and terror.

Gothic preoccupations are evident as much in the machinery as in the settings. A full list of the elements employed in these plays would perhaps include every item of the paraphernalia used by Gothicists since Walpole. Bells toll—always when the scene is darkest; nearly every play has at least one entrance to or exit from castle, convent, or cavern through a secret door and a subterranean passage; Radcliffean winding stairways and grated windows abound. Even so, preoccupation with physical machinery of this sort is overshadowed by preoccupation with the idea of the supernatural. Though there is no "real" manifestation of the supernatural, almost every scene toys with the idea. Heroes, heroines, villains, and the minor characters are almost constantly restive in their belief that immortal shadows are about them. With Joanna Baillie, the supernatural seems not a preoccupation, but an obsession.

The dramatist's attitude toward ruins would identify her with the Gothic Revival even though no other Gothic features marked her plays. Similarly, even if physical settings bore no resemblance to the conventional ones, the content of descriptive passages would associate her with that Revival. Reading at random, we come upon such passages as these; in *Romiero:*

> There is within the precincts of this wood
> An old abandon'd chapel, where the dead
> Rest undisturb'd. No living tenant there,
> But owlet hooting on the ruin'd tower,
> Or twitt'ring swallow in his eaves-screen'd nest,
> Will share the dismal shelter.[5]

In the same play:

> A ghost was seen by some benighted men,
> As they report it, near the ancient chapel,
> Where light pour'd through the trees, and
>   strangely vanish'd.[6]

In *Henriquez:*

> By unfrequented paths
> Through rugged wilds I've traveled many a league:
> Three irksome days and nights in that deep grove,
> The ruin of an ancient sepulchre,
> Like some unhallow'd spirit, I have haunted...[7]

In the same:

> The light from every lattice stream'd,
> Lamps starr'd each dusky corridor, and torches
> Did from the courts beneath cast up the glare
> Of glowing flame upon the buttress'd walls

And battlements, whilst the high towers aloft
Show'd their jagg'd pinnacles in icy coldness,
Clothed with the moon's pale beams.[8]

In *The Dream:*

Methought I was returning from the mass, through the cloisters that lead from the chapel, when a figure, as I have said, appeared to me, and beckoned me to follow it ... so wonderfully it rose in stature and dignity as it strode before me, that, ere it reached the doors of the stranger's burying vault, I was struck with unaccountable awe ... It entered, and I followed it. There, through the damp mouldering tombs, it strode still before me, till it came to the farther extremity, as nearly as I could guess, two yards westward from the black marble monument; and then stopping and turning on me its fixed and ghastly eyes, it stretched out its hands....[9]

Such descriptions, prevalent in every play, supplement the physical representations, and through the combination is achieved a totality of Gothic atmosphere.

As typically Gothic as settings and machinery is the protagonist in each play. Though most of these pieces were written for the announced purpose of illustrating the working, in each, of a single passion, the most striking marks on every protagonist are those which, in the eighteenth century, distinguished the Gothic villain and, in the early nineteenth, the Byronic hero. Miss Baillie was clearly fascinated by this figure. Her comments on the staging of plays show how concerned she was to have the character properly presented. She was especially disturbed by the lighting facilities. The footlights were most distressing, because "the lights hit the under-part of the chin, the nostrils, and the under curve of the eye-brows, turning of course all the shadows upwards." Hence, "whenever an actor ... comes near the front of the stage, and turns his face fully to the audience, every feature immediately becomes shortened, and less capable of any expression, unless it be of the ludicrous kind."[10] Possibly the lighting system annoyed others in the general audience; but to any Gothicist it must have been intolerable, for it was the central figure of the Gothic play who was most injured by this kind of lighting. Brooding gloom could scarcely be projected when footlights turned up the corners of a mouth, the point of a nose, and the brows. Joanna recommended that the roof of the stage be brought forward and that a row of lamps with reflectors be placed there. By thus bringing light from above, she believed the stage might achieve such illumination—

That the eye may look hollow and dark under the shade of its brow; that the shadow of the nose may shorten the upper lip, and give a greater character of sense to the mouth.[11]

We may sympathize with Joanna's demand for lighting that would emphasize the hollowness and darkness of the eye "under the shade of its brow" when we observe the focus of her own descriptions of her central figures. Such lines as these introduce her brooding protagonists; from *De Monfort:*

> But Monfort, even in his calmest hour,
> Still bears that gloomy sternness in his eye...[12]

From *Ethwald:*

> Mark'd you the changes of the stripling's eye?
> Brooding in secret, grows within his breast
> That which no kindred owns to sloth or ease.[13]

From *The Dream:*

> The Count seems gloomy and irresolute.[14]

From *Romiero:*

> ...but he did fix his eyes
> With such a keen intenseness on my face,
> I fear'd...[15]

From *Henriquez:*

> When he came forth again, I watch'd his eye,
> And it was calm, though gloomy.[16]

From *Rayner:*

> ... I met him, dark and thoughtful,
> With melancholy and unwonted gait
> Slow saunt'ring through lone, unfrequented paths,
> Like one whose soul from man's observing eye
> Shrinks gall'd, as shrinks the member newly torn
> From every slightest touch.[17]

Given the dramatist's emphasis upon these features, the rest can be filled in. All of Miss Baillie's protagonists are haughty, impulsive, and emotionally violent. They strike "gloomy postures" and "thoughtful poses" by habit. The people, places, and objects which they cannot see without startling reactions are numerous. They "start back in great agitation." They are obsessed by the supernatural "idea." All retain vestiges of former magnificence, mental and physical, despite events which have shattered their nerves and set them stalking in lone places. Strongly attractive in their agony, some of them are on the border line between villain and hero; others, as De Monfort, have crossed it.

To close this hasty summary of Joanna Baillie's plays in general, before turning to *Orra,* it seems advisable to let her speak in her own defense on a point of first importance. Joanna's Gothic dramas are precisely of the kind long buried under the term "German." Several were written just at the height of English adaptation and translation from the German school. Are her plays German? Her own words will serve as the final comments of this study upon that subject. In the preface to *Rayner,* a typical Gothic play, she wrote:

> A play with the scene laid in Germany, and opening with a noisy meeting of midnight robbers will, I believe, suggest to my readers certain sources from which he will suppose my ideas must have certainly been taken. Will he give me perfect credit when I assure him, at the time this play was written, I had not only never read any German plays of any kind, but was even ignorant that such things as German plays of any reputation existed? I hope—I am almost bold enough to say, I know that he will.[18]

One reader, at least, after nearly a century and a half, finds no cause to disbelieve.

ORRA

Orra is the tragedy "on the passion of fear." It has been reserved for individual treatment as a work at once typical of the author's relation to Gothic drama and outstanding among her tragedies for its exploitation of Gothic elements and its achievement of Gothic atmosphere.

It might be possible to name in advance the sources of fear chosen by the dramatist in her tragedy on that passion. In an age which found Gothic castles and convents, banditti, caverns, underground passages, vaults, and galleries in bookstalls and on the stage, it was inevitable that she should frighten her own heroine with the properties of the Gothic school. Aware of the possibility that "the principal character could not be actuated by this passion without becoming so far degraded as to be incapable of engaging the sympathy and interest of the spectator or reader," the author took precautions:

> I have, therefore, made Orra a lively, cheerful, buoyant character, when not immediately under its influence, and even extracting from her superstitious propensity a kind of wild enjoyment, which tempts her to nourish and cultivate the enemy that destroys her.[19]

Mrs. Radcliffe might have written a similar description of any of her persecuted maidens, who, induced by the prospect of "wild enjoyment," go exploring by flickering lamplight in the places most likely to terrify them. Orra seems at once a typical Gothic heroine and a deliberate analysis of the type.

The terror that drives Orra mad is Gothic terror. Steeped in tales of the supernatural, she finds herself the principal figure in a situation identical with the heroine's plight in any one of these stories. Refusing to marry Hughobert's booby son Glottenbal, she is confined (on the advice of the villainous Rudigere) in a ruined castle. She is told tales of horror that are calculated to break her resistance and thus bring about her acceptance of Glottenbal. Theobald and his banditti rescue her at last, but fear has driven her mad.

In the hands of Dibdin or Lawler, the play might have been burlesque, with the scene contemporary and the heroine driven out of her wits by too regular attendance in the Gothic theater. But for Miss Baillie this was no matter for burlesque. She laid her scene in the fourteenth century and surrounded her heroine with the very objects of terror that the tales Orra had heard presumably contained. The atmosphere is throughout as somber as that in a novel by Mrs. Radcliffe. Joanna's intense moral purpose, her firm conviction that drama should instruct, not entertain, makes grim business of the whole action.

"His brow is dark," says another character of Rudigere before the villain appears on the stage. It is he who schemes to break the heroine's resistance by concentrating on her particular weakness. He inquires of an attendant,

> Has Orra oft of late requested thee
> To tell her stories of the restless dead,
> Of spectres rising at the midnight watch?[20]

Orra describes her reaction to tales of horror:

> Yea, when the cold blood shoots through every vein:
> When every pore upon my shrunken skin
> A knotted knoll becomes, and to mine ears
> Strange inward sounds awake, and to mine eyes
> Rush stranger tears, there is a joy in fear.[21]

She is removed to a ruined castle, that terror may do its work. But the result exceeds the purpose of Hughobert, for banditti are about. A robber reports to his captain:

2nd Outlaw.
> A train of armed men, some noble dame
> Are close at hand, and mean to pass the night
> Within the castle.

Franko.   ... Some benighted travelers,
          Bold from their numbers, or who ne'er have heard
          The ghostly legend of this dreaded place.
          ... Within those walls
          Not for a night must travelers quietly rest,
          Or few or many. Would we live securely,
          We must uphold the terrors of the place:
          Therefore, let us prepare our midnight rouse.
          See, from the windows of the castle gleam
          Quick passing lights, as though they moved within
          In hurried preparation; and that bell,
          Which from yon turret its shrill 'larum sends,
          Betokens some unwonted stir. Come, hearts!
          Be all prepared, before the midnight watch,
          The fiend-like din of our infernal chace
          Around the walls to raise.[22]

The scene shifts to the castle and "A Gothic room, with the stage darkened." Orra, entering with her attendant and already feeling the effects of fear, describes her surroundings:

          Advance no further; turn, I pray!
          This room
          More dismal and more ghastly seems than that
          Which we have left behind. Thy taper's light,
          As thus aloft thou wav'st it to and fro,
          The fretted ceiling gilds with feeble brightness;
          While over-head its carved ribs glide past
          Like edgy waves of a dark sea, returning
          To an eclipsed moon its sullen sheen....
          ... Alas! how many hours and years have past
          Since human forms around this table sat,
          Or lamp or taper on its surface gleam'd!
          Methinks I hear the sound of time long past
          Still murmuring o'er us in the lofty void
          Of those dark arches, like the ling'ring voices
          Of those who long within their graves have slept.
          It was their gloomy home; now it is mine.[23]

Though the point is incidental, the fundamental Gothic anachronism is here so conspicuous as to require some comment. Like other Gothicists, Joanna Baillie seems to have lost her sense of time. Orra, who is very obviously a young lady of Miss Baillie's own generation, transported to the fourteenth century, speaks of "time long past" and of those who "long within their graves have slept"; the ruin was "their gloomy home." Obviously, the dramatist was representing the thoughts, not of a fourteenth-century maiden, but of an early nineteenth-century one. In Joanna's time—and Orra's—the scene was indeed "long past." But in the age in which Orra has supposedly been placed, it is strange of find her, a medieval woman, speculating in this fashion. It is, of course, no more strange than that in the fourteenth century there should have been a Gothic "ruin" at all, since Gothic architecture was then as contemporary as Chaucer. Gothicists, however, were not antiquaries. They were interested not in revealing the attitude of fourteenth-century people toward fourteenth-century castles, but in revealing that of late eighteenth- and early nineteenth-century people toward them.

To the other sources of Orra's fear must be added the villain, Rudigere. Trusted by the heroine's guardian to see that no real harm comes to her, he seizes the opportunity to further his private ends. He enters the "dismal and ghastly" Gothic chamber, drives away the attendant "with a fierce, threatening look," and menaces Orra with his attentions until her desperate fury drives him off. At midnight "the cry of hounds is heard without at a distance, with the sound of a horn." Orra, in terror, rushes into the chamber in which Rudigere sleeps, the villain having ousted the attendant who was to sleep in the room adjoining Orra's. Fear of Rudigere competes with fear of the supernatural; at length she awakens him, and again is menaced by his villainous designs.

Meanwhile Theobald, an obscure banneret who loves Orra, has left Hughobert's castle to rescue her from the prison of terror. In a dark wood he is attacked by a robber. Franko intervenes, recognizing Theobald as a childhood friend, for the hero bears on his arm "That mark which from mine arrow thou receiv'd/ When sportively we shot." The captain of the robbers offers his aid:

> From these low caves, a passage underground
> Leads to the castle—to the very tower
> Where as I guess the lady is confin'd.[24]

His plan is "to be the spectre-huntsmen for a night, and bear her off, without pursuit or hindrance." Franko shows Theobald two keys:

> ... this doth unlock
> The entrance to the staircase, known alone
> To Gomez, ancient keeper of the castle,
> Who is my friend in secret, and deters
> The neighb'ring peasantry with dreadful tales
> From visiting by night our wide domains.
> The other doth unlock a secret door,
> That leads us to the chamber where she sleeps.

Meanwhile the heroine's terror increases. She stands with Cathrina, an attendant, gazing into the night from the ramparts of the castle, and speaks solemnly:

> ... Mysterious night!
> What things unutterable thy dark hours
> May lap!—What from thy teeming darkness burst
> Of horrid visitations, ere that sun
> Again shall rise on the enlighten'd earth![25]

Again the dramatist's sense of time seems to have failed, for Orra suddenly cries:

> Look there! Behold that strange gigantic form
> Which yon grim cloud assumes: rearing aloft
> The semblance of a warrior's plumed head!

Perhaps one of the ghostly stories of which Orra was fond was Walpole's *Otranto*, whence comes this plumed head. The heroine returns to her apartment, and Rudigere enters. After repeating his earlier attempts to overcome her, he presents the usual ultimatum:

> ... Thou knowst my fix'd resolve;
> Give me thy solemn promise to be mine.
> This is the price, thou haughty, scornful maid,
> That will redeem thee from the hour of terror.[26]

He departs with a final threat: "The hour is near at hand!" Orra's imagination works on, raising visions of horror. It is the midnight hour that she dreads, for then she expects return of the ghostly hounds and hunters. Cathrina joins her, and, as they watch the sandglass which indicates the approach of midnight, offers entertainment:

> I'll tell thee some old tale, and ere I've finish'd,
> The midnight watch is gone. Sit down, I pray.

Orra requests a story of something "touching the awful intercourse which spirits with mortal men have held at this dread hour." Cathrina begins to tell of a man who was compelled "to pass the night in a deserted tower." She continues until Orra's "shrunk and sharpen'd features are of the corse's colour." So the midnight hour passes, and Orra, "bold and buoyant grown," consents to be left alone. At once her terrors return. She strives to open the door, but does not know its secret; as she paces the floor, "A horn is heard without, pausing and sounding three times, each time louder than before." Orra strives desperately to open the door to free herself, and then—

(after a pause in which she stands with her body bent in a cowering posture, with her hands locked together, and trembling violently, she starts up and looks wildly round her.)

> There's nothing, yet I felt a chilly hand
> Upon my shoulder press'd. With open'd eyes
> And ears intent I'll stand. Better it is
> Thus to abide the awful visitation,
> Than cower in blinded horror, strain'd intensely
> With every beating of my goaded heart.

(Looking around her with a steady sternness, but shrinking again almost immediately)

> I cannot do it! on this spot I'll hold me
> In awful stillness.
> The icy scalp of fear is on my head;
> The life stirs in my hair; it is a sense
> That tells the nearing of unearthly steps,
> Albeit my ringing ears no sounds distinguish.

(Looking round, as if by irresistible impulse, to a great door at the bottom of the stage, which bursts open, and the form of a huntsman, clothed in black, with a horn in his hand, enters and advances towards her. She utters a loud shriek, and falls senseless to the floor.)[37]

The huntsman is Theobald, and Franko enters soon after, but their way of rescue has proved too much: Orra is insane.

The final act brings Hughobert to the ruined castle. He has discovered Rudigere's treachery, and now orders the villain seized and taken to prison:

> Full well upon the ground
> Mayst thou decline those darkly frowning eyes,
> And gnaw thy lip in shame.[38]

Rudigere stabs himself, and in his last torment serves, like other villains, to illustrate the consequences of evil upon the perpetrators of it.

The last scene shows "The forest near the castle; in front a rocky bank crowned with a ruined wall overgrown with ivy, and the mouth of a cavern shaded with bushes." Orra, brought here by Theobald and the robbers, emerges from the cave "with her hair and dress disordered, and the appearance of wild distraction in her gait and countenance." Gothic horrors have destroyed her mind. The last lines of the play, uttered by the mad heroine, suggest that she might have read too much of Matthew Gregory Lewis:

> See! from all points they come; earth casts them up!
> In grave-clothes swath'd are those but new in death;
> And there be some half bone, half cased in shreds

Of that which flesh hath been; and there be some
With wicker'd ribs, through which the darkness scowls.
Back, back!—They close upon us.—Oh! the void
Of hollow unball'd sockets staring grimly,
And lipless jaws that move and clatter round me
In mockery of speech!—Back, back, I say!
Back, back!"[29]

CHAPTER XII

GOTHIC SURVIVAL IN LITERARY DRAMA

THE PURPOSE of this final chapter is to suggest the extent and the nature of Gothic manifestations in selected plays by major romantic poets. There is no attempt here to present these dramas in all of their complex relationships. Wordsworth, Coleridge, Scott, Byron, and Shelley brought to their works, from the age and from themselves, much that must be omitted here. Their dramatic works have been illuminated in other volumes and monographs by consideration of the currents and crosscurrents of the age, the literary and philosophical implications involved in the nebulous romanticism, and the intellectual and emotional inclinations, attitudes, and convictions of the poets.[1] I shall therefore view the plays in a light in which they have hitherto not been specifically examined. Strictly, the purpose is twofold: to extend an account of the Gothic into the literary drama of the early nineteenth century, and to resurvey certain literary dramas against the background of Gothic tradition on the stage.

LITERARY PLAYS BY WORDSWORTH AND COLERIDGE

THE BORDERERS

Wordsworth's *Borderers,* like the other plays to be examined, has generally been related, but rather haphazardly, to Gothic tradition.[2] The reference has been, however, to Gothic fiction, not to Gothic drama. It seems more logical and proves more instructive, since the work is in dramatic form, to refer it to the dramatic tradition.

Of the major dramas of the romantic poets, this is one of the least Gothic. When it is viewed against its proper background,

---
[1] For notes to chap. xii, see pages 256–257.

both the extent of Wordsworth's debt to the conventional Gothic materials, methods, motifs, and purposes, and the nature of his departure from these show clearly. The points of conformity to the usual pattern are obvious, and a short summary will suffice for them. The points of departure demand a somewhat closer analysis.

The familiar pattern is followed, first, in the deliberate development of mystery and the equally deliberate withholding of the solution. Until the second scene of the fourth act, when Oswald discloses the truth of the past event, the reader and all but one of the principal characters are excluded from knowledge of even the most essential facts. More than one critic has found Wordsworth dramatically inept because he failed to make everything clear in the preliminary exposition. But perhaps the poet should not be blamed, for he was following the prevailing dramatic technique of his time. Virtually every Gothic playwright after Walpole studiously withheld that secret which was the key to motivation, character, and action. In *The Mysterious Mother* the dramatist reserved it and compounded the mystery until the last scene of the last act; in other plays the truth was usually divulged somewhat earlier, but perhaps never in the first act and rarely in the second. When Wordsworth wrote his play, the Gothic species was at the very height of its popularity.[a] Not the poet, then, but the kind of drama itself, in which exposition made only darkness visible, should bear the blame.

Second, the conventional pattern is followed in the settings. The most striking of these are "The Area of a half-ruined Castle—on one side the entrance to a dungeon," and "A desolate prospect—a ridge of rocks—a Chapel on the summit of one—Moon behind the rocks—night stormy—irregular sound of a bell." As in earlier plays, the surroundings become vital agents, closely involved in the thoughts and feelings of the characters.

Again, and very conspicuously, the pattern is followed in that the primary subject of the play is the agony of remorse. That the treatment of remorse differs somewhat from the conventional does not alter the essential fact that remorse is the subject.

Finally, it is followed in the use of a robber motif; in the presence of an unknown (Oswald) among the band of robbers; in the use of machinery such as creaking trees and tolling bells; in the theme of persecution of innocent and helpless individuals (Idonea and Herbert); in its portrait of a tyrant who inhabits a fearful castle (Lord Clifford, who, though he does not actually appear, is as effectively represented through description); and in numerous minor details.

The evidence of technique, settings, characters, and machinery suggests that Wordsworth sought to work out an idea within the established frame of the Gothic play. But in the very fact that he proceeded from an *idea* which he attempted thus to expound lies a principal cause for his departure from the traditional Gothic path. The fundamental difference between *The Borderers* and a typical Gothic play is that of purpose. The only idea which prompted Gothic playwrights was achievement of the utmost in mystery, gloom, and terror. For Wordsworth, on the other hand, the Gothic frame was a vehicle, not a destination. His use of the *modus operandi* of the Gothic school implies merely that he accepted the convenient contemporary fashion, perhaps without much thought, as a suitable way to communicate his more important idea.

Wordsworth was the first to use the Gothic mode for a purpose other than the mere exploitation of the elements which composed it. It matters little here what his purpose was.[*] It is sufficient to affirm that it was a philosophical rather than a theatrical one. He aimed to expose and damn the Godwinian thinking of which he had earlier been a disciple. For this purpose, the Gothic school furnished backdrop and properties.

At the same time, *The Borderers* shows another, though related, difference from the conventional Gothic play. This lies in the treatment of remorse and in the involvement of the poet himself. In the typical Gothic play, the study of remorse—whatever may have been the deficiencies of its execution—had always been objective. The villain whose body and mind were made to show the ravages of conscience was an objective figure. He originated as an object of terror. He grew through decades of interpretation by famous actors. His gloom intensified to an agony that perhaps pleased the censor and invited sympathy from the public. Thoughout the period of growth and change, he remained impersonal. He was a property of playwrights, no less than were a subterranean passage and a winding staircase. His remorse was a part of him, transferable with himself from playwight to playwright. The individual author projected his own mind and his own spiritual problems into this figure no more than he imposed his own personality upon a turret or a gallery. Whatever else he may have been, the Gothic protagonist was not a receptacle to be filled from a poet's self. He was a ready-made property upon which individual writers made only external alterations.

But in *The Borderers* the figure became subjective. As he used the framework of the conventional species as a structure within which to expound a philosophical idea, so Wordsworth used the Gothic protagonist as a receptacle for his personal remorse, perhaps over abandonment of Annette Vallon and his child.[5] In identifying his own with the traditional remorse of a theatrical type, Wordsworth began the personalizing of the Gothic villain that was the final step in the evolution of the Byronic hero.

REMORSE

The focus of Coleridge's *Remorse*, like that of *The Borderers*, is on the special agony which had afflicted a generation of villains. In one way, the two plays, written at almost the same time, complement each other by approaching the same problem from opposite directions. Both are analytical studies of remorse. But while Wordsworth's problem was how to eliminate that agony, Coleridge's was how to awaken it in one who seemed incapable of feeling it. In *The Borderers,* Oswald's Godwinian project to render Marmaduke incapable of remorse failed, and Marmaduke's final declaration that he will suffer agony until death mercifully sets him free is Wordsworth's assertion that experience is important and valid, and his rejection of a system which taught how to escape the consequences of bitter experience. In *Remorse,* the position of the remorseless Don Ordonio is in direct opposition to that of Marmaduke. Oswald actively attempts to make Marmaduke incapable of remorse; Don Alvar, the hero of *Remorse,* strives to make his brother Don Ordonio capable of it. In Wordsworth's play, the villain tries to destroy the hero's remorse, and fails; in Coleridge's play, the hero tries to arouse the villain's remorse, and succeeds. Thus, proceeding from opposite directions, both poets reached the same conclusion. Philosophical analysis by two great minds approved the trait that had been for a generation a principal subject of dramatic spectacle.

Like Wordsworth, Coleridge took over the frame of the conventional Gothic play within which to work out his problem. A bare summary of the plot exposes more familiar trappings than are apparent in a comparable summary of *The Borderers.* The central figure is Don Ordonio, son of Valdez and brother of Don Alvar. "Long years" before, he had, as he supposed, caused the assassination of his brother. In reality, the Moor, Isidore, ordered to slay Don Alvar, had at the crucial moment discovered circumstances which caused him to stay his hand. Don Alvar, long captive on a foreign shore, returns at the opening of the play. Disguised as a Moresco chieftain, he has two goals—to find whether there is truth in the rumor of his wife's marriage to Don Ordonio, and to find a means of awakening remorse in his brother, "that I may save him from himself." Isidore, commanded by Don Ordonio to appear as a sorcerer and convince Teresa that Alvar is dead, so that one of her objections to remarriage will be eliminated, directs the villain to "a stranger near the ruin in the wood" who had issued a mysterious promise "to bring the dead to life again." Don Ordonio fails to recognize the stranger as his brother, and Alvar agrees to come to the castle and execute the villain's commands. Instead, when Teresa, Valdez, and the villain are assembled, he presents an "illuminated picture" (not unlike those in "Monk" Lewis' plays) which shows his own "assassination." The inquisitors interrupt the scene; Don Ordonio is thrown into "great agitation," and Alvar is confined in a dungeon. Fearing that the Moor will disclose the truth, Don Ordonio entices him to a cave and murders him, but is observed by Isidore's wife. She leads the friends of her dead husband in an assault on the castle. Meanwhile Teresa, who had been caught by "something" in the aspect of the "stranger," ventures, like a Radcliffean maiden, into the dungeons to free him. She finds and recognizes her husband, and the two have barely time to embrace before Ordonio enters. Though now much shaken by conscience, he attempts to slay his brother. The blow misses, and he attempts to kill himself, but is prevented by Don Alvar. The Moors break down the gates, and Isidore's widow slays the unresisting—and remorseful—murderer of her husband.

Settings include "The sea-shore, with a view of the Castle," "A wild and mountainous country," "A Hall of an Armoury, with an Altar at the back of the stage," "The interior of a Chapel, with painted windows," "A Cavern, dark except where a gleam of moonlight is seen on one side at the further end of it," and "The interior court of a Saracenic or Gothic Castle, with the iron gate of a Dungeon visible." These represent no departure from tradition.

Among the characters, Don Ordonio, Alvar, and Teresa are familiar. The villain is thus described by Teresa when Valdez urges marriage:

> ... I have no power to love him.
> His proud forbidding eye, and his dark brow,
> Chill me like dew damps of the unwholesome night.[6]

Before the audience knows of his villainy, a brief scene exhibits his guilty marks:

Alhadra.	My lord, my husband's name
	Is Isidore. (Ordonio starts) You may remember it:
	You left him at Almeria.
Monviedro.	Palpably false!
	This very week, three years ago, my lord,
	...
	You were at sea, and there engaged the pirates,
	The murderers doubtless of your brother Alvar—
	... What? is he ill, my lord?
	How strange he looks!
Valdez.	(Angrily) You press'd upon him too abruptly
	The fate of one on whom, you know, he doted.
Ordonio.	(Starting as in sudden agitation) O Heavens!
	I? doted?—(then recovering himself)
	Yes, I doted on him. (Walks to end of stage)
Monviedro.	The drops did start and stand upon his forehead ...[7]

Alvar, the hero, closely resembles his predecessors. Like them, he is quickly removed to a dungeon, where he remains until the end. He has "that within" which identifies him, even through his wanderer's garb, as no commoner. Finally, like heroes, heroines, and other wronged Gothic figures, he is eager to bring to repentance and to forgive the vicious criminal who has injured him. As we have seen, it is this particular characteristic which becomes the subject of the play. Don Alvar's determination is not to have revenge, but to arouse in his brother's hardened heart the remorse that will save him from perdition. When the villain, sword in hand, approaches to kill him, the hero delivers a lecture on Gothic villainy in general:

> What then art thou? For shame, put up thy sword!
> I fix mine upon thee, and thou tremblest!
> I speak, and fear and wonder crush thy rage,
> And turn it to a motionless distraction!
> Thou blind self-worshipper! thy pride, thy cunning,
> Thy faith in universal villany,
> Thy shallow sophisms, thy pretended scorn
> For all thy human brethren—out upon them!
> What have they done for thee? have they given
>   thee peace?
> Cured thee of starting in thy sleep? or made
> The darkness pleasant when thou wak'st at midnight?
> Art happy when alone? Can'st walk by thyself
> With even step and quiet cheerfulness?
> Yet, yet thou mayst be saved—[8]

It is somehow delightful to find Coleridge, who partially identified himself with his hero, doing exactly as we would expect—lecturing, even as an assassin approaches. Don Ordonio is literally talked into repentance by Alvar, whose care is "Chiefly, chiefly, brother, my anguish for thy guilt." The villain is at last brought into line with all his dramatic ancestors; the agony that has been encased in him finds release, and he cries,

> O horror! not a thousand years in heaven
> Could recompense this miserable heart,
> Or make it capable of one brief joy!

Teresa is in the Radcliffean tradition of the heroine who explores by dim light in dark places. Mysteriously attracted to the "sorcerer," she visits the dungeons to release him:

> (Enter Teresa with a taper)
> It has chilled my very life—my own voice scares me;
> Yet when I hear it not I seem to lose
> The substance of my being—my strongest grasp
> Sends inwards but weak witness that I am.

> I seek to cheat the echo.—How the half sounds
> Blend with this strangled light! Is he not here?
> O for one human face here—but to see
> One human face here to sustain me.—Courage!
> It is but my own fear! The life within me,
> It sinks and wavers like this cone of flame,
> Beyond which I scarce dare look onward! Oh!
>   (shuddering)
> If I faint? If this inhuman den should be
> At once my death-bed and my burial vault?
> (faintly screams as Alvar comes from the recess)[*]

The direction "faintly screams" suggests one difference between *Remorse* and a typical Gothic play; in a "tragedy" by Lewis, the direction would likely have been "shrieks." Like the other major poets of his time who attempted drama, Coleridge subdued the louder Gothic tones. Like them, also, he raised the Gothic above itself through finer poetry. And, like Wordsworth, Byron, and Shelley, he left certain very obvious marks of his own personality on the formerly impersonal dramatic kind.

SCOTT AND GOTHIC DRAMA

The main contribution of Scott to Gothic drama was indirect. Between 1816 and 1823 fifteen of his novels were adapted—some of them half a dozen times—by playwrights who frantically sought to capitalize on their popularity. Among the many adapters was Daniel Terry, whose version of *Guy Mannering* appeared at Covent Garden in 1816. After witnessing its performance, Scott referred to the dramatizing of his novels as the art of "Terryfying." After several adaptations had appeared, he commented, "I believe my muse would be Terry-fyed into treading the stage even if I wrote a sermon."[10] The various adaptations have been studied elsewhere,[11] and though the author was not especially concerned with Gothic matters, his detailed discussions of setting, action, atmosphere, and technique have naturally included them. It is perhaps worth repeating that the adapters invariably emphasized not the realistic scenes and the character studies, but the wild and highly "romantic." Very obviously, all of the adapters had been educated in the Gothic school. Scott's poems, too, especially *The Lady of the Lake,* were frequently adapted, and these dramatizations have been catalogued in the same study.

Scott's own first attempt at drama was a translation of Goethe's *Götz,* published unacted in 1799. Thereafter he assisted Terry in adapting *Guy Mannering,* and wrote *Halidon Hill, Auchindrane, The Doom of Devorgoil, The House of Aspen,* and *MacDuff's Cross.*[12] In all of these the Gothic heritage is apparent. In *Devorgoil* and *Aspen,* which I shall examine, it is dominant.

In these latter are mixed Scottish superstition, melodramatic technique which makes us think of Lewis' *One O'Clock,* German materials from Goethe, Schiller, and Kotzebue,[13] and a great deal that is more strictly associated with the Gothic Revival. Ruins are prominent in both. The settings of *Devorgoil* include "A wild and hilly country—exhibiting the Castle of Devorgoil, decayed, and partly ruinous"; "A ruinous Anteroom in the Castle"; and various "decayed chambers." The settings in *Aspen* are more elaborate. They include "An ancient Gothic chamber in the Castle of Ebersdorf"; "A woodland prospect... in the background the ruins of the ancient castle of Griefenhaus"; "The wood of Griefenhaus, with the ruins of the castle"; and "The subterranean Chapel of the Castle of Griefenhaus. It seems deserted and in decay. There are four entrances, each defended by an iron portal.... In the centre of the Chapel is a ruinous Altar, half sunk in the ground, on which lie a large book, a dagger, and a coil of ropes, beside two lighted tapers. Antique stone benches of different heights around the Chapel. In the back scene is a dilapidated entrance into the sacristy, which is quite dark."[14]

Gothic haunted chambers and German diablerie are burlesqued in the early scenes of *Devorgoil.* The absurd Gullcrammer, foolish and conceited, is sent to bed in a chamber declared haunted and is especially warned to watch out for "Owlspiegle," the fantastic goblin fond of shaving off hair and beards. Gullcrammer lies abed, wind rustles the tapestries, the lone taper flickers, and a bell tolls. With a fool instead of a distressed damsel as subject, the scene appears to ridicule Mrs. Radcliffe's favorite situation. Katleen and Blackthorn, for mischief, dress in weird costumes to represent Owlspiegle and an attendant goblin; they enter, shave Gullcrammer's head, sing comic-diabolical songs, and disappear through a trapdoor. To this point, the mood is hilarious; but as the pranksters are returning to their own apartments they pass through "A Gothic Hall, waste and ruinous," where they encounter a real ghost:

> Black. Art thou not afraid,
> In these wild halls while playing feigned goblins,
> That we may meet with real ones?
> Kat. Not a jot.
> My spirit is too light, my heart too bold,
> To fear a visit from the other world.
> Black. But is not this the place, the very hall,
> In which men say that Oswald's grandfather,
> The black Lord Erick, walks his penance round?
> Credit me, Katleen, these half-moulder'd columns
> Have in their ruin something very fiendish ...[35]

They hear a rustling, and "a figure is imperfectly seen between two of the pillars." Blackthorn flees, but Katleen stands her ground, and the apparition addresses her:

> I come, by Heaven permitted; quit this castle:
> There is a fate on't—if for good or evil,
> Brief space shall soon determine. In that fate,
> If good, my lineage thou canst nothing claim;
> If evil, much mayst suffer.—Leave these precincts.

Black Erick's spirit leaves a key, admonishing the heroine to "wait the event with courage." When "the event" arrives, the key prevents a catastrophe, and the "doom" of Devorgoil is averted in a spectacular scene involving a scroll, an old suit of mail, a mysterious iron door with a rusty lock, thunder, lightning, and unearthly music.

The House of Aspen belongs with plays which blend the secret-tribunal motif with Gothic settings, machinery, and characters.[16] The preoccupation with Gothic ruins has already been indicated, and also prominent are a Byronic hero who "shuts himself up for days in his solitary chamber"; a persecution theme which involves a distressed maiden; and numerous elements of the traditional paraphernalia of terror. On the whole, this is perhaps the most elaborately Gothic play written by a major author.

Until the third act there hangs over the action that same dark mystery which had prevailed in Gothic drama since *The Mysterious Mother;* probably, if specific debt could be ascertained, *Aspen* would be found to owe most to that first of the species. Isabella's guilt in the assassination of her first husband—the past event which had long preceded the action of the play—had caused her to "drag out years of hidden remorse," and her son, naturally inclined to gloom, is first agonized to find his mother guilty and then horrified to realize that as a member of the secret tribunal he must bring her to trial and certain execution. The last act is singularly devoted to theatrical spectacle, and suggests the strong influence of the most violent Gothic playwrights. George, the son, refusing to bring his mother to trial, accuses himself before the tribunal and is executed as an oathbreaker. The mother, blindfolded, is brought in, accused, and forced into the sacristy where her son's body lies. There she is to await the executioner's dagger. Rudiger, her present husband and the father of George, is dragged before the court. He is shown his son's body, and, as he watches, Isabella, wounded mortally, enters and throws herself on the corpse. Rudiger is thrust into the sacristy to await his own death, and Bertram, henchman of Roderic, the familiar gloomy villain, follows him. But at this instant the Duke of Bavaria, a *deus ex machina,* appears and saves the remaining victim.

In Scott's plays, as in *The Borderers* and *Remorse,* crude Gothic elements are refined by a surer hand. Though some of the most horrific aspects of action and machinery persist, superior poetry, keener analysis of motives, and deeper penetration into the human heart tend to raise the works from the class of subliterary concoctions into that of literary compositions. Scott's plays are nearer the Gothic tradition than are those by his great contemporaries, not only because he included more of the familiar materials, but also because he preserved the Gothic impersonality. Wordsworth, in his play, worked out a personal problem; Coleridge indulged his habit of analysis and lecture; Shelley idealized his principal characters; and Byron read himself into the whole Gothic tradition. Scott, in very conspicuous contrast, omitted himself entirely.

SHELLEY'S CENCI

It is not remarkable that Shelley's *Cenci* bears marks of the Gothic school." On the contrary, it is at first surprising that it does not bear more of them. As a child and as a student at Eton, Shelley devoured tales in the chapbooks picked up at the bookstalls." The influence of these "shilling shockers" remained until the end of his life and is demonstrable in all of his works excepting the shorter lyrics. Furthermore, he wrote four distinctly Gothic pieces: *Zastrozzi* (1810), *St. Irvyne* (1811), *The Assassins* (1814), a fragment of a romance, and *The Coliseum* (1818–1819), another fragment. These show full awareness of the native Gothic and the German traditions. The two completed works revolve about the center which attracted the poet's attention until his death—tyrannical persecution of the innocent and the defenseless. This had been a Gothic theme since *Otranto*.

The chapbooks read in youth were not the only forces which directed his mind to the tyrant-victim relationship. Shelley's political, social, and religious philosophy developed under the tutelage of his father-in-law. Godwin, in *Caleb Williams,* had expanded the tyrant-victim formula of the Gothic novel to serve a broader purpose.[19] In the typical novels, tyrants persecuted unhappy ladies for the mere purpose of exciting terror in the reader. There were no broader implications, political, social, or otherwise: whatever they wrote, Horace Walpole, Clara Reeve, and Ann Radcliffe did not write propaganda. But in *Caleb Williams* the simple tale of persecution was transformed into a social instrument. Personal persecution became social oppression. The tyrant-victim relationship became an oppressor-oppressed one.

In the Cenci manuscript Shelley saw, very naturally, the theme which Gothic fiction and Godwinian philosophy had alerted his senses to perceive. Beatrice's story conformed to the pattern he had traced in *Zastrozzi* and *St. Irvyne.* It accorded also with the more significant concept of oppressor and oppressed. He visited the Cenci palace, and his observations there reveal his association of that structure with the primary setting of Gothic romance:

> The Cenci palace is of great extent; and ... there yet remains a vast and gloomy pile of feudal architecture in the same state as during the dreadful scenes which are the subject of this tragedy. The palace is situated in an obscure corner of Rome ... and from the upper windows you see the immense ruins of Mount Palatine half hidden under their profuse overgrowth of trees ... One of the gates of the palace formed of immense stones and leading through a passage, dark and lofty and opening into gloomy subterranean chambers, struck me particularly.[20]

He next studied a portrait which he believed to be that of Beatrice. He was moved by the fact that the subject seemed "sad and stricken down in spirit" and by "the fixed and pale composure upon the features." This might have been a portrait of any imaginary Gothic heroine; to Shelley it was also a symbol of the oppressed:

> The crimes and miseries in which she was an actor and a sufferer are as the mask and the mantle in which circumstances clothed her for her impersonation on the scene of the world.[21]

Shelley was therefore drawn to the subject of his tragedy through the channels of Gothic fiction and Godwinian philosophy. Theme, story, setting, and principal characters all accorded with his double background of terror-Gothic and social-Gothic. It was inevitable, then, that he should have been moved to retell the story, and equally inevitable that his retelling should bear marks of the Gothic school. So much is certain and even obvious.

But somewhat less obvious are the reasons why *The Cenci*, made from raw materials perfectly suited to Gothic composition and by a poet with an unusual Gothic background, does not more completely resemble the typical Gothic play. Probably the main reason is that Shelley, though he knew Gothic fiction, was ignorant of Gothic drama. Indeed, he knew almost nothing of any contemporary drama. Late in his life he saw some Italian operas, but earlier he had attended the theater perhaps half a dozen times in all. Kean's Hamlet infuriated him, and Peacock had to detain him forcibly in his seat after he had witnessed two acts of *The School for Scandal*. He never saw, and almost certainly never read, a Gothic play. He was therefore quite unequipped to dramatize a Gothic story in the contemporary fashion. The raw materials themselves suggested the mould into which the taste of the times would have liked them poured, but Shelley had no such mould. He attempted deliberately, as he wrote to Leigh Hunt, to write a drama "of a more popular kind," but the specialized techniques of Gothic plays, developed in the preceding half-century, were unfamiliar to him. He lacked formula for the construction of that kind of play which both the nature of his materials and his own background indicated.

The theater's loss, of course, was literature's gain. Lacking acquaintance with Gothic dramatic models, the poet turned to others which he knew intimately—Greek and Shakespearean tragedies. The marks of *Macbeth,* especially, are so emphatic upon *The Cenci* that in certain passages a reader might momentarily wonder whether he has not picked up the wrong volume. The result of modeling upon dramatic masterpieces was a tragedy infinitely superior to the typical Gothic play, and doubtless superior to that which Shelley might have written had he been close to the Gothic theater; but the tragedy was not of the kind which the raw materials indicated and which the poet expressly aimed to write. Had he used the narrative form, he would likely have composed a Gothic novel along conventional lines. Unaware of the Gothic stage, however, and intimate with the highest dramatic models, he created a great tragedy in which the close affinity of the materials with the Gothic was nearly obscured.

A second force which tended to obscure the relation of *The Cenci* to the Gothic species was that of poetic genius. More than Wordsworth's, Coleridge's, or Scott's, Shelley's power of language and his rare imagination transmuted the gross materials. It is universally agreed that some passages in *The Cenci* are unsurpassed outside Shakespeare as dramatic poetry.

Further, Shelley's habitual idealization of character, here especially invited by the closeness of the subject to his heart, led him to lift out of type the principal figures in the tragedy. The idealization of villainy in Count Cenci and of persecuted innocence in Beatrice wrought changes upon the conventional types of villain and heroine. Though Count Cenci's actions are those of the typical Gothic tyrant, his reactions are not. The consequences of evil, emphasized so heavily by Gothic playwrights, are not represented in any of his words or through any physical manifestations.[22] Being evil incarnate, Cenci takes pleasure in evil, and the torture of remorse so characteristic of the Gothic villain is quite unknown to him. Beatrice, who is at once victim and rebel, is similarly exalted and thus lifted out of type. She does not and cannot know the terror which it was the original function of the Gothic heroine to feel and to transmit. Though her position is precisely that of the harassed maiden, idealization raises her above a capacity for terror. Only during the scenes directly before and after Count Cenci's assault, when she is momentarily stripped of idealization, does she closely identify herself with the familiar type of persecuted heroine.[23]

This much, to summarize, may be stated of the relation of *The Cenci* to Gothic drama. The theme of persecution aligns it with Gothic tradition in both fiction and drama. The principal characters are Gothic types idealized. Some scenes, especially those before and after Cenci's attack on Beatrice, would fit unaltered into a Gothic play. Several descriptive passages paint settings which were favorites of Gothic writers after Mrs. Radcliffe.[24] But Shelley's unawareness of the contemporary theater, his intimacy with dramatic masterpieces, and his poetic power prevented full achievement of his lower aim to write a play "of a more popular kind." Aided by Shakespearean and classical drama, his art elevated the Gothic to such an unprecedented height that, though it achieved triumph, it suffered obscuration.

Byron's Manfred

Though it was composed before *The Cenci, Manfred* has been reserved for final discussion because it best represents the high romantic expression, in dramatic form, of the Gothic spirit. *Manfred,* in some measure at least, gives point to the study of many earlier theatrical pieces which are intrinsically worthless, and toward review of *Manfred* my examination of these has more or less naturally been aimed. Byron's tragedy might be described as a consummation of Gothic evolution on the stage. The crude Gothic machinery seems, as we look backward, to have been building toward the high romanticism of these Alpine summits, mists, and spirits. The crude Gothic protagonists of nearly fifty years passed into this most striking portrait of the Byronic hero.

It is with this hero, who has remained both baffling and fascinating, that we are chiefly concerned, for it is Manfred who is the play, and to interpret his agony is to interpret both him and the tragedy.

What ails this Manfred, then, alone at midnight in his Gothic gallery:

> My slumbers—if I slumber—are not sleep,
> But a continuance of enduring thought,
> Which then I can resist not: in my heart
> There is a vigil, and these eyes but close
> To look within.[25]

Poised to leap from a Jungfrau precipice:

> To be thus—
> Gray-hair'd with anguish, like these blasted pines,
> Wrecks of a single winter, barkless, branchless,
> A blighted trunk upon a cursed root,
> Which but supplies a feeling of decay—[26]

Offered a cup of "ancient vintage" to thaw his veins:

> Away! away! there's blood upon the brim!
> Will it then never—never sink in the earth?[27]

What ails him, that the Dependant voices doubt and mistrust:

> ...night after night, for years,
> He hath pursued long vigils in this tower,
> Without a witness...to be sure, there is
> One chamber where none enters: I would give
> The fee of what I have to come these three years
> To pore upon its mysteries.[28]

And that he cries of

> The innate tortures of that deep despair
> Which is remorse without the fear of hell.[29]

What ails Manfred? In answer, the play offers only hints which veil rather than expose; there is a broken-off, deliberately unended line:

> The sole companion of his wanderings
> And watchings—her, whom of all earthly things

> That lived, the only thing he seem'd to love,—
> As he, indeed, by blood was bound to do,
> The lady Astarte, his—[30]

There is an agonized self-reproach, a shriek of anguish the cause of which is left undescribed:

> If I had never lived, that which I love
> Had still been living; had I never loved,
> That which I love would still be beautiful,
> Happy and giving happiness.[31]

These are half-answers only, which darken, not illuminate, the mystery.

From outside the play, from Byron's life, letters, and other compositions, we learn of *Weltschmerz,* of the poet's lame foot and hurt pride, of incest, *Faust,* and Chateaubriand's *René.*[32] Were these the sources of Manfred's agony? They are not the only ones. To them must be added the most important of all— Manfred's dramatic ancestry. More specifically, must be added his inheritance from the Gothic villain whose half-century of theatrical agony evolved him. The shadowed places in the delineation of Manfred can best be lighted by understanding of that heritage.

The essentials of Manfred are visible in the history of this villain. His manner of feeling, thought, and action was patterned before Byron was born. The motive for his agony is more readily perceived by examination of the protagonist in any one of a dozen plays before 1800 than by analysis of *Manfred* itself or by compilation of the facts and legends of Byron's life. Manfred, a theatrical figure which Byron knew well[33] and with which he identified himself, could have been essentially as he is represented in the play even though the poet's foot had been sound and his pride unhurt, and though there had been no *Faust,* no *René,* and no incest. It is true that he might have been an objective rather than a subjective creation, though Wordsworth had earlier changed him in that respect. He would certainly have lacked some qualities imposed by Byron's personality, but in all essentials he could have been as he is.

It is not in Byron's life, then, or in the tragedy itself that we shall find the cause of Manfred's agony. Byron's own "explanation" of the character must itself be interpreted by reference elsewhere: "... a kind of magician, who is tormented by a species of remorse, the cause of which is left half unexplained."³ The other half must be sought in dramatic tradition.

Over each play examined in preceding chapters the same question hovered, and no playwright permitted the audience to forget or to relax investigation: What ails the villain? This was asked by Martin, a friar, concerning the protagonist of the first Gothic play:

> What is this secret sin, this untold tale,
> That art cannot extract, nor penance cleanse?
> ... Then whither turn
> To worm her secret out?

It was in Solerno's mind in Greatheed's *The Regent,* as he tells how the villain had stood,

> ... with folded arms
> And forehead all convulsed, and quiv'ring lip.

Characters and audience alike asked it of Ferrand, Boaden's villain in *Fontainville Forest,* who cried,

> Now every heart with glowing rapture beats
> Save mine alone, where like a vulture, guilt,
> Continual gnawing, keeps me on the stretch.

It was precisely the question for which the provost in *Julian and Agnes* demanded answer from Alfonso, the strange wanderer who

> ... commun'd with his soul and talkst with guilt
> Lonely on unknown heights, where none ere gazed.

And it was asked of Bertram by the prior in Maturin's Byronic drama:

> ...full well I deemed no gentler feelings
> Woke the dark lightning of thy withering eye.
> What fiercer spirit is it tears thee thus?
> Show me the horrid tenant of thy heart!

For all of these sufferers except the last, the answer was the same: secret knowledge of past evil. One had committed incest with her son. Another had assassinated his benefactor. Another had chained his wife to a rock and left her to die. Another had married two women and slain the brother of one. In the period between Walpole and Byron scores of similar figures had perpetrated similar acts, contained their guilt in their bosoms, and suffered cruel remorse. In every case the full truth of the past event, though deliberately withheld by the dramatist as long as his skill allowed, was ultimately divulged—not "left half unexplained." Why did Maturin and Byron resort to vagueness?

So long as the Gothic protagonist remained a *villain*, it was possible finally to expose his guilt fully and clearly. It was even possible, however unspeakable his crime, to win a portion of sympathy for him by magnifying the personal effects of his remorse. Thus a villain could become a hero-villain, no matter how black his crime, if the dramatist smote him with sufficient remorse to compensate and if a great actor made a magnificent show of that agony. But when the villain was transformed, through this very agony, to *hero*, the dramatist was confronted by a seemingly insoluble dilemma. How could a creature guilty of such crime as Gothic villains committed be offered as a hero? And if he were not guilty of enormous evil, how could that remorse which was his distinguishing quality be motivated?

Lewis, as we have seen, found one solution. His Adelmorn believed himself guilty of murder, but was in the end proved innocent. Thus the playwright motivated the exhibition of intense remorse, and at the same time was able to keep Adelmorn's title of "hero" unimpeachable. But the device required to make Adelmorn think himself a murderer was so elaborate as to be impracticable; despite the playwright's care, we are never convinced that the hero could really have thought himself the cause of his uncle's death. And had a second playwright immediately borrowed Lewis' deceptive method, the Drury Lane audience, always quick to be enraged, might have given him cause to doubt whether his trouble had been worth while. A third might have fared even worse.

In any event, Lewis did succeed in motivating remorse without having to convict his hero of a villain's crimes. In contrast, Maturin evaded the problem altogether. The remorse of Bertram made spectacular but unmotivated histrionics. Bertram was guilty of no past crime. He suffered merely because his dramatic forbears proved attractive in suffering. That these had legitimate cause and Bertram none the playwright seems to have considered irrelevant.

Byron's solution in *Manfred* was more effective than either Lewis' overelaborate device or Maturin's complete evasion, and was obviously inspired by Gothic tradition. To move the unsurpassed and prolonged agony of his hero, the poet needed to suggest a crime of immense proportions. A minor infraction such as would not blacken the hero's name would have been absurdly out of ratio. Byron's way was to leave the cause of remorse "half unexplained." It was to extend the familiar Gothic technique to the very last lines of the tragedy: to hint, break off, and hint again, but never to speak the ugly fact in unmistakable words. Walpole's countess in *The Mysterious Mother,* after five acts of veiled suggestion and mysterious implication, at last says bluntly that she yielded her body to her son. Just so, the crimes of villains in other Gothic plays were ultimately divulged, after long speculation, in naked words. Manfred's deed, we are led to suppose, was as appalling as any of theirs, who were villains; yet Manfred remains a hero, whose heroic reputation was preserved by extending the traditional Gothic ambiguity. Byron never lifted the dark veil which envelops him and the past event where the truth lies, and thus what might have been irreparably ugly, when boldly displayed, retained the fascination of profound mystery. Fleeting glimpses by half-light revealed a hero where full illumination would have disclosed a villain.

Manfred, intriguing in his "half unexplained" remorse, is the theatrical villain transformed into a hero and enriched by his passage through the mind of Byron. Struggling on precipices, conversing with spirits, and invoking demons, he is quite at home among the properties of Gothic machinery which had evolved with him. Projected into a rarer atmosphere by the imagination of a great poet, the crude conventional figure and the crude convential paraphernalia which over several decades had gathered around a castle ruin achieve distinction and triumph. The objective tyrant of tradition, who was invented as an agent of terror whose sole function was to frighten sensitive maidens in galleries and vaults, is here subjective and poetic, a receptacle which contains some of the personal being of the immediate creator. The original mechanical properties of haunted rooms and fearful ghosts have here become mystic properties of a metaphysical realm, their grossness obscured by Alpine clouds. Yet only the height to which they have at last ascended is new. Neither the transformed villain nor the lovelier machinery through which he now moves is essentially changed. The emphatic and unmistakable marks of half a century of theatrical tradition remain to dominate them both.

APPENDIX

A LIST OF GOTHIC PLAYS

THE CHRONOLOGICAL list which follows is intended to be complete from 1768 to 1810, and only representative thereafter to 1823. In the first two decades are included plays chiefly Gothic and others characterized in part by Gothic elements; thereafter only those in which Gothic elements predominate are listed. Plays read in the Larpent Collection in the Henry E. Huntington Library are marked "Larpent"; plays not so marked are available in printed collections. The plays of Joanna Baillie have caused the only problem in chronology, since the publication dates do not accurately represent the dates of writing, which were usually considerably earlier.

The Mysterious Mother. Tragedy, 5 acts. Horace Walpole, published 1768.
Almida. Tragedy, 5 acts. Dorothy Celesia. Drury Lane, January 1769. Larpent.
The Grecian Daughter. Tragedy, 5 acts. Arthur Murphy. Drury Lane, February 1771.
Eldred, or The British Father. Tragedy, 5 acts. John Jackson. Haymarket, July 1775. Larpent.
The Heroine of the Cave. Tragedy, 5 acts. Paul Hiffernan. Drury Lane, March 1775.
Percy. Tragedy, 5 acts. Hannah More. Covent Garden, December 1777.
The British Heroine. Tragedy, 5 acts. John Jackson. Covent Garden, May 1778.
The Law of Lombardy. Tragedy, 5 acts. Robert Jephson. Drury Lane, February 1778.
The Fatal Falsehood. Tragedy, 5 acts. Hannah More. Covent Garden, May 1779.
Albina, Countess of Raimond. Tragedy, 5 acts. Hannah Cowley. Haymarket, July 1779. Larpent.
Zoraida. Tragedy, 5 acts. William Hodson. Drury Lane, December 1779. Larpent.
Dissipation. Comedy, 5 acts. Miles Peter Andrews. Drury Lane, March 1781. Larpent.
Elmira. Tragedy, 5 acts (anon., application 1781, unacted). Larpent.
The Count of Narbonne. Tragedy, 5 acts. Robert Jephson. Covent Garden, November 1781.

Banditti; or, Love in a Labyrinth. Comic opera, 3 acts. John O'Keefe. Covent Garden, November 1781. Larpent. (Altered as *The Castle of Andalusia.* Covent Garden, November 1782.)
The Mysterious Husband. Play, 5 acts. Richard Cumberland. Covent Garden, 1783.
Lord Russel. Tragedy, 5 acts. William Hayley. Haymarket, August 1784.
Carmelite. Tragedy, 5 acts. Richard Cumberland. Drury Lane, December 1784.
The Nunnery. Farce, 2 acts. William Pearce. Covent Garden, April 1785. Larpent.
Coeur de Lion. Comic opera. Leonard MacNally. Covent Garden, October 1786.
Coeur de Lion. Musical Entertainment. John Burgoyne. Drury Lane, October 1786.
The Enchanted Castle. Pantomime, 1 act. Miles Peter Andrews. Covent Garden, December 1786. Larpent.
Julia; or The Italian Lover. Tragedy, 5 acts. Robert Jephson. Drury Lane, April 1787.
Vimonda. Tragedy, 5 acts. Andrew McDonald. Haymarket, September, 1787. Larpent.
The Regent. Tragedy, 5 acts. Bertie Greatheed. Drury Lane, March 1788. Larpent.
The Battle of Hexham; or Days of Old. Play with music, 3 acts. Colman the Younger. Haymarket, August 1789.
The Haunted Tower. Opera, 3 acts. James Cobb. Drury Lane, November, 1789.
The Crusade. Opera, 3 acts. Frederic Reynolds. Covent Garden, May 1790.
The Kentish Barons. Play, 3 acts. Francis North. Haymarket, June 1791. Larpent.
The Midnight Wanderers. Comic opera, 2 acts. William Pearce. Covent Garden, 1793. Larpent.
The Ward of the Castle. Comic opera, 3 acts. "Miss Burke." Covent Garden, October 1793. Larpent.
The Castle of Otranto. Play, 3 acts (application by Stephen Kemble). Newcastle, November 1793. Larpent.
Fontainville Forest. Play, 5 acts. James Boaden. Covent Garden, March 1794. Larpent.
Netley Abbey. Operatic farce. William Pearce. Covent Garden, April 1794. Larpent.
The Sicilian Romance; or The Apparition of the Cliff. Play, 3 acts. Henry Siddons, Covent Garden, May 1794. Larpent.

The Mysteries of the Castle. Dramatic tale, 3 acts. Miles Peter Andrews. Covent Garden, January 1795. Larpent.
The Adopted Child. Musical drama, 2 acts. Samuel Birch. Drury Lane, May 1795.
The Secret Tribunal. Play, 5 acts. James Boaden. Covent Garden, June 1795. Larpent.
The Iron Chest. Drama, 3 acts. Colman the Younger. Drury Lane, March 1796.
The Days of Yore. Drama, 3 acts. Richard Cumberland. January 1796. Larpent.
Almeyda, Queen of Granada. Tragedy, 5 acts. Sophia Lee. Drury Lane, April 1796. Larpent.
Don Raymond; or The Castle of Lindenburgh. Ballet pantomime, 2 acts. Anon. Covent Garden, March 1797. Larpent.
The Italian Monk. Play, 3 acts. James Boaden. Haymarket, August 1797. Larpent.
The Castle Spectre. Drama, 5 acts. M. G. Lewis. Drury Lane, December 1797.
Raymond and Agnes; or The Bleeding Nun of Lindenberg. Melodrama, 3 acts. H. W. Grosette. Covent Garden, June 1797.
The Mysterious Marriage; or, The Heirship of Roselva. Play, 3 acts. Harriet Lee (unacted) 1798. Larpent.
The Inquisitor. Play, 5 acts. Thomas Holcroft. Haymarket, June 1798. Larpent.
The Cambro-Britons. Play, 3 acts. James Boaden. Haymarket, July 1798. Larpent.
The Outlaws. Comic opera, 2 acts. Andrew Franklin. Drury Lane, October 1798. Larpent.
Aurelio and Miranda. Play, 5 acts. James Boaden. Drury Lane, December 1798. Larpent.
The Black Forest. Dramatic romance, 3 acts. Samuel Birch. Covent Garden, December 1798. Larpent.
Feudal Times. Drama, 2 acts. Colman the Younger. Drury Lane, January 1798. Larpent.
The Castle of Montval. Tragedy, 5 acts. Thomas Sedgwick Whalley. Drury Lane, April 1799. Larpent.
Villario and *Theodora.* Tragedies, 5 acts (written 1799, published, unacted 1814). Sophia Burrell.
Edmond, Orphan of the Castle. Tragedy, 5 acts (anon., published, unacted 1799).
Fortune's Frolic. Farce, 2 acts. John Till Allingham. Covent Garden, May 1799.

The Castle of Sorrento. Opera, 2 acts. Henry Heartwell. Haymarket, July 1799.
The Red Cross Knights. Play, 5 acts. Joseph George Holman. Haymarket, August 1799.
The Secret Castle; or, Henry and Edwy. Farce, 2 acts. Manchester, 1799(?). Larpent.
De Monfort. Drury Lane, April 1800; *Ethwald, Orra, The Dream, Romiero, Henriquez, Rayner, The Family Legend:* Bath, 1811; *The Separation, Witchcraft.* Joanna Baillie (published 1798-1812).
Julian and Agnes. Tragedy, 5 acts. William Sotheby. Drury Lane, April 1801. Larpent.
Adelmorn, the Outlaw. Romantic drama, 3 acts. M. G. Lewis. Drury Lane, May 1801.
Alfonso, King of Castile. Tragedy, 5 acts. M. G. Lewis. Covent Garden, January 1802.
A Tale of Mystery. Melodrama, 2 acts. Thomas Holcroft. Covent Garden, November 1802.
The Mystic Cavern. Tragedy, 5 acts. anon. Norwich, May 1803. Larpent.
The Harper's Daughter. Tragedy, 5 acts. M. G. Lewis. Covent Garden, May 1803. Larpent.
A Tale of Terror. Dramatic Romance, 3 acts. Henry Siddons. Covent Garden, May 1803. Larpent.
The Maid of Bristol. Play, 3 acts. James Boaden. Haymarket, August 1803. Larpent.
Valentine and Orson. Pantomimical romantic melodrama, 2 acts. Thomas John Dibdin. Covent Garden, April 1804. Larpent.
The Hunter of the Alps. Musical drama, 2 acts. William Dimond. Haymarket, July 1804.
Angelina; or Wolcot Castle. Musical drama, 2 acts. Mary Goldsmith (?). 1804 (?). Larpent.
St. Margaret's Cave. Play, 5 acts. George Charles Carr. York and Hull, 1804 (?). Larpent.
The Venetian Outlaw. Drama, 3 acts. Robert William Elliston. Drury Lane, April 1805. Larpent.
Rugantino; or The Bravo of Venice. Melodrama, 3 acts. M. G. Lewis. Covent Garden, 1805. Larpent.
The Towers of Urbandine. Play, 5 acts. George Charles Carr. York and Hull, 1805. Larpent.
Adrian and Orrila. Play, 5 acts. William Dimond. Covent Garden, November 1806. Larpent.
Alberto and Lauretta; or The Orphan of the Alps. Melodrama, 2 acts. Thomas J. Lynch. Haymarket, December 1806. Larpent.

Edgar; or Northern Feuds. Play, 5 acts. George Manners. Covent Garden, May 1806. Larpent.
The Curfew. Play, 5 acts. John Tobin. Drury Lane, February 1806.
The Wood Daemon; or, The Clock Has Struck. Melodrama, 2 acts. M. G. Lewis. Drury Lane, April 1807.
Adelgitha; or, The Fruits of a Single Error. Tragedy, 5 acts. M. G. Lewis. Drury Lane, April 1807. Larpent.
Faulkner. Tragedy, 5 acts. William Godwin. Drury Lane, December 1807.
Boniface and Bridgetina. Burlesque melodrama, 2 acts. T. J. Dibdin. Covent Garden, March 1808. Larpent.
The Mysterious Bride. Play, 3 acts. Lumley St. George Skeffington. Drury Lane, June 1808. Larpent.
The Forest of Hermanstadt; or, A Princess and no Princess. Melodrama, 3 acts. T. J. Dibdin. Covent Garden, October 1808. Larpent.
The Exile. Opera, 3 acts. Frederic Reynolds. Covent Garden, November 1808. Larpent.
Venoni; or, The Novice of St. Mark's. Melodrama, 3 acts. M. G. Lewis. Drury Lane, December 1808. Larpent.
Raymond and Agnes; or, The Bleeding Nun. Melodrama, 2 acts. M. G. Lewis (application Norwich, November 1809). Larpent.
The Haunted Village. Comic burletta. anon. Pavilion, November, 1809. Larpent.
The Edict of Charlemagne; or, The Free Knights. Opera, 3 acts. Frederic Reynolds. Covent Garden, February 1809.
Bad Neighbors; or, The Earl and the Baron. Melodramatic opera, 3 acts. Samuel James Arnold. Lyceum, September 1810. Larpent.
The Bridal Ring. Dramatic Romance, 2 acts. Frederic Reynolds. Covent Garden, October 1810. Larpent.
The Lady of the Lake. Melodrama, 3 acts. Edmund St. John Eyre. Edinburgh, January 1811. Larpent.
Timour the Tartar. Melodrama, 2 acts. M. G. Lewis. Covent Garden, April 1811.
The House of Morville. Play, 5 acts. John Lake. Lyceum, February 1812. Larpent.
The Aethiop. Drama, 3 acts. William Dimond. Covent Garden, October 1812.
The Italian Husband. Play, 3 acts. Edmund St. John Eyre. Haymarket, August 1812. Larpent.
The Harper's Son and the Duke's Daughter. Melodramatic romance, 2 acts. T. J. Dibdin. Surrey, December 1812. Larpent.
Remorse. Tragedy, 5 acts. S. T. Coleridge. Drury Lane, January 1813.

The Forest Knight. Burletta, 2 acts. anon. Sans Pareil, November 1813. Larpent.
The Earls of Hammersmith; or, The Cellar Spectre. Burlesque, 1 act. Dennis Lawler. Olympic, January 1814. Larpent.
The Wandering Boys; or, The Castle of Olival. Drama, 2 acts. John Kerr. Covent Garden, February 1814. Larpent.
The Woodman's Hut. Melodrama, 3 acts. Samuel James Arnold. Drury Lane, April 1814. Larpent.
Hortensia. Tragedy, 5 acts. anon. publ. unacted 1815.
Bobinet the Bandit; or, The Forest of Montescarpini. Melodrama, 2 acts. anon. Covent Garden, December 1815. Larpent.
Bertram; or, The Castle of St. Aldobrand. Tragedy, 5 acts. C. R. Maturin. Drury Lane, May 1816.
Terrors of Conscience. Melodrama, 2 acts. anon. application 1816. Larpent.
Right of Might; or, The Castle of Ellangowan. Play, 3 acts. anon. Covent Garden, February 1816. Larpent.
The Broken Sword. Melodrama, 2 acts. William Dimond. Covent Garden, October 1816. Larpent.
Manuel. Tragedy, 5 acts. C. R. Maturin. Drury Lane, March 1817.
The Fate of Taranto. Play, 3 acts. William Dimond. Covent Garden, April 1817. Larpent.
Edwin, Heir of Cressingham. Tragedy, 3 acts. Edward Fitzball. Norwich, April 1817. Larpent.
The Falls of Clyde. Melodrama, 2 acts. George Soane. Drury Lane, October 1817.
The Lord of the Castle. Melodramatic Romance, 2 acts. anon. Sans Pareil, October 1817. Larpent.
The Bride of Abydos. Tragick Play, 3 acts. William Dimond. Drury Lane, 1818.
The Bravo's Son. Melodrama, 2 acts. anon. Bath, March 1819. Larpent.
Fredolfo. Tragedy, 5 acts. C. R. Maturin. Covent Garden, May 1819.
Montrose; or, Second Sight. Melodramatic Romance, 3 acts. T. J. Dibdin. Edinburgh, July 1819. Larpent.
The Bride of Lammermoor. Caledonian Romance, 2 acts. T. J. Dibdin. Surrey, July 1819. Larpent.
The Ruffian Boy. Melodrama, 2 acts. T. J. Dibdin. Surrey, 1819.
Evadne; or, The Statue. Tragedy, 5 acts. R. L. Sheil. Covent Garden, 1819.
The Phantom; or, Montoni. Tragedy, 3 acts. R. L. Sheil. Covent Garden, May 1820. Larpent.
Giraldi; or, The Ruffian Boy. Melodrama, 3 acts. Edward Fitzball. Norwich, April 1820. Larpent.

Warlock of the Glen. Melodrama, 2 acts. C. E. Walker. Covent Garden, December 1820.

St. Cuthbert's Eve; or, The Tomb of Monteith. Burletta, 3 acts. George Herbert Rodwell. Adelphi, October 1820. Larpent.

The Phantom Bride; or, The Castilian Bandit. Melodrama, 2 acts. C. Z. Barnett. Royal Pavilion, 1820 (?).

The Child of Mystery; or, The Ruby Cross. Musical Burletta, 2 acts. anon. Olympic, February 1821.

The Bandit of Bohemia. Romantic Drama, 3 acts. C. E. Walker. Drury Lane, September 1821. Larpent.

The Bride of Lammermoor. Drama, 3 acts. John William Calcraft. Edinburgh, May 1822. Larpent.

Melmoth, The Wanderer. Melodramatic Romance, 3 acts. Benjamin West. Royal Coburg, July 1823.

Frankenstein. Melodramatic opera, 3 acts. Richard Brinsley Peake. Lyceum, July 1823. Larpent.

NOTES TO CHAPTER I

[1] The volumes most useful to me have been these: E. A. Baker, *A History of the English Novel*, vol. 5 (London, Longmans, 1924); Edith Birkhead, *The Tale of Terror* (London, Constable, 1921); Jakob Brauchli, *Der Englische Schauerroman* (Weida, 1928); Alice Killen, *Le Roman Terrifiant* (Paris, 1901); K. K. Mehrotra, *Walpole and the English Novel* (Oxford, 1938); Eino Railo, *The Haunted Castle* (London, Routledge, 1927); Montague Summers, *The Gothic Quest* (New York, Columbia University Press, 1938); and P. Yvon, *Le Gothique et le Renaissance Gothique en Engleterre* (Paris, 1931).

[2] J. M. S. Tompkins, *The Popular Novel in England* (London, Constable, 1932), p. 248.

[3] A single article, Willard Thorp's "The Stage Adventures of Some Gothic Novels," *Publications Modern Language Association*, XLIII, 476–486, deals with adaptations. It does not recognize the existence of a school of Gothic drama, but discusses "Gothic novels dramatized."

[4] A similar point has been touched, though obliquely, by George Sampson in *The Concise Cambridge History of English Literature* (London, Macmillan, 1941), p. 537: "It was through Percy's *Reliques* that the Middle Ages really came to have an influence in modern poetry, and this was an effect far greater than that of Ossian (which was not medieval) or that of *The Castle of Otranto* (which was not poetical)." My point is not that the Gothic novel did not influence poetry to some extent, but that study of prose fiction has not shown how Gothic materials, transformed, passed into poetry.

[5] I do not forget Scott, some of whose prose pages are filled with Gothic materials and motifs. It is to be noted, however, that mystery, gloom, and terror are never the dominant effects in a novel by Scott, and Montague Summers, in his *Gothic Bibliography* (Fortune Press, 1941), deliberately omits all of Scott's novels.

[6] Allardyce Nicoll, *Late Eighteenth Century Drama* (Cambridge, 1927), and *Early Nineteenth Century Drama*, 2 vols. (Cambridge, 1930).

[7] John Genest, *Some Account of the English Stage* (London, Carrington, 1832).

[8] See, for example, W. S. Dye, *A Study of Melodrama in England, 1800–1840* (State College of Pennsylvania, 1920). This writer treats a number of Gothic plays without establishing that a Gothic dramatic genre existed.

[9] These manuscripts are catalogued by Dougald MacMillan, Larpent Plays in the Henry E. Huntington Library (San Marino, California, 1939).

[10] This question was raised and discussed in some detail by C. F. McIntyre, "Were the Gothic Novels Gothic?," *PMLA*, XXXVI, 644–667.

[11] This important fact is convincingly substantiated by Kenneth Clark, *The Gothic Revival* (London, Constable, 1928).

[12] Clark, *op. cit.*, though primarily a student of architecture, gives unqualified credit to the poets for the whole movement toward Gothic architecture in the latter eighteenth century.

[13] *Letters on Chivalry and Romance* (Oxford, 1911).

[14] See A. E. Longueil, "The Word Gothic in 18th Century Critcism," *Modern Language Notes*, XXXVII, 453–460.

[15] This has been the universal impression. It is true that Walpole built a Gothic castle and surrounded himself with relics of the Middle Ages. But it is true also that these gave him a nightmare, out of which, by his own admission (Letter to the Rev. Wm. Cole, March 9, 1765), *Otranto*. Basic to an understanding of Walpole and the Gothic school in both fiction and drama is the realization that he was not the foremost rebel from the conventional attitude toward medievalism, but its foremost exploiter.

[16] Almost any page of a Gothic piece will verify this statement. Note especially Aikin's Fragment, *Sir Bertrand* (London, J. Johnson, 1792), which was written specifically to illustrate the Gothic exploitation of terror; in it the "medieval" hero is conspicuously unaccustomed to medieval surroundings. It is very apparent that the inhabitants of Gothic castles in novels and plays are not at home; only the villains belong, and even they some-

times react to galleries, turrets, and vaults as though they had never seen them before. Perhaps the most glaring anachronism occurs in Joanna Baillie's *Orra*, as we shall see in Chapter XI, below.

[17] These are common opinions; see especially Birkhead, *The Tale of Terror* and Railo, *The Haunted Castle*.

[18] *Op. cit.* Here elements are considered, separated from the more important preoccupations and purposes.

[19] See, for example, *The Cambridge History of English Literature*, vol. 11, where far the greatest space is given to the reasons for dramatic inferiority, and relatively little to discussion of individual plays.

[20] In *Late Eighteenth Century Drama* and *Early Nineteenth Cenury Drama*, vol. 2.

[21] See W. P. Harbeson, *Elizabethan Influence on the Tragedy of the Late 18th and Early 19th Centuries* (Lancaster, Pa., 1920). This study suggests, very curiously, that Elizabethan influence was slight.

[22] Here is a typical summary of the dramatic history: "... the English drama of the latter 18:th century, viewed in broad outlines, followed the fiction. The spectator is taken into scenes of domestic life where the absence of the grander elements of tragedy is compensated with tender and always well-bred sentimentality. Out of this *milieu*, but under the freshening influence of classical comedy, there arose the dramatic masterpieces of the age, the comedies of Sheridan and Goldsmith." Niilo Idman, *Charles Robert Maturin* (London, Constable, 1920), p. 122.

NOTES TO CHAPTER II

[1] That is, "An attempt to blend the two kinds of Romance, the ancient and the modern." (Preface to the 2d ed., 1765.) This, however, was a studied afterthought. It conflicts with the author's statement that he wrote in the white heat of excitement after a dream at Strawberry Hill, where he had gone to sleep with his head "full of Gothic fancy."

[2] Mehrotra, Summers, and Baker call particular attention to Smollett's and Leland's works. Summers' introduction to his edition of Walpole's novel states, "That *The Castle of Otranto* had a predecessor in no way impugns Walpole's position." Others agree that Walpole's was the first novel of its kind. I note that the resemblance between certain passages in Smollett and Walpole was observed as early as 1792, in Aikin's *Essays*, p. 125.

[3] All were admonished that the tragedy should not fall into the hands of Garrick and Johnson.

[4] By McIntyre, *loc. cit.*

[5] Gothic playwrights themselves were well aware that theirs was a dramatic kind different from the Elizabethan. Jephson, Andrews, and Boaden felt that they had no precedents for what they were attempting.

[6] Though Congreve's famous "vaulted aisle" passage would fit unaltered into any Gothic play, the single speech is but a minute portion of the whole work, the preoccupations of which are other than mystery, gloom, and terror.

[7] These, and similar statistics elsewhere in this survey, are drawn from Genest, *op. cit.*

[8] Nicoll, *Late Eighteenth Century Drama*, p. 92.

[9] *Douglas*, I, 1.

[10] Obviously, this theme was not "new." The Gothicists' universal adoption of it illustrates their characteristic seizure of materials appropriate to their purpose.

[11] *Douglas*, V, 1.

[12] *Ibid.*, III, 2.

[13] *Ibid.*, II, 1.

[14] *Ibid.*

[15] Home's *Dramatic Works* (1822), introduction.

[16] The difference between the conventional eighteenth-century attitude toward medievalism and the romantic nineteenth-century attitude (anticipated by Leland) may be strikingly illustrated by comparing a Gothic novelist's description of a ruin with one of Scott's descriptions. Though Mrs. Radcliffe saw beauty in the ruin, it was always mixed with terror, and terror predominates in the effect of her descriptions; other Gothicists

preferred terror to the exclusion of all else. In sharp contrast is this typical description from Scott: "It was one hour after midnight, and the prospect around was lovely. The grey old towers of the ruin, partly entire, partly broken, here bearing the rusty weather-stains of ages, and there partially mantled with ivy, stretched along the verge of the dark rock which rose on Mannering's right hand. In his front was the quiet bay, whose little waves, crisping and sparkling to the moonbeams, rolled successively along its surface, and dashed with a soft and murmuring ripple against the silvery beach." (*Guy Mannering*, chap. iii.)

[17] *The Countess of Salisbury*, V, 2.
[18] *Ibid.*, I, 1.

NOTES TO CHAPTER III

[1] Doubtless, however, *The Mysterious Mother* influenced later plays, for the privately printed copies fell into "unscrupulous" hands and several editions were advertised without Walpole's consent. Numerous plays toward the end of the century indicate specific debt, and later Byron's *Manfred* clearly betrays influence of what Byron called "the last tragedy in the language."

[2] Walpole's postscript in the first "authorized" version of the play treats the classical "rules" with veneration.

[3] *The Mysterious Mother*, epilogue.
[4] *Ibid.*, Postscript.
[5] *Ibid.* The author later noted a similar story in Margaret of Navarre's *Heptameron*.
[6] *Ibid.* Italics mine.
[7] Though no Elizabethan dramatist used this story, two plays of the late seventeenth and early eighteenth centuries were based on it: the anonymous *Fatal Discovery* (1697) and *Innocence Distress'd* (1703). The scenes were laid, respectively, in Venice and Muscovy. That Gothic atmosphere was not implicit in the story, but was entirely the result of Walpole's favorite predilection is evident from the fact that neither of these earlier plays suggests the remotest Gothic qualities.

[8] *The Mysterious Mother*, I, 1.
[9] *Ibid.*
[10] *Ibid.*, I, 3.
[11] *Ibid.*, II, 2.
[12] There were exceptions, of course, as in *The Winter's Tale*, but these are rare, and, so far as I know, confined to comedy and tragicomedy.
[13] *The Mysterious Mother*, II, 2.
[14] Such anachronisms and even worse incongruities were common. Home's *Fatal Discovery*, for instance, shows Ossianic characters cavorting before a Grecian temple. The mélange was typical and significant, for it emphasizes the unsettled condition of drama and the hasty groping in every direction for dramatic materials.

[15] *The Grecian Daughter*, I, 1.
[16] *Ibid.*, IV, 2.
[17] *The British Father*, I, 1.
[18] *Ibid.*, III, 6.
[19] *Dramatic Works* (New York, Harper, 1852), p. 502.
[20] *Ibid.*
[21] *Percy*, I, 1.
[22] *Ibid.*, III, 1.
[23] *Ibid.*, I, 1.

NOTES TO CHAPTER IV

[1] Walpole advised Jephson on the adaptation, and his classicism is evident in the finished work. That Jephson himself cared little for dramatic laws is apparent in his later plays.

[2] To Seymour Conway, November 12, 1781.

³ *London Chronicle,* November 18, 1781.
⁴ *British Theatre* (London, 1898), Vol. 20, p. 38.
⁵ *Julia, or The Italian Lover* appeared in 1787.
⁶ See chap. v.
⁷ *The Count of Narbonne,* I, 1.
⁸ *Ibid.,* II, 1.
⁹ Note Byron's Manfred thirty-five years later: "Away! away! there's blood upon the brim!"
¹⁰ *The Count of Narbonne,* II, 1.
¹¹ *Ibid.,* V, 1.
¹² Though the debt is obvious, here, as elsewhere in Gothic plays, it goes no deeper than the language. Gothicists imitated or stole from Shakespeare in most of their moments of crisis. But the purpose of Hamlet's meeting with the ghost is quite different from that of Raymond's meeting with what seems a ghost. Hamlet's shock and seeming horror is incidental; Raymond's terror is the end itself.
¹³ *The Count of Narbonne,* I, 1.
¹⁴ The only exception, to my knowledge, occurs in Andrew McDonald's *Vimonda* (1787), where the hero stabs the villain after he has himself been poisoned and is dying.
¹⁵ The heroes of Scott's novels illustrate both tendencies in early nineteenth-century heroes. Ivanhoe, Quentin Durward, Peveril, and Tressilian, to name a few, evince the negative qualities of the eighteenth-century type. Who has not wished to give all of these—and Ivanhoe particularly—a beating for ineffectuality, incompetence, and plain stupidity? Ravenswood, on the other hand, a true child of the Gothic villain, remains attractive even to the modern reader.
¹⁶ *The Count of Narbonne,* I, 1.
¹⁷ *Ibid.*
¹⁸ *Ibid.*
¹⁹ The most revealing account of theatrical conditions of the time is Boaden's *Life of Kemble,* 2 vols. (London, 1825). Genest, too, records numerous cases of the damning of a play as result of petty circumstances apart from the merits of the play.
²⁰ *The Castle of Andalusia,* II, 1. Since there are no important differences between this and the manuscript of *Banditti,* references are to the printed version.
²¹ The usually helpful sources fail to give much information about this play. Genest does not list *The Enchanted Castle,* but records a performance of *The Castle of Wonders* in 1809. Professor Nicoll lists only *The Enchanted Castle,* which seems to be the same as the Larpent *Castle of Wonders.*
²² *The Castle of Wonders,* Larpent Collection, preface.
²³ See chap. vi.
²⁴ Genest, *op. cit.,* Vol. 6, pp. 586–587.
²⁵ Boaden, *op. cit.,* Vol. 2, p. 15.
²⁶ *The Haunted Tower,* I, 3.
²⁷ *Ibid.,* III, 2.
²⁸ *Ibid.,* III, 4.

NOTES TO CHAPTER V

¹ Outstanding among these are *Lord Russel* (Hay. Aug. 1784), by William Hayley, and *Julia; or The Italian Lover* (D. L. April 1787), by Jephson.
² *The Days of Yore* (C. G. Jan. 1796), a play which makes very elaborate use of medievalism for purposes of gloom and terror; *The Mysterious Husband* (C. G. Jan. 1783), which was evidently suggested by Walpole's tragedy; and *Joanna of Montfaucon* (C. G. Jan. 1800), an "adaptation" of Kotzebue's play.
³ *The Carmelite,* I, 1.
⁴ *Ibid.*
⁵ *Ibid.,* V, 1.
⁶ Genest, *op. cit.,* Vol. 6, p. 591.

Evans: *Gothic Drama from Walpole to Shelley*

[7] A striking illustration of this principle is cited in chap. viii, in connection with Lewis's *The Castle Spectre*.
[8] *Vimonda*, I, 1.
[9] *Ibid.*, II, 2.
[10] *Ibid.*, IV, 1.
[11] *The Regent*, I, 2.
[12] *Ibid.*, IV, 2.
[13] *Ibid.*, II, 1.
[14] *Ibid.*, IV, 2.
[15] *Ibid.*
[16] *Ibid.*, V, 1.
[17] *Kentish Barons*, I, 2.
[18] *Ibid.*, II, 1.
[19] *Ibid.*, II, 4.
[20] *Ibid.*
[21] That the Gothic playwrights had Shakespeare's great characters—and the fame of their contemporary actors in those parts—in mind constantly, is attested by the great number of imitated Shakespearean lines uttered by the Gothic villains. These playwrights could not create whole Hamlets, Iagos, Richards, or Macbeths, but they could reproduce some of the more violent actions and reactions of these.
[22] Boaden, *op. cit.*, Vol. 1, p. 338.
[23] Another play, *Terrors of Conscience* (anon. 1816) in the Larpent Collection also emphasizes the obsession with remorse by its title. Almost any Gothic play, including Byron's *Manfred*, would have been appropriately named with Coleridge's or this title.

NOTES TO CHAPTER VI

[1] Identity of the translator is not known with certainty. Genest suggests that it was possibly Holcroft.
[2] Obviously the materials which they used came from various lands, but not from a Gothic or horrific school in other lands. Ann Radcliffe, for example, preferred the Italian scene and was partly inspired by paintings of it; yet the manner in which she used the foreign scene was thoroughly English.
[3] Besides these, I have found a play called *Lucinda*, anonymous and undated, in the Duncombe series of acting plays. Neither Genest nor the *Biographia Dramatica* records it, and it is not listed by Professor Nicoll. It is very obviously adapted from *A Sicilian Romance*. Possibly it was produced in America, never in England.
[4] Boaden, *op. cit.*, Vol. 2, p. 96.
[5] With the lone exception of her last novel, *Gaston De Blondeville*, in which there is a "real" appearance of the supernatural.
[6] *Fontainville Forest*, II, 1.
[7] *Ibid.*, I, 1.
[8] *Ibid.*, I, 4.
[9] *Ibid.*, II, 1.
[10] This kind of trickery had been practiced earlier, even in *The Mysterious Mother* (IV, 1, where the chant of friars is deliberately represented as a supernatural chorus). It was comparatively rare, however, before Mrs. Radcliffe's influenced the stage.
[11] *Fontainville Forest*, II, 4.
[12] *Romeo and Juliet*, IV, 3.
[13] *Fontainville Forest*, II, 5.
[14] *Ibid.*, III, 2.
[15] *Ibid.*, IV, 2.
[16] Boaden, *op. cit.*, Vol. 2, p. 97.
[17] *Ibid.*, p. 98.
[18] *Ibid.*, p. 119.

[19] Outstanding among Gothic plays using the Inquisition as primary motif is Holcroft's *The Inquisitor* (Hay. June 1798).
[20] The Larpent Collection includes two manuscripts of the play, one under each title.
[21] *The Sicilian Romance*, I, 1.
[22] *Ibid.*
[23] *Ibid.*, I, 2.
[24] *Ibid.*, II, 1.
[25] *Ibid.*, II, 2.
[26] *Ibid.*
[27] *Ibid.*, III, 1.
[28] In the burlesque *Banditti* (1781) the hero turned outlaw; possibly, but very improbably, Siddons may have borrowed from O'Keefe rather than from Schiller.
[29] By Reynolds, who was to have half the earnings and none of the fame as author.
[30] Boaden, *op. cit.*, Vol. 2, p. 137.
[31] This action does not represent an exception to the rule that Gothic heroes never effectively thwart the villains. As the scene is arranged, it is apparent that Carlos is a very minor factor in the interruption of Montoni's purpose.
[32] *The Mysteries of The Castle*, I, 2.
[33] *Ibid.*, II, 1.
[34] It was this very tendency of the Gothic novelists to take themselves too seriously which particularly invited Jane Austen's ridicule in *Northanger Abbey*.

NOTES TO CHAPTER VII

[1] Indeed, the Gothic species flourished in England even before there *were* any horrific elements to borrow from Germany. Goethe's *Götz* and Schiller's *Räuber*, the first works of their kind in Germany, followed *Otranto* by nine and seventeen years respectively. English novelists and dramatists maintained a full ten-year lead in the development of mystery, gloom, and terror materials.
[2] *Biographia Literaria* (Macmillan, 1926), p. 359.
[3] *Zapolya*, rejected by Byron in 1816.
[4] Agnes Murphy, *Banditry and Chivalry in German Fiction, 1790–1830* (University of Chicago Press, 1935), p. 2.
[5] *Ibid.*, p. 25.
[6] *Ibid.*, p. 5.
[7] *Ibid.*, p. 9.
[8] *Ibid.*, p. 28.
[9] *Ibid.*, p. 29.
[10] *Ibid.*, p. 32.
[11] Boaden, *op. cit.*, p. 143.
[12] See Summers' *op. cit.*, p. 129.
[13] Or, as often, of the Inquistion. The two institutions served the same purpose in Gothic plays.
[14] *The Secret Tribunal*, I, 2.
[15] *Ibid.*, III, 3.
[16] *Ibid.*, III, 4.
[17] *Ibid.*, IV, 1.
[18] See V. Stockley, *German Literature as Known in England, 1750–1830* (London, George Routledge and Sons, Ltd., 1929), app., and F. W. Stokoe, *German Influence in the English Romantic Period* (Cambridge University Press, 1926), app., and W. Sellier, *Kotzebue in England* (Leipzig, 1901).
[19] It does not seem necessary to discuss *The Rovers* among Gothic burlesques. Gothic motifs are scarcely touched by Canning and Frere, whose ridicule was directed at Kotzebue, Schiller, and especially at an anonymous *Stella*, translated in 1798. The many strong attacks by English reviewers on the immorality of *Stella* indicate once more the strictness of moral rules applied to drama. The play was never acted, possibly because the censor would not license it. See Stockley, *op. cit.*, p. 132.

NOTES TO CHAPTER VIII

[1] Genest, *op. cit.*, Vol. 1, p. 333.
[2] The *Biographia Dramatica* records a conversation between Lewis and Sheridan. The two had a dispute, and Lewis offered to bet all the money *The Castle Spectre* had earned that he was right; Sheridan replied that he could not afford to wager so much, but would bet "all it is worth."
[3] *The Castle Spectre* (1797), preface.
[4] *Ibid.*, I, 1.
[5] *Ibid.*, I, 2.
[6] *Ibid.*
[7] *Ibid.*
[8] *Ibid.*, II, 1.
[9] *Ibid.*
[10] *Ibid.*, III, 3.
[11] *Ibid.*, II, 1.
[12] *Ibid.*, IV, 1.
[13] *Ibid.*, IV, 2.
[14] *Ibid.*
[15] Genest, *op. cit.*, Vol. 1, p. 334.
[16] S. M. Ellis, *Life of Michael Kelly* (cited by Genest).
[17] *The Castle Spectre*, V, 2.
[18] *Ibid.*, V, 3.
[19] *Ibid.*, IV, 1.
[20] *Adelmorn, the Outlaw*, III, 1.
[21] *Ibid.*, II, 2.
[22] *Lacey's Acting Plays* (London, 1871).
[23] Joshua Pickersgill, *The Three Brothers, A Romance* (London, John Stockdale, 1803). *The Deformed Transformed* was founded partly on Goethe's *Faust*.
[24] *One o'Clock*, III, 2.
[25] *Ibid.*
[26] *Alfonso* (1801), preface.
[27] *Adelgitha* (1807), preface.
[28] Note that Walpole laid the scene of *The Mysterious Mother* "in what age and country I chose," and Hannah More chose the time of Percy and Douglas for her discussion of a contemporary problem.
[29] *Adelgitha* (1807), note.
[30] Lewis, of course, as author of *The Monk*, was an especial target for the censor's suspicion. He published his *Alfonso* before he would allow it to be acted, to forestall and protect himself against any possible accusations of "offensive" matters which might, without his knowledge, find their way into the acting version. Earlier, he had been in trouble with the censor over *The Castle Spectre*, partly because he allowed his heroine to stab the villain.
[31] Cited in Genest, *op. cit.*, Vol. 6, p. 342.
[32] Joanna Baillie, who would not have pressed the claim, would be his only rival.
[33] Reference is specifically to his association with and influence on Byron and Shelley, both of whom were his personal acquaintances, and both of whom heard his tales and translations.

NOTES TO CHAPTER IX

[1] James Frederick Mason, *The Melodrama in France from the Revolution to the Beginning of the Romantic Drama*, cited by Dye in *A Study of Melodrama in England from 1800 to 1840*, p. 2. See also A. R. Thompson, "Melodrama and Tragedy, *PMLA*, XVIII, 810–835.

[2] Martin Griffin, *Melodrama* in his *Collected Works*, Vol. CXLI, 564–568. This appears to represent standard opinion. (Italics mine.)
[3] To these might be added *Valentine and Orson* (C. G. April 1804), by T. J. Dibdin; *The Forest of Hermanstadt* (C. G. Oct. 1808), by the same author; *Alberto and Lauretto* (Hay. Dec. 1805), by Thomas J. Lynch; *The Travelers Benighted* (Hay. Sept. 1811), anonymous; *Bobinet the Bandit* (C. G. Dec. 1815), anonymous; *Terrors of Conscience* (application 1816), anonymous; and, of course, the many dramatizations of Scott's novels.
[4] Those most marked by Gothic preoccupations are *Adrian and Orilla* (C. G. Nov. 1806), *The Fate of Taranto* (C. G. April 1817), *The Aethiop* (C. G. Oct. 1812), and *The Broken Sword* (C. G. Oct. 1816). The last-named play is most remarkable for its inclusion of virtually all of the conventional Gothic elements.
[5] *The Foundling of the Forest*, I, 1.
[6] *Ibid.*, I, 2.
[7] *Ibid.*, I, 5.
[8] *Ibid.*, I, 6.
[9] *The Woodman's Hut*, I, 1.
[10] *Ibid.*, I, 2.
[11] *Ibid.*, I, 5.
[12] *Ibid.*, II, 2.
[13] Cottages became prevalent in melodramas, and by 1820 were used more frequently than castles. With this shift of location came gradually a shift of emphasis. Gothicists had used dilapidated structures to excite mystery, gloom, and terror. Melodramatists of the later period described the poverty of the cottage, and sought to rouse pity. Moncrieff, Fitzball, and Planché were among the many playwrights who exploited the new humanitarianism, often with the very settings through which earlier writers had exploited terror.
[14] Yet in numerous plays of the later nineteenth century Gothic materials and motifs continued to dominate. Moncrieff's *The Monk's Cowl* and *Mount St. Bernard* are examples between 1830–1840, as are several plays by George Almar, *Knights of St. John, The Rover's Bride*, and others. In 1851 appeared the anonymous *Pauline*, filled with chapels, vaults, night views of ruined castles, and so on. In the 1860's there seems to have been something of a revival of Gothic horror plays, of which W. E. Suter's *The Accusing Spirit; or The Three Travelers of the Tyrol, The Angel of Midnight*, and *The Outlaw of the Adriatic* are striking examples.
[15] *Boniface and Bridgetina*, I, 1.
[16] *The Earls of Hammersmith*, I, 1.
[17] *Ibid.*, I, 2.

NOTES TO CHAPTER X

[1] Others of this period, besides the plays by Lewis which have been discussed, were *A Tale of Terror* (C. G. May 1803), by Henry Siddons, *St. Margaret's Cave* (York and Hull, 1804), by George Charles Carr, and *The House of Morville* (Lyceum, Feb. 1812). There were so many more that selection of the best possible pieces for discussion has been very difficult.
[2] *Julian and Agnes*, III, 2.
[3] *Ibid.*
[4] *Ibid.*, IV, 1.
[5] The other was *St. Margaret's Cave*.
[6] *The Towers of Urbandine*, I, 1.
[7] *Ibid.*, II, 2.
[8] *Ibid.*, II, 3.
[9] *Ibid.*, III, 2.
[10] *Ibid.*, III, 4.
[11] *Ibid.*, IV, 1.
[12] *Ibid.*, IV, 5.
[13] *Ibid.*, V, 3.
[14] *Ibid.*, V, 5.

[15] Genest, *op. cit.*, Vol. 8, p. 37.
[16] Nicoll, *Early Eighteenth Century Drama*, pp. 164–165. Professor Nicoll acknowledges the presence of horrific elements, but does not relate the play to a Gothic school of drama.
[17] Harbeson, *op. cit.*, p. 42.
[18] *The Curfew*, I, 2.
[19] *Ibid.*, III, 3.
[20] *Ibid.*, V, 3.
[21] Summers, *A Gothic Bibliography*, preface.
[22] *Melmoth* was dramatized as "a Melo-Dramatic Romance" in three acts by Benjamin West, and appeared at the Royal Coburg Theatre in 1823. It was acted in Baltimore, Maryland, in 1831.
[23] *Bertram, Fredolfo* (C. G. May 1819), and *Manuel* (D. L. March 1817). The latter play was written to supply Kean with a mad role; he could not play *King Lear*, for George III was mad, so Maturin provided a nonroyal madman.
[24] In the *Quarterly Review*, October, 1810.
[25] Sheil wrote three other plays which have Gothic marks: *The Apostate* (C. G. 1817), *Evadne; or The Statue* (C. G. 1819), which was based on Shirley's *The Traitor*, and *The Phantom; or Montoni* (C. G. 1820), which drew its main character from *Udolpho*.
[26] *The Correspondence of Sir Walter Scott and Charles Robert Maturin*, eds. F. E. Ratchford and W. M. McCarthy (University of Texas Press, 1937); May 29, 1814.
[27] Murray to Scott, December 25, 1815.
[28] *Monthly Magazine* (1815), V, 451.
[29] *British Review* (1816), VIII, 64.
[30] Cited by Helene Richter, *Geschichte der englischen Romantik* (Halle, 1911), Vol. I, 299.
[31] *Bertram*, I, 2.
[32] *Ibid.*, II, 1.
[33] *Ibid.*, II, 3.
[34] *Ibid.*, II, 4.
[35] Niilo Idman, *Charles Robert Maturin* (London, Constable, 1923), p. 120.
[36] See, for example, S. C. Chew, *The Dramas of Lord Byron* (Johns Hopkins Press, 1915): "The play is essentially Byronic... the protagonist is another Lara, though Maturin borrowed the hero-villain type not so much from Byron as from Mrs. Radcliffe" p. 12. Of course Maturin knew *Lara*, but the hero of that poem was already fully developed before Byron wrote.

NOTES TO CHAPTER XI

[1] As one evidence of this need, I quote a statement by S. C. Chew, *op. cit.*, pp. 5–6: "At the foundation of Joanna Baillie's theories and practice in the drama was a reaction from the 'Gothic' vogue, very similar to that which later led Byron to the 'regular' drama." On the contrary, Joanna Baillie ranks second only to Lewis as a Gothic dramatist. It is as difficult to understand Professor Chew's remark about Miss Baillie, when we remember *De Monfort, The Dream*, and *Orra*, as to understand that about Byron when we remember *Manfred* and *Werner*.
[2] I have given Miss Baillie a brief chapter by herself, since it seems difficult to place her works either with "acting" or "literary" drama. They seem to fall between the two. The author very obviously attempted to make them actable, but *De Monfort*, the only one brought to the stage and the one which would have seemed most likely to succeed, failed badly.
[3] All are included in the *Dramatic Works* (London, 1851).
[4] *Ibid.*, introd. x.
[5] *Romiero*, II, 3.
[6] *Ibid.*, IV, 3.
[7] *Henriquez*, I, 1.
[8] *Ibid.*, II, 2.

[9] *The Dream*, I, 3.
[10] *Dramatic Works*, p. 234 (note).
[11] *Ibid.*
[12] *De Monfort*, I, 1.
[13] *Ethwald*, Pt. I, I, 1.
[14] *The Dream*, I, 2.
[15] *Romiero*, II, 2.
[16] *Henriquez*, IV, 4.
[17] *Rayner*, I, 1.
[18] *Dramatic Works*, p. 389.
[19] *Ibid.*, p. 229.
[20] *Orra*, I, 2.
[21] *Ibid.*, II, 2.
[22] *Ibid.*, III, 1.
[23] *Ibid.*, III, 2.
[24] *Ibid.*, III, 4.
[25] *Ibid.*, IV, 1.
[26] *Ibid.*, IV, 3.
[27] *Ibid.*
[28] *Ibid.*, V, 1.
[29] *Ibid.*, V, 2.

NOTES TO CHAPTER XII

[1] I have found most useful E. S. Bates, *A Study of Shelley's Drama The Cenci* (Columbia Univ. Press, 1908); Chew, *op. cit.*; E. de Selincourt, *Oxford Lectures on Poetry* (Clarendon Press, 1934), chap. vii; Nicoll, *Early Nineteenth Century Drama;* and U. C. Nag, "The English Theatre of the Romantic Revival," *19th Century*, CIV, 384-398. Besides these, and the more general accounts of English drama, are chapters on these plays in critical biographies of the individual poets.

[2] But the main emphasis has been on its relation to the poet himself, as though the play occupied no position with regard to any tradition. It seems to me that this kind of study needs to be supplemented with outside references, even though the play is of importance chiefly because it portrays a stage in the poet's evolution.

[3] In the two years, 1795-1797, a dozen Gothic plays were performed at the Covent Garden and Drury Lane theaters, including some of the outstanding specimens.

[4] For discussions of Wordsworth's purpose, see O. J. Campbell and P. Mueschke, "The Borderers as a Document in the History of Wordsworth's Aesthetic Development," *Modern Philology*, XXII, 465-482, and Selincourt, *op. cit.*, pp. 157-179.

[5] For opposite points of view, see Campbell and Mueschke, *op. cit.*, who argue in the affirmative, and George W. Meyer, *Wordsworth's Formative Years*, pp. 174 ff., where a contrary opinion is stated. See also E. Legouis, *William Wordsworth and Annette Vallon* (London, Dent, 1922).

[6] *Remorse*, I, 2.
[7] *Ibid.*
[8] *Ibid.*, V, 1.
[9] *Ibid.*

[10] John Lockhart, *Life of Scott* (Boston, Houghton, 1901), Vol. 2, p. 233.

[11] H. A. White, *Sir Walter Scott's Novels on the Stage* (Yale University Press, 1927). I have included in the appended list of Gothic plays only a few of the adaptations, in which Gothic qualities were so prominent that it seemed they must be included. Perhaps as many as twenty or twenty-five titles might have been listed as Gothic melodramas.

[12] All were published between 1822 and 1830, and all are contained in Scott's *Poetical Works* (Boston, Houghton, 1900), Vol. 5.

[13] Scott acknowledged great influence from the German writers (*House of Aspen*, preface). His plays had been written around 1800, and he gave as reason they had not been staged at once the opinion that the burlesque *The Rovers* had laughed German drama

Evans: Gothic Drama from Walpole to Shelley 257

from the stage. At about the same time, Joanna Baillie disclaimed all German influence on her "Plays of the Passions." The works of both suffered from the effects of. *The Rovers*, and erroneously, for that burlesque ridiculed the "real" German drama, not that Gothic drama to which "German" became attached. It was partly the confusion of terms, prevalent then as now, which kept Scott's plays from the stage.

[14] It is perhaps superfluous to draw attention once more to the conventional settings of Gothic drama. Yet these are the most striking features of Scott's two Gothic plays, and clearly indicate their line of descent. These are *not* the settings of the German drama which was ridiculed by Canning and Frere. Except for the confusion of terms, *The Rovers* should not have kept Scott's plays from being acted.

[15] *The Doom of Devorgoil*, III, 1.

[16] After Boaden had introduced the Secret Tribunal to the Gothic stage, several playwrights seized it, and apparently attempted to outdo one another in showing its horror. Unquestionably the most elaborate and terrifying exploitation of this institution was achieved by Frederic Reynolds, author of many horrific plays, in *The Edict of Charlemagne; or The Free Knights* (C. G. Feb. 1809). Compared with it, Scott's play is mild.

[17] Bates, *op. cit.*, the most detailed examination of *The Cenci*, indicates no awareness that the drama is related to Gothic tradition. The study of the tragedy has generally centered on its relation to the poet's mind, and its revelation of his views.

[18] See W. W. Watts, *Shilling Shockers of the Gothic School* (Cambridge, Mass., 1932), and of course Dowden's *Life of Shelley*, 2 vols. (New York, 1896), for discussions of the poet's early reading.

[19] *Caleb Williams* was adapted for the stage by Colman the Younger as *The Iron Chest* (D. L. March 1796). The social purpose is virtually lost in the stage version. There is merely the spectacle of a hero (Wilford) hounded by spies of the man on whose black secret he had stumbled.

[20] Quoted by Bates, *op. cit.*, p. 19.

[21] *Ibid.*

[22] Note: I love
    The sight of agony, and the sense of joy,
    When this shall be another's and that mine.
    And I have no remorse and little fear . . .
And:
    I am what theologians call
    Hardened; . . . (I, 1)
No Gothic villain ever talked or thought so.

[23] *The Cenci*, II, 1, and III, 1.

[24] Note especially Beatrice's description of the pass in which Count Cenci was to be ambushed (III, 1); also the officer's report of finding "this ruffian and another" (III, 4).

[25] *Manfred*, I, 1.

[26] *Ibid.*, I, 2.

[27] *Ibid.*, II, 1.

[28] *Ibid.*, III, 3.

[29] *Ibid.*, III, 1.

[30] *Ibid.*, III, 3.

[31] *Ibid.*, II, 2.

[32] For the sources of Manfred, see Chew, *op. cit.*, chap. iv. These are summarized in the following statement: "Study of the sources of *Manfred* has shown that there are three chief elements in the character of the protagonist, distinct but related to each other. These are the themes of Prometheus, Don Juan, and Faust." (Pp. 74-75.)

[33] Byron's service on the Drury Lane committee should not be forgotten. He could scarcely have avoided familiarity with the traditional Gothic villain. When he wrote to Scott (who then sent him *Bertram*), he referred to five hundred plays, no one of which he "could think of accepting." Among these were undoubtedly a great many of the Gothic species.

[34] To John Murray; dated Venice, February 15, 1817.

www.ingramcontent.com/pod-product-compliance
Lightning Source LLC
Chambersburg PA
CBHW021659230426
43668CB00008B/675